Bounder!

Graham McCann is the bestselling and critically acclaimed author of *Spike and Co.*, *Dad's Army*, *Frankie Howerd*, *Morecambe & Wise* and *Cary Grant*. He is one of Britain's foremost writers on entertainment. He lives in Cambridge.

'A magnificent book … If people are saying I never know what to get you at Christmas, have a look at the wonderful *Bounder!* … Well done, Graham McCann!' *Danny Baker*

GRAHAM McCANN

Bounder!

The Biography of Terry-Thomas

First published in Great Britain 2008
by Aurum Press Ltd, 7 Greenland Street, London NW1 0ND
www.aurumpress.co.uk

This paperback edition first published in 2009 by Aurum Press.

Copyright © 2008 by Graham McCann

A catalogue record for this book is available from the British Library.

ISBN 978 1 84513 441 9

10 9 8 7 6 5 4 3 2
2013 2012 2011 2010 2009

Typeset by Saxon Graphics Ltd, Derby
Printed and bound in Great Britain by CPI Bookmarque, Croydon

For
Richard Briers,
Richard Hope-Hawkins
&
Glyn Roberts

In this age, the mere example of non-conformity, the mere refusal to bend the knee to custom, is itself a service. Precisely because the tyranny of opinion is such as to make eccentricity a reproach, it is desirable, in order to break through that tyranny, that people should be eccentric. Eccentricity has always abounded when and where strength of character has abounded; and the amount of eccentricity in a society has generally been proportional to the amount of genius, mental vigour, and moral courage which it contained. That so few now dare to be eccentric marks the chief danger of the time.

John Stuart Mill

They say that the only way to find truth is to deny oneself, but I would rather have a bash at finding it the luxury way. Wouldn't you? You see, one's hope of finding it is so small that it seems silly to go after it the hard way, doesn't it?

Terry-Thomas

Contents

Acknowledgements

I TAKE SPECIAL pleasure in expressing my gratitude to Richard Briers for his kindness and advice, as well as to two other great Terry-Thomas admirers and archivists, Richard Hope-Hawkins and Glyn Roberts; their help, and trust, improved this book immeasurably. Jonathan Cecil was another remarkably generous and insightful advisor, and, among other interviewees, I am particularly indebted to Barry Cryer, Sarah Miles and Eric Sykes.

I am also grateful to the staff of the following institutions: the BBC Written Archives Centre at Caversham; the National Archives at Kew; the London Metropolitan Archives; the British Library, Newspaper Library and Sound Archive; the Theatre Museum in London; the Margaret Herrick Library in California; the National Film and Sound Archive of Australia; the British Film Institute Library; and the University of Cambridge Library. I am pleased to acknowledge, in addition, the assistance and encouragement from everyone at Aurum – especially my editor, Karen Ings, and Graham Coster and Dan Steward – as well as my agent, Mic Cheetham, and Nigel Adams, Wendy Ashman, Peter Eaton, Steve Gove, David Jones, Richard McCann, Irene Melling, Tony Osborne, Christopher Potter and Richard Webber. Special thanks go, as always, to Silvana Dean, Dick Geary and my dear mother, Vera McCann, for their essential friendship and support.

Prologue

The point I am trying to make is that you
must give the ruddy thing a chance ...

THERE HE IS, out on the tennis court, ready to play the first game of his match against a frightfully nice, terribly well-brought-up, but rather gullible sort of young fellow. *Thwack!* The frightfully nice young fellow, blinded by the sunlight, hits his first serve straight into the net. He tries again: *Thwack!* Double fault: Love-fifteen ('Hard cheese!'). *Thwack!* Another limp serve droops straight down into the net ('Hard cheese!'), followed by a second that actually manages to make it over the net – at last – and deep into the other side of the court. 'Out!' cries the young fellow's crafty opponent – 'but I'll take it!' *Thwack-whizz!* Love-thirty ('Hard cheese!'). The next serve also ends up in the net ('Hard cheese!'). The next one fails to materialise at all ('*Oh!* Hard *cheese!*'). Love-forty. The frightfully nice young fellow takes a deep breath, tosses up the ball and tries his very best to save the game: *Thwack!* 'Out! Hard cheese!' The second serve flies off sideways and ends up rattling into the wire fence. *Thwack-ping!* 'Oh, I *say!*' crows his tormentor. 'Smashing *cricket* stroke! Well, that's, ah, one-love. *Sure* you wouldn't like that handicap?'

This is *School For Scoundrels'* Raymond Delauney, otherwise known, *mutatis mutandis*, as *The Naked Truth*'s Lord Mayley, otherwise known as *I'm All Right, Jack*'s Major Hitchcock, otherwise known as *Those Magnificent Men in Their Flying Machines*' Sir Percy Ware-Armitage, Bart, otherwise known as *It's a Mad, Mad, Mad, Mad World*'s Lt-Col. J. Algernon Hawthorne – but always known, to his watching audience, as the one and only Terry-Thomas.

Terry-Thomas was – and remains – British cinema's favourite fake.

With his sly little moustache, his broad gap-toothed grin, his garish waistcoats, his ostentatious cigarette holders and his bright-eyed, gleefully 'up-to-something' way of saying 'Hell-*o*!', he was blatantly all form and no content, a comically inverted image of the conventional English gent. He was, in short, an absolute bounder.

What *is* a bounder? A bounder is not quite the same kind of character as a cad, a wastrel, an *arriviste* or a *parvenu*. Unlike his tougher cousin the cad, the bounder is not the type of person who is wilfully callous and cruel. Unlike the wastrel, the bounder is no hopeless slave to aimless profligacy. Unlike the *arriviste* – who is desperate to get somewhere – or the *parvenu* – who is desperate to stay there – the bounder is content just to nip in and out of there and elsewhere without ever being called on to pay the full price of admission.

A bounder is, in short, a crafty tall story – a distinctively English kind of free rider. He is a man who is prepared, in order to ensure that he gets his own way, to bend the rules of whatever is considered to be the proper type of adult behaviour, and slip a shiny shoe or two beyond the bounds of gentlemanly good grace. He is neither good nor bad, but merely childishly self-obsessed: a chronically mischievous, uncomplicatedly flawed and unashamedly sybaritic old rascal.

There have been plenty of bounders – half-baked and full-blown – in real life. Take B.J.T. 'Bosie' Bosanquet, for example: a very well-connected sporting Old Etonian and Oxford Blue, with a weakness for billiards, banking and long leisurely lunches, who popularised that most bounderish of cricketing actions, the notorious 'wrong 'un', or, as it also came to be known, the *googly* – a ball delivered with an orthodox leg-break action which, with a deviously unorthodox twist of the wrist at the moment of release, bounces towards the batsman from an impertinently unexpected *off*-break angle. 'Bad form!' gasped the watching gentlemen. 'Ding-*dong*!' giggled the watching bounders.

Take, as another example, none other than Bosie's very own son, Reginald Bosanquet, who read the news on British television for ITN during the 1970s. Dubbed 'Reggie Beaujolais' by a grateful *Private Eye*, this thrice-married soft-cheeked sybarite with the lop-sided grin became notorious for the tipsiness of his delivery, the woozy look of his wig and the louche nature of his on-screen exchanges with a succession of attractive young female colleagues. During bulletins he would disregard most of the urgent instructions that reached him via his earpiece, sniggered while reporting on an elderly lady's kitten that was rescued by the Army from high up a tree only to then be accidentally run over by their own truck, and sometimes hiccuped in the middle of sober political stories (thus inspiring the euphemism 'completely newscastered'). Away from the screen, he socialised with undisguised relish, demanding plenty of chilled white wine 'drunk from a pewter or silver goblet',[1] and was once discovered looking tired and emotional alongside a similarly worse-for-wear Oliver Reed deep in the bowels of the Royal Albert Hall (when both men should have been upstairs in the audience for a major television industry event), studying – so they claimed – 'the inner workings of the heating system'.[2] Late on in his broadcasting career, Bosanquet even had the nerve to slur his saucy way through a 'funky' pop record called 'Dance With Me': 'Dance, now, ladies ... Let me see you all *dance* ... There, *that's* it, that's *good* ... I feel rather splendid at present ...'[3] 'Unprofessional!' snapped the gentlemen. 'Unmissable!' sniggered the bounders.

Then there was the writer, musician, painter, raconteur and cofounder of the Bonzo Dog Doo-Dah Band, Vivian Stanshall – a sly young wag from Oxfordshire who kept his wit uncorrupted by commerce, fled from every job that threatened to become even remotely 'proper', and dedicated himself unreservedly to a lush life of imaginative and elaborate larks. On one celebrated occasion (which was then reprised at irregular intervals), he wandered into an unsuspecting London tailor's shop and started admiring a particular pair of sturdy-looking woollen trousers; his accomplice arrived, posing as another customer, and insisted that he wanted to purchase the very same item of clothing. The two men contested the issue fiercely by pulling at one leg each until, much to the watching tailor's horror, the trousers tore in half – at which point a one-legged actor (hired by Stanshall) hopped into the shop and exclaimed excitedly, 'Ah – just what I've been looking for!'[4] 'Juvenile!' moaned the gentlemen. 'Delightful!' cheered the bounders.

It was the same sort of thing, on the screen, with Terry-Thomas – only more so. He was never, in truth, a particularly *good* on-screen bounder, in the sense that his bounding was so easily bated, but his obvious incompetence – in addition to his unashamed incorrigibility – only served to make him all the more endearing.

In *School for Scoundrels*, for example, he tries to charm his way into the affections of his chum's new girlfriend ('Oh, hel-*lo*, hell-*oh*, hell-*ohhh*! Where did you find *this* lovely creature?') – first by showing off at his regular posh restaurant ('It's an *honest* little wine, especially if it's allowed to *breathe* for a while. Unless, of course, the grapes have had too much of the Dordogne *wind* – in which case they have a tendency to *sulk*. I think you'll *like* it!'), and then by cheating his way to a win over his fair-minded rival at tennis ('Hard *cheese*, old boy!') – but he still ends up being beaten by, of all things, a simple show of sincerity ('Just a minute! Something's gone wrong! *Stop that I say!*').

Similarly, in the rather harsher context of *Too Many Crooks*, he sets out to stash a tidy sum far away from the prying eyes of the men at Her Majesty's Treasury, and tries his best to appear blithely unconcerned when informed that his kidnapped wife will be cut into little pieces unless he coughs up the lion's share of the cash ('Start *slicing*, old fruit!'). By the close of the movie, however, he finds himself outwitted by a bunch of incompetent blackmailers ('I *fell* for it!'), and stuck not only firmly under the thumb of his defiantly uncut wife but also sharply in the sights of his newly acquired son-in-law (whose profession turns out to be none other than that of the deeply dreaded tax inspector).

Sometimes, such as in *Carlton-Browne of the F.O.*, he gets to play the kind of dim-witted and repressed English character for whom the business of bounding, though it undoubtedly holds some appeal, ends up being deemed a dare or two too far. Even when portraying such craven and quietly frustrated poor coves as these, however, he still manages to provide us with at least the odd tantalising glimpse of the corruptible old rogue who lurks within. Licking his lips and knocking back another strong glass of something-or-other as he watches a scantily clad table-dancer have her pert little bottom smacked, 'CB' allows himself to sit back and reveal the giveaway gap-toothed grin: 'Good *show*!' he whispers gratefully as the woman jumps down nearby and scampers off into the night.

Terry-Thomas would not have objected to being styled a bounder off the screen as well as on it – indeed, he often seemed to actively encourage such a patently one-dimensional portrayal – but, in truth, he was a far more admirable, interesting and complicated creature than that. No one, it seemed, was ever entirely sure who, essentially, he really was – even his own family was puzzled by how and why he came to seem so dazzlingly *sui generis* – but 'T-T' was the kind of enigma who engaged far more than he enraged. Whatever he was up to, it was fascinating for the rest of us to watch him go about it.

He contained contradictions, but in the kind of way that seemed, somehow, to make sense. Terry-Thomas was a self-made toff, a class-bound critic of the class system, a deft filleter of dubious privilege who took out all of the spiky conceit and left in only the fleshy fun. He was drawn not to the haughtiness (which is why he regarded the likes of the 'extremely snooty' Rex Harrison, who would ignore you if 'he didn't think that you were in his class', with a fair amount of disdain)[5] but rather to the hedonism. The promise of pleasure was what drove him on.

Born into a relatively unexceptional lower-middle-class English family from darkest Barnet, he began transforming himself at a very early age into a defiantly dandified kind of young gadabout. Like an anglicised version of West Egg's Jay Gatsby, the man who became 'T-T' would seem to have sprung 'from his Platonic conception of himself'.[6] He was not, he later acknowledged, the first Teddy Boy, but he did actually become, he declared proudly, 'the first Terry Boy'.[7]

It was from staid conventions that he went on to bound so determinedly beyond – all of those grim, fatalistic and class-based attitudes and outlooks that were suffocating so many once-bright British lives. 'I shall not be cowed' was always his motto,[8] and he really meant it, ignoring all of the snorts of derision at his knowingly *faux* way of speaking, dressing and behaving, and simply pushing ahead with his pursuit of a singularly pleasurable style of life.

He did more than just have fun, however, beyond the various boundaries over which he breezed. In addition to the crucial contribution he made in the movies to the Boulting Brothers' smart little post-war social satires, he also brought an impressively innovative wit and spirit to the fledgling era of British television. *How Do You View?* – his pioneering debut series from the late 1940s and early 1950s – was the first small-screen comedy show to really acknowledge, explore and exploit the medium that conveyed it, attempting everything from sharp comic close-ups to surprise shots of the cameras and crew. It was not Michael Bentine (with *It's a Square World*), Spike Milligan (with *Q*) or the *Monty Python* team who first taught television how to trick and twist and tease – it was actually Terry-Thomas.

Then he blazed a trail for other British comic actors in America, where he carved out a long and lucrative career for himself (not by mocking his compatriots, but rather by celebrating their splendid capacity for self-mockery). Appearing on US television alongside the likes of Judy Garland, Bing Crosby, Danny Kaye, Don Rickles and Lucille Ball, and in Hollywood movies with such stars as Jack Lemmon, Spencer Tracy, Jayne Mansfield, Rock Hudson, Doris Day and Jerry Lewis, he became every American's idea of how a mischievous English gent should look, sound and behave.

Although he was never given to remorseless self-analysis, he none the less always knew, on some conscious and comfortably workable level, what he was really up to, and why he was bothering to do it. Form became his content, and style his substance, as an ironic response to the heavy-lidded banalities of his time. As the critic D'Aurevilly once observed, 'Dandyism is the product of a bored society',[9] and Terry-Thomas, with his own inimitable brand of sartorial frivolity, cocked a snook at the chronically dull sobriety of post-war Britain ('If I chose to spend my bus fares on a carnation,' he once said defiantly, 'that, I considered, was my business'[10]). Even in plain old black-and-white, he was always the incorrigibly 'colourful' character, sending up the pretensions of the many 'temporary' gentlemen of the era while still appreciating the sheer rebelliousness of their cheek. Acknowledging 'how absurd' his public persona was, he said that it was his 'good luck' that he was 'able to earn a great deal of money by sending up pompous Englishmen, the sort of people to whom I had been exposed a lot as a young man. But I wasn't one of them. I suppose really I've cashed in on playing the lower-middle-class pretending to be upper-class.'[11]

That was Terry-Thomas: the actor who was so good at acting like an actor – not a *stage* or *screen* actor, but rather the kind of *social* actor who we all, to varying extents, are: a prosaic self-publicist, a show-off of (what we like to think of as) our best and most appealing self. Whenever we see him do it, we laugh at the persistence of our own childish vanity, and we warm to the memory of our own childish cheek and *joie de vivre*.

He may have died in 1990, but, in various ways, his influence has continued right through to this day. A role model for the urbane and worldly wise raconteur, an inspiration to the classier kind of ironist, a shining example for the budding individualist and an excellent guide for those who dream of being wittily silly, the spirit of T-T still engages with a wide range of tastes, attitudes, ambitions and ages. The children's television glove puppet, Basil Brush, for example, is an acknowledged terylene tribute to the spirit of Terry-Thomas (as are both Dustin Hoffman's depiction of the eponymous anti-hero in *Hook*, and, at least in vocal terms, Rupert Everett's portrayal of the devious and vainglorious Prince Charming in *Shrek 2*).[12] Ronnie Corbett's enduringly popular rambling anecdotes on BBC1's *The Two Ronnies* and elsewhere are another happy *hommage* to T-T. Similarly, successive generations of light-hearted iconoclasts have warmed to his indomitable addiction to fun, citing him as a kindred irreverent spirit. When, for instance, the British comedian Vic Reeves was invited by the makers of a television commercial for a mobile phone company to select his ideal recipient of a casual call, he had no hesitation in choosing Terry-Thomas: 'If I had a One-2-One with Terry-Thomas,' Reeves revealed, 'I'd find out if he really was a bounder ... I hope he was!'[13]

In London during March 1999, a National Film Theatre season of Terry-Thomas movies attracted not only lovers of old English cinema, 1950s comedies and Boulting Brothers social satire, but also a surprising number of young T-T fanatics. 'People have been turning up in evening dress,' said a delighted NFT spokesperson, 'with false moustaches and carrying cigarettes in long holders. And everyone has been trying to steal the cardboard cut-outs of Terry which are dotted around the foyer. We've never had a response like it.'[14] Traces of T-T have turned up in some of the most unlikely places: in 1998, for example, the big beat band Propellerheads featured a sample of his voice in the single named after one of his catchphrases, 'Bang On!',[15] and when the former middleweight and super-middleweight world champion boxer Chris Eubank was asked how on earth a black British sportsman from East Dulwich ended up wearing a bowler hat, a monocle, a cravat, a brightly coloured waistcoat, jodhpurs and spats on a regular basis, he explained that his role model had been none other than Terry-Thomas.[16] More predictably, the comedian Paul Whitehouse was another performer who tipped his hat at the memory of T-T by modelling one of *The Fast Show*'s resident characters, the 13th Duke of Wybourne, on the enduring image of Terry-Thomas: with his slightly rumpled dinner jacket, an opened bottle of champagne and a wicked glint in his eye, the raffish 13th Duke would always turn up, as if by accident, at various halls of residence, dormitories and French maids' finishing schools, and, standing in the middle of a room full of sleeping girls, would grin lasciviously at the camera and whisper, 'What? *Me?* Here? With *my* reputation?'

Terry-Thomas's own reputation, however, though still reasonably sound and secure, could actually do with another, much closer, look. It currently rests solely on the lustre of the shiny surface, and discourages us from exploring the hidden depths that lurked beneath. Here, however, was far more than a mere gap-toothed grin and a glinting eye. Here was also a delightfully shrewd actor, a strikingly clever comedian and a deceptively complicated human being. What follows, therefore, while celebrating the appeal of the familiar icon, will also seek to appreciate the achievement of the relatively unfamiliar figure who brought the bounder to life.

CHAPTER ONE

Hell-*o*!

I shall not be cowed.

THE PERSON WHO would one day become known to the world as Terry-Thomas was born on 10 July 1911, tiny, plain and unhyphenated, as Thomas Terry Hoar Stevens in what in those days was the relatively humdrum London suburb of North Finchley.[1] He would always claim to have come into the world on 14 July 1911 inside a house called 'Glenfern' in Nether Street, but, as his birth certificate confirms, the erroneous coincidence with Bastille Day seems merely to have served a subsequent humorous purpose ('The French, you may have noticed, celebrate my birthday by dancing in the streets'[2]). He actually emerged inside a smart little Victorian maisonette situated a couple of streets away from Nether Street, on the other side of what is now Finchley Central tube station, at 53 Lichfield Grove, Church End.

It is not clear why he ever felt moved to attempt such a modest deception, because, by his own admission, he always believed that he should have been born in a far better class of borough, and not merely a fractionally more fashionable sort of street. Apparently an out-and-out snob 'even as a nipper', the fledgling Thomas Stevens felt that he was the victim of some kind of frightful genetic mix-up: instead of growing up in a golden, glamorous, glorious part of England – which was where, more or less right from the start, he felt that he had been pre-programmed to pop up – this brown-haired and hazel-eyed little boy found himself stuck in the mundane, mediocre, lower-middle-class milieu of Finchley. It did not seem fair. It did not seem right.

It was not just dull old Finchley, however, that bothered young

Thomas Stevens; it was his family, too. His father, Ernest Frederick Stevens, certainly struck him as something of a disappointment. Although Ernest's own parents, Frederick and Julia, had been a 'jolly well-off' couple who had settled in Shepherd's Hill (which in those days was regarded as one of the smartest streets in Highgate), he was himself always struggling to live up to such lofty social and material standards.[3] A bowler-hatted butcher (or, as he might have preferred to be called, a 'provision merchant') at Smithfield Market, the lean and neat Ernest Stevens was (his son would grudgingly acknowledge) 'a stylish person up to a point', in the sense that he sported a conservative but 'immaculate' dress sense and invariably smelled 'like a first-class railway carriage', but, alas, the hoped-for *haute bourgeois* effect was forever compromised by a 'flat, toneless, London accent with very little character'.[4]

The precociously snobbish young Tom (as most of his family would always call him) was slightly more positive about his gregarious, gap-toothed and 'voluptuous' mother, Ellen Elizabeth (née Hoar), who, as one of the twelve doted-upon children of a fairly well-respected Islington horse dealer, always did her best to look and sound like 'a well-behaved duchess'.[5] He very much liked the fact that, in this respect, she did her best – her best, however, still left him distinctly unimpressed.

He suspected, in fact, that the feeling was probably mutual. Having already produced three lusty sons (John, Richard and William) since their marriage began in 1903, it seems that Ernest and Ellen had then gone and 'done their nut' trying for a daughter, and so the gender of baby number four had caused, supposedly, 'a general feeling of disappointment'.[6] Even the belated arrival (four years later in 1915) of the longed-for baby girl, Mary, failed to convince young Tom that he was really, truly wanted.

He was wrong. Both of his parents loved him. It was just that, as time went on and his nascent personality began to take shape, they found him a little *odd*.

Thomas Terry Hoar Stevens was indeed a little odd. Even *he* thought that he was a little odd. If, however, 'not being odd' meant fitting in with Finchley, then, as far as he was concerned, his oddity was not the problem.

Normality was the problem, and he was having none of it. Tom Stevens was adamant that he did not belong in such an 'extraordinarily rough' environment, living among such 'positively coarse' people who spoke in such 'nondescript' accents. He belonged, he reasoned, somewhere nicer, somewhere brighter, somewhere smarter: somewhere *posh*.[7]

The desire to be 'posh' certainly played a key role in the rise of his sense of restlessness, but so too (and perhaps even more so) did the need to be really happy. It seems that hardly anyone within the Stevens household, deep down, was genuinely happy with his or her little lot.

The quietly dapper and dutiful Ernest, for example, was a repressed extrovert with slicked-down hair, a severe side-parting and dark little eyes that seemed full of doubt and suspicion, and his true 'sportive' personality only really crept out when he took part, as an occasional supporting dancer, singer and actor, in the various productions of his local amateur theatrical company.[8] His wife Ellen, on the other hand, was a far more immediately engaging kind of character ('with a gift', according to her son, 'for getting on intimate terms with total strangers in under ten seconds'[9]), but she too had grown frustrated by how far what was real still fell short of her own ideal, forever hiding herself, as a consequence, behind a façade made up of the manners and accent of the 'grander' sort of person whom she knew she could never really become.

Even Tom, young and naïve though he was, could sense that something was going seriously wrong with his parents' marriage, and, as the years went by, he watched the two of them with secret feelings of sadness as they drifted slowly but inexorably further apart. Father had his interests; and mother had her interests; and seldom did they overlap and find a common cause. Neither seemed particularly content with the way that things were going, but both appeared more or less resigned to the drift of their discreetly unhappy fate.

Both of them, for example, had begun to drink a relatively excessive amount of alcohol on an increasingly regular basis, but more often than not they did so separately rather than together, and more to deaden the pain than to lift the spirits. Ernest, who was 'exclusively a whisky-and-soda man', struck his youngest son as someone who simply 'liked getting sloshed'.[10] Ellen, on the other hand, appeared less selective: 'She drank

anything. Regularly. But I never once saw her anywhere near intoxicated. Well-behaved duchesses naturally took great care never to be
seen to be tiddly.'[11]

Religious differences, among other things, had contributed to the
tensions that had risen up between them. Whereas Ernest remained a
decidedly earthbound 'non-practising agnostic' for whom a game of golf
at the North Middlesex was about as close as he ever came to commun-
ing with non-material matters, Ellen was an increasingly committed
convert to Roman Catholicism (and, much to Ernest's irritation, she
was becoming financially 'very lavish to Rome'[12]). Rarely, on a spiritual,
moral or practically any other kind of parental issue, did the two of them
see eye-to-eye.[13]

Young Tom did his best to link them back together through laughter,
acting the gap-toothed 'giddy goat' whenever he sensed it was most
likely to achieve the intended cheerful effect. He danced and sang, did
impressions, told jokes, recited comic monologues, invented 'frightfully
clever' bits of slapstick and generally played the fool. More often than
not it worked – 'My family thought I was the funniest person in the
world'[14] – but what light relief it provided proved disappointingly shallow
and short-lived. Although his father would respond to Tom's clowning
with the odd indulgent chuckle, he remained 'a somewhat remote
figure' to his son,[15] and the impact on Ellen seemed only marginally less
superficial.

The mood only lightened slightly during the holiday season because
such occasions were treated more like 'getaways' than 'get-togethers'.
Every summer, Ernest would rent a house (and a limousine with which
to get there) for a two-month family holiday at the cosy old seaside village
of Combe Martin in North Devon, but, on each occasion when his wife
and children departed, he always stayed behind at their home in Finchley and carried on clocking-in at work. Motions were gone through,
appearances were kept up, but no more than half of either heart was
actually invested in the relationship. The marriage was clearly destined
to end, eventually, in divorce, but not before young Tom and the others
had become accustomed to the kind of harsh familial coldness that
hovered above and around them.

It was from this domestic melancholy, as well as from the supposed social mediocrity, that Tom came to crave an escape. Acting like an 'only child' in spite of the fact that he was living with four siblings – 'I don't recall joining in my brothers' games or ever going out with them,' he would later admit. 'While they liked to do things together I tended to be a loner'[16] – his young life seemed defined by what it lacked. He thought of the hall door of his own home, through whose mosaic of multi-coloured glass he could glimpse a strange world of mauve skies, scarlet trees and blue lawns (which, if he moved his head a fraction to one side or the other, would suddenly become a world of green skies, golden trees and auburn lawns), and wished that the transparent reality outside would become so instantly and exotically beguiling.

There was simply not enough coloured glass about in Finchley to keep young Tom contented. He had tried being a loner, but just being alone failed to spirit him away from the flat sights and sounds of Finchley, and he wanted to do so much more merely exist in misanthropic isolation. He wanted the freedom to find a fresh life.

Such a life ought to be, he felt, much more like the kind of lives that leapt out from the pages of short stories by P.G. Wodehouse: light, bright, playful souls in spats who flitted gaily back and forth from metropolitan clubs to country estates, moving briskly on from one memorable adventure to the next. The more that he read about it, and thought about it, the more Thomas was sure that he would be far more at home as a denizen of a place like the Drones, swapping gossip with the likes of Tuppy Glossop, dispensing romantic advice to Bingo Little and playing sly little pranks on the pompous Oofy Prosser. The fact that such a place was fictional, he reasoned, was relatively inconsequential; he believed in it enough to think of it as real. The course of his own life, he hoped, would supply its confirmation.

Like some stubborn short-trousered existentialist, therefore, he resolved to recreate himself in accordance with his own nascent tastes and fast-budding ambitions, shunning anything that threatened to thwart his crafty self-completion. Even when his mother, with a spectacular lack of tact, warned him that he lacked the kind of looks that were most likely to attract a truly desirable wife, he merely shrugged his shoulders, rolled his tongue over the gap in his teeth and kept on hoping that nurture would improve on nature.[17] When he was about ten, for example, he started changing the way that he spoke ('I realized that good speech automatically suggested that you were well-educated and made people look up to you'[18]), modelling his delivery initially on the crisply modulated tones he associated with the Berkshire-born stage and cinema actor Owen Nares.

The somewhat frail, long-faced and wavy-haired Nares – one of England's most popular matinee idols of the time – sounded as though he had spent all of his adult life ensconced inside one of London's snootiest gentlemen's clubs, and this was precisely the kind of 'exclusive' metropolitan sound that young Thomas was now so keen to acquire – even if his early attempts to do so were more likely to elicit ridicule than respect. 'Tom,' one of his startled aunts exclaimed at the start of an unsolicited family visit, 'why do you have such a *peculiar* way of talking?'[19] 'That intrigued me,' he later said of her knowingly barbed remark, 'because I thought that *she* had.'[20] This was the first of many little shockwaves set off by his sudden and seemingly inexplicable transformation. His second cousin Richard Briers, for example, who was born in 1934, would recall growing up in an extended family that continued to wonder from where on earth this extraordinary 'T-T' creature had actually come:

> The odd thing was that he really was just a middle-class boy from Barnet. Exactly the same background as me except his family had money and mine didn't. His father was in the butchery trade, and had a perfectly ordinary, natural, standard English accent – as everyone else in our family did – and yet Terry, for some unknown reason, developed this sort of P.G. Wodehouse, Bertie Wooster, kind of character and way of speech. And what was even odder was: he never dropped it. Because other actors often put on different kinds of voices, and put on different dialects, but when the curtain comes down they become themselves again. But in Terry's case it stayed with him. He always spoke like that![21]

He was, as all of the rest of those around him soon discovered, virtually unembarrassable, so sure was he of the wisdom of his audacious reinvention. While most of the rest of Finchley conformed to all of the standard class conventions, the teenaged Tom Stevens skipped, strolled and swanned along to an unorthodox range of paradiddled sounds emanating from a very different, and, in his opinion, a vastly superior, kind of drum.

He was always prepping up on the various 'posh' toffs and show-offs who appeared willing to put themselves up on public view. He went to nearby Golders Green to see the new shows that were staged at the Hippodrome, and took in the latest Hollywood movies at the local Odeon; sometimes, when he had enough pocket money, he would catch a tram to the West End to sample some of the latest plays and musicals at the Coliseum. Always, wherever he went, he would be studying each performer and learning to mimic whatever they did, wore or said that struck him as suitably urbane, bright and elegantly apt.

One of the earliest sartorial stimulants, both on and off the cinema screen, was the debonair swashbuckler Douglas Fairbanks Snr – an American star renowned for his devotion to bespoke London tailoring (evening clothes from Hawes & Curtis of Jermyn Street; suits from Anderson & Sheppard of Savile Row; shirts from Beale & Inman of New Bond Street; shoes from John Lobb of St James's Street; and monogrammed velvet slippers from Peal & Co. of Burlington Arcade). Young Tom Stevens – who loathed the plain old clothes that he kept being given ('As a fourth child, everything I had was fourth-hand'[22]) – yearned to look as smart and as suave as the very famous Fairbanks ('an infallible way of attracting attention in England', he reasoned[23]).

He also fancied getting himself a pair of suede shoes, like those he spotted the English actor-manager Sir Gerald du Maurier wearing; and a daring midnight blue dinner coat, like those he heard that the then Prince of Wales, the future Edward VIII, was now starting to champion; and, while he was at it, one of those exotic-looking monocles, just like the one the self-mockingly severe Austrian movie director and actor Erich von Stroheim was known to sport. He could afford none of these things at present, but he was already dreaming of the day when he would be able to.

School came only belatedly, and proved to be no match for such a determined individualist. Although he exhibited an early aptitude for memorising any lines or lyrics that aided his efforts as an infant entertainer (William Makepeace Thackeray's light-hearted seafaring saga 'Little Billee' was one such childhood favourite[24]), he had remained unusually resistant to his parents' notion of 'knuckling down' and learning something for his general 'betterment', let alone studying something seemingly just for its own sake. An initial 'attempt' was made to educate him at a small local co-ed prep school, situated at the back of an enticingly pretty little garden stuffed full of loganberries, and run by a vivacious young woman named Norah Pratt, who 'loved kids and knew how to handle them'.[25] She took to Tom right from the start, indulging him in his oddity and encouraging him to cultivate his own peculiar act. He, in turn, loved her, but still loathed learning, and so his more formal academic work continued to fail to impress.[26]

He was soon moved, as a consequence, to a more 'organised' institution nearby (Fernbank School in Hendon Lane), and then, at the age of thirteen, he was sent on (thanks to some deep digging into the parental coffers) to a public school: Ardingly College, near Haywards Heath, in West Sussex. This red-bricked, three-storey and fairly austere Victorian educational establishment (whose motto is *'Beati Mundo Corde'* – 'Blessed are the pure in heart') was, his family felt, a far more impressive, imposing and 'ceremonious' sort of place, as well as a far better bet to shape young Tom into a slightly more 'sensible' sort of pupil, primed more reliably for a conventional adult life.

Ardingly, Tom would later confess, certainly came as 'something of a shock' to his still relatively delicate system.[27] It was a proper school. It had rules. It had blackboards. It had regular lessons. It had a set of stern-looking, gown-wearing tutors. It also had more than its fair share of *bona fide* swots and toffs.

Faced with this intimidating context and challenge, Tom Stevens decided, after a brief but intense period of callow panic, to respond with a bold, undiluted and sustained show of *chutzpah*. Instead of fading away meekly into grey, therefore, he resolved to explode into the full spectrum of colours. He found artful little ways to embellish his drab house uniform, caught the ear with his accent and the eye with his antics and generally did his very best to be found out playing the fool. Consenting only to be 'just exposed' to such edifying subjects as Latin, History, Geography 'and things', and soon dropping out of the school's sober little drama group (where his addiction to ad-libbing had caused a certain amount of friction), he devoted the vast majority of the rest of his waking hours to the school jazz band – initially as the boy who 'plonked the ukulele', then as an unpredictable comedy dancer and percussionist, and ultimately as a conductor.[28] Sport was fairly acceptable, he declared, so long as the weather remained suitably clement (catching trench foot playing cricket on a sodden pitch at kindergarten had left him, he explained, 'allergic' to the rain[29]). Only what struck him as fun was taken remotely seriously. 'My stay there,' he would go on to say of his unorthodox Ardingly years, 'was distinguished only by the time I spent marching up and down the fine court as a defaulter in the Officers' Training Corps, and by my revolutionary dress sense.'[30]

It was, none the less, a fairly inspirational place for an impressionable and upwardly mobile young show-off to start mastering his characterful art. The school's surroundings struck him as 'beautiful',[31] the many double-barrelled surnames as exciting and the rich mix of well-bred eccentrics as very endearing. He also took great pleasure in studying the array of crusty old eccentrics among the academic and administrative staffs, and paid particular attention to the many clipped and flat-lipped exclamations that came from his own house master, Major Plum-Crawford. 'Boy,' Plum-Crawford would bark in any real or imaginary crisis, 'go and get your *garse masque*.'[32] All of this, he felt sure, was edging him ever closer to the reality of his longed-for Wodehousian world.

He was enjoying his unorthodox education. Although the sum total of his formal academic achievements at Ardingly would not amount to more than one 'best in school' performance in an Officers' Training Corps exam (unless one also counts the solitary time when he managed to come top of his Carpentry class), there were plenty of extra-curricular highlights for him to savour elsewhere. The chief reason for this was the fact that his peers among the student jazz fraternity had picked him out as a special kind of 'character'. 'I would do anything to attract attention,' he later admitted. 'The satisfaction I got when I made people laugh was indescribably potent.'[33] The more that he larked about, he noticed, the louder and longer that those who watched him appeared to cheer. They even honoured him with his first bit of 'bill-matter', dubbing him 'The funny chap with the gift of the gap'.[34]

Such a reaction was just the sort of thing that he was after, and, for the remainder of his stay at Ardingly, he devoted himself to 'skylarking around'. Emboldened even further by a clandestine romance he had recently started back in Finchley with his family's new housekeeper – a slim-hipped, raven-haired and very confident young Cornish woman called Miss Kate Dixon, who would go on to sneak away his virginity one sultry but silent summer night in 1927[35] – he began to act more like a carefree man than a dutiful boy, and, rather than bow and scrape in the presence of his supposed superiors, he took undisguised pleasure in straining their patience. Most members of staff were definitely not impressed – especially when, at the end of a school concert in the presence of a fair number of very important parents, he conducted the national anthem to a syncopated tempo while pulling a succession of silly faces over his shoulder (Ardingly's 'peeved' headmaster made it eminently clear that he considered such antics to have been in 'very bad taste'[36]) – but they let him get away with it, and his fellow students kept urging him on.

He departed, branded an academic 'duffer',[37] shortly before his seventeenth birthday in the summer of 1928. Stuffing his belongings into the boot of his father's smart-looking hired car, he brushed back his brilliantined hair, flashed a gap-toothed grin at the block of rust-red sharp-arched buildings and bid his venerable old school a breezy little 'Pip-Pip!' That period of his life, as far as he was concerned, was now, without the slightest delay, well and truly over, and he sat back and relaxed as the motor chugged its way back to London. School was out, nothing else was planned and, regardless of whatever anyone else might have been thinking or hoping, the future was still most definitely on hold. There were certainly no regrets on his part about the apparent waste of an expensive education, and he duly 'loafed around contentedly' in the sunshine for the next month or two 'while [his] family held earnest discussions'.[38]

All kinds of potential solutions were sketched out for young Tom by various anxious relations. One scenario would have seen him dispatched to a Brazilian coffee plantation. Another suggestion was to send him away to a sheep station in Australia. A third, more obviously perfunctory, proposal was for him to make himself available for some sort of expedition to the Antarctic. The general consensus certainly seemed to favour him going somewhere a very long way away and then staying there for a good number of years.

It was probably in defiance of this desire that he agreed instead to accept his father's far more pragmatic advice and join him at Smithfield Market in London as a fifteen-shillings-a-week junior transport clerk with the Union Cold Storage Company. He knew that he would almost certainly hate every minute of it, but at least it struck him as better than, or not quite as bad as, counting beans in Brazil or shearing sheep in Australia.

In submitting to his father's prosaic advice, however, he feared that he might also be in danger of submitting to his father's plain and methodical style of life (whose only spot of excitement seemed to come at the moment each year when the sound made by the hanging of his hat on the stand in the hall changed from the 'donk' of a bowler to the 'plonk' of a boater), and so he duly did his best to make the prospect of a long-term career at Smithfield seem almost comically far-fetched. He made no attempt to blend in. In fact, he did all that he possibly could to stand out from the common crowd.

From his very first day in Smithfield Market (an environment best known in those days for its grubby white blood-stained smocks and cheap grey ash-flecked suits), he turned up for work, straight-backed and six foot tall, sporting an olive-green pork-pie hat, a taupe double-breasted suit decorated with a clove carnation, a multi-coloured tie and yellow washleather gloves, twiddling a long cigarette holder with one hand and twirling a silver-topped malacca cane with the other (the overall effect, he would later declare proudly, marked the 'first, fine, florid rapture' of his adult dandyism[39]). His bemused clerical colleagues – stooped in sober shades of grey, black or brown – called him 'the man with the carpet slippers', because, like Sir Gerald du Maurier before him, he now sported a pair of those 'revolutionary' brown suede shoes. His austere managing director, more sternly, informed him that he looked 'like a juvenile lead in a musical comedy' – to which Tom replied (with an exaggerated arch of the eyebrows and a sly little gap-toothed grin), 'Oh, how *awful!*'[40]

Undeterred by the less than positive reaction, he carried on regardless: 'I never stopped farting around.'[41] He did impersonations of the Hunchback of Notre Dame 'at the drop of a hat', strutted around like Erich von Stroheim (using as a prop the monocle he had made from a watchglass 'lost' by his father), mocked his superiors behind their backs and seized on every other opportunity to make 'the chaps chuckle'.[42] He started telling strangely compelling little stories about a set of characters who existed only within his own imagination, such as Colonel Featherstonehaugh-Bumleigh ('a charming fellow but an awful ass') and Cora Chessington-Crabbe ('a frightfully flirtatious little filly'), and used them more and more to make the 'boring office days bearable'.[43] He also joined the firm's amateur dramatic society, and immediately became one of its keenest members, volunteering for anything he could and making all kinds of bold and hopeful suggestions. He made his debut playing the portly, pompous and irascible Lord Trench in *The Dover Road* at London's little Fortune Theatre in Russell Street, and revelled in the applause his performance brought. 'The buffoon in me was released,' he would declare, and, from this point on, there was no hope of curbing his clowning.

He started clocking-in whenever it suited him – 'I felt that my impeccable appearance more than compensated for my habitual late arrival at the office'[44] – and relied on his bosses, many of whom were involved in producing the shows in which he now starred, to continue turning a blind eye: '[My chief] told me, one day, that he really ought to sack me for incompetence,' Tom later admitted. 'But he could not afford to lose me from his cast.'[45] Rather than sack him, in fact, his immediate superior chose instead to promote him (from docile office clerk to mobile meat seller) and make much better use of his crafty charm.

The unlikely elevation worked – after a fashion. Freed from the oppressive confines of the dozy office, he was able to flit around and

about town as an engagingly exotic individual, as well as slip off whenever seemed necessary to place a bet or two, play a spot of poker or
pontoon and plot his next evening performance. A fair amount of meat
was sold, but, more importantly, one big ham was handed some invaluable local exposure.

His first professional engagement, as an entertainer, arrived on 11
April 1930 when, at the age of eighteen, he appeared (billed as 'Thos
Stevens') as a 'cheerer-upper' at a social evening organised by the Union
of Electric Railwaymen's Dining Club in South Kensington. He was
paid thirty shillings for his efforts, but received precious few laughs from
his boozy audience. After repairing his 'damaged ego' by playing a
couple of small but noticeable parts in rehearsals of a Gilbert and Sullivan operetta produced by the Edgware Operatic Society, followed by a
succession of week-long runs at the Scala Theatre, he devoted an increasing amount of his time to the serious business of being a show-off. 'He
was an extraordinary creature,' Richard Briers reflected. 'He was never
trained to act. He was never trained to sing. He was never trained to do
anything. He just *did* it!'[46]

Upon reaching the age of twenty-two in the summer of 1933, Tom
Stevens finally found something that he had in common with his
employers at Smithfield Market: he came to the conclusion that selling
meat was never going to be his metier, and they agreed with him completely. He was thus brusquely 'booted out' – after being given a decidedly limp golden handshake – and then redeployed as an electrical engineer in a shop run by a good friend of one of his older brothers.

True to form, he made no attempt to 'become' an electrical engineer.
As usual, he just *posed*. The pose, on this occasion, was not good enough
– or at least not *safe* enough – to allow him to pass for a proper engineer,
but it proved good enough to get him another role as a travelling electrical salesman. Putting on his best hat and jacket and his cheekiest smile,
he duly sauntered from door to door, trying to sell 'electrical instalments'
to people whose homes were fitted only for gas, and radio plugs to people
who did not yet own a wireless. Few of the potential customers upon
whom he called were won over by his sales patter to the extent that they
reached for their wallets or purses, but it seems that many of them were

still thoroughly charmed by his extraordinary *chutzpah*: 'Your salesman is quite a card, isn't he?' wrote one highly amused (female) consumer. 'He even sang songs at the piano for me, played down at the bottom end, too. Just like a professional he was!'[47]

Prosaic electrical talk, however, soon began to eat into his valuable entertaining time, and so he moved on to what he hoped would prove more amenable forms of employment while continuing to moonlight playing the ukulele for a local jazz band called the Rhythm Maniacs. He tried his hand at being an insurance agent for the Norwich Union, but left after little more than a week ('my heart wasn't in it'[48]). Turning, rather more logically, to dancing as an approximation of a proper profession, he brushed up on his technique and began giving 'exhibitions' in partnership with the vivacious sister of the musical star Jessie Matthews, as well as attending weekly tea dances at his local Dickins & Jones department store and sometimes helping out at the popular Ada Foster School of Dance in nearby Golders Green. What little cash came his way went straight on embellishing his image. 'He'd get a bus into town and then he'd stroll down Park Lane,' Richard Briers would recall. 'Everyone knew him because of the way he dressed – you couldn't miss him! And the odd taxi driver used to say: "'Allo, Terry, do you wanna lift?" And Terry would say: "No, thank you – it's such a lovely day, I'll walk!" He hadn't got a bob in the world! The money was all spent on the clothes.'[49]

The closest that the dandy came to forging a full-time career in this particular field was a spell as a professional ballroom (or '*adagio*') dancer at the Cricklewood Palais de Danse, but, in spite of the lure of all the slim-hipped and long-legged women in their stockings and posh frocks (and the daydream of becoming a gigolo), he failed to summon up the requisite degree of effort and dedication. There were too many rules, he realised, and no real room for improvisation (let alone the bounder's anarchic antics), and so, yet again, he gave up and tried something else.

The thing that he tried next was to find work as a film extra. Now in his mid-twenties, he finally fled from Finchley and moved in with a friend of his named John Barnes, who had a smart little mews flat overlooking Lord's cricket ground in the far more upmarket area of St John's Wood. Barnes was a fellow dandy, 'cough-drop' and 'a bit of a card', and so he (with his bowler hat and brolly, Velázquez moustache and 'an Oxford accent that you could cut with a knife') and his new flatmate (who at this stage was turning himself out in a black homburg hat, black coat, houndstooth trousers, pearl-grey waistcoat and the obligatory clove carnation) soon became one of the most eye-catching double-acts about town.[50]

Barnes was already on call as a film extra, earning a guinea a day for his modest efforts, or thirty shillings if required to don a dinner jacket or tails. When, therefore, he found that an invitation to appear on set clashed with a rather more enticing offer of a long weekend in the country, his flatmate was only too happy to pop down to Pinewood and step in to take his place.

Right from the start, Tom felt entirely at home in the film environment. 'It wasn't really like work to me,' he later reflected. 'I got an enormous kick out of it: playing poker, drinking Champagne-and-Guinness for elevenses and telling the crowd funny stories during the long waits between takes.'[51] His father, upon hearing of this latest attempt to forge yet another new career, was appalled – 'If you think because you've played a ukulele and spent a few years fooling around on the amateur stage you can now earn your living in show business,' Stevens Snr warned his son, 'you must be crazy'[52] – but, as usual, young Tom remained totally undeterred. Spurred on by 'a lot of cocky faith in myself', he kept going back for more of the same, responding to whatever task was up for grabs by nodding excitedly and claiming: 'Yes, I'm frightfully good at it.'[53]

He stood around in crowds. He listened to other people talking. He picked things up and then put them back down, and sometimes put things down and then picked them back up. He even stood off camera and provided the sound of a cow.[54] In contrast to all of his previous jobs, in the movies he was happy to start at the bottom, accept everything that was on offer and wait patiently for the chance to make a mark. He knew where he was going, and was ready to enjoy the journey.

His first – uncredited – speaking part came late in 1935, in a movie (to be released the following year) called *Once in a Million*, when he was heard to shout 'A *thousand!*' during an auction scene (he promptly had some publicity cards made, describing himself as the man who had said "A *thousand!*"'[55]). He was also glimpsed during 1936 being stabbed to death by an angry Saxon (essayed by his fellow extra and future star Michael Wilding) in the Jack Buchanan period comedy *When Knights Were Bold*; tumbling head-first into a water tank (permanently damaging his hearing as a consequence) in the musical *This'll Make You Whistle*; dancing in both the Jessie Matthews vehicle *It's Love Again* (he was the one sashaying past the star while casting an indignant look in her direction) and the Stanley Lupino vehicle *Cheer Up* (in which he got the chance to share the screen, albeit fleetingly, with the leading lady, Jean Colin); getting drunk in Vic Oliver's variety revue *Rhythm in the Air*; and cropping up (uncredited as usual) later that same year in the film adaptation of the H.G. Wells science-fiction novel *The Shape of Things to Come*.

More bits and pieces followed, as well as the odd credited appearance in such low-budget movies as the comedy short *Sam Goes Shopping* (in which he played a dapper but callow beau about town) and the patriotic drama *For Freedom* (which saw him pop up in the distinctly undemanding part of a newsreader).[56] He also tried his hand – by way of a hobby – at writing a young man's guide to modern sexual etiquette, and managed to produce several pages of pertinently practical axioms (e.g. 'Always have an extra pillow handy. This can be slipped under the lady's bottom at the appropriate moment and will permit even closer contact'[57]) before deciding that much more empirical research would be needed (especially on the subject of 'deep-bosomed women') before the project could have any hope of being completed.[58] John Barnes (craving a slightly quieter life than the one now being enjoyed by his increasingly concupiscent friend) moved out of the St John's Wood flat, and a succession of 'jolly eager girls' – most of them budding starlets from Elstree, Denham, Pinewood and various sets elsewhere – moved in. Things were looking up, and, as he had always planned, he was having fun.

Always appreciative of the importance of a distinctive image, and increasingly eager to accelerate the pace of his progress, he decided that the time was now right to acquire a somewhat 'snappier' and more stylish-sounding name. 'Thomas Stevens' was, he reasoned to himself, far too stiff and stuffily suburban, whereas 'Tom' or 'Thos' sounded more suitable for a member of the supporting cast than it did for a would-be leading man. 'A name is awfully important,' he would reflect, 'and I had lots of struggle before I eventually found the right one.'[59] He tried for a short time – presumably out of desperation – the extraordinary sobriquet of 'Mot Snevets' ('Tom Stevens' spelt backwards) before returning rapidly to his senses. He then tried on for size the stage name of 'Thomas Terry' (the adoption of which, he feared, might be misinterpreted as an attempt to pass himself off as a relation of the illustrious thespian Ellen Terry) before settling, for the time being, on 'Terry Thomas' (the defining hyphen would take another nine years to arrive).[60]

The most eventful year so far for the newly named Terry Thomas occurred in 1938, when, in addition to his labours as a movie extra, he not only made his debut on radio but also married the woman who had recently come into his life. The radio debut took place on 6 June, when (for a fee of four guineas) he contributed a twee little turn to the BBC's afternoon tea dance programme called *Friends To Tea*; it was, he would later exaggerate, 'a dismal failure', but it led, none the less, to further occasional engagements at Broadcasting House.[61] The wedding occurred a little earlier in the year, when, following the proverbial whirlwind romance, he married a tall, thin, dark-haired and vivacious South African ballet dancer and choreographer named Ida Florence (or, as she preferred to be called, 'Pat') Patlanski.[62]

Patlanski, who had only recently arrived in London from her hometown of Johannesburg (where her father, Philip, owned an hotel and she had run a small ballet school), first encountered Terry Thomas in the autumn of 1937, when she was looking for someone to partner her in her Spanish-style dancing act. 'Look, I don't think I'll do for you because I can't really dance flamenco,' he confessed. 'My style is capering around in Cricklewood.'[63] She assured him, however, that what she needed was someone who could be funny rather than technically adept at flamenco, and so the two of them agreed to form a new cabaret double-act called 'Terri and Patlanski'.

Terri and Patlanski were in demand right from the start. They were lively, they were funny, they were different and they were good. 'Terri' would stride on to the stage, and, speaking with a cod-Spanish accent, he would say: 'Ladeez and gentlemen. The dance you just see is the tango. When a Spaniard make *loff* he is a caballero. A gentleman. But when a Mexican make *loff* he takes his *partnerrrr* and *tearrrrs* her to pieces. One minute, I show you …'[64] 'Patlanski' would then come on and be torn to pieces by the passionate Terri.

It was only a matter of weeks before the two of them were tearing each other to pieces, in a far more affectionate sort of way, in private. Pat struck Terry as 'a very neat, vibrant, well-read and enthusiastic little female', whose greater experience and worldly wisdom slightly unnerved but also excited him.[65] Terry struck Pat (who was almost nine years his senior and already twice-divorced[66]) as one of the most amusing, self-mocking and dapper-looking young men in London. Early in 1938, as a consequence, they decided to formalise their union, on the morning of 3 February, by marrying in a Marylebone register office (where, curiously, both of them lied about their age – he claiming, perhaps rather gallantly, to be thirty-one – when he was actually twenty-six – and she thirty-two – when she was really thirty-five). The couple eschewed going off on a conventional honeymoon in favour of 'a legal, Mexican-style romp' in the former bachelor flat at St John's Wood.[67]

The stage act lasted only a couple of months, but the marriage proved a little more enduring. After moving into their first home of their own (at 29 Bronwen Court, off Grove End Road, again in St John's Wood), the couple took whatever work cropped up on the cabaret circuit, while Terry sometimes supplemented, and sometimes diminished, their meagre finances by playing regular late-night sessions of roulette, pontoon and poker in various London clubs. A greater degree of stability was attained at the end of the summer, when Don Rico, the male leader of a women's touring orchestra, took on Pat as a pianist and then added Terry to act as a compère.

It soon became evident, however, that one or two cracks had already begun to appear on the surface of this still-infant marriage. The arguments – which had initially been rare and insignificant – were now far more frequent and unpleasantly intense ('There had been no screaming matches before we were married,' Terry would recall, but afterwards, he reflected ruefully, his wife took to flying 'into the most shocking rages'[68]), and in place of the love that had drawn the pair of them so quickly together came a hatred that would drive them just as rapidly apart.

Pat, Terry discovered, had been having casual affairs since the earliest days of their marriage, so now he too began to think relatively little of being unfaithful ('Talk about tit for tat,' he later lamented[69]). The problem with Pat, he felt, was that she distinguished far too neatly and conveniently between casual extra-marital sex and committed intra-marital love and affection. The problem with Terry, she felt, was that he had an immature – almost adolescent – attitude toward sexual relation-ships (his undisguised excitement at being invited to preside over the El Morocco Club's saucy 'striptease auctions', for example, left her dis-tinctly unimpressed[70]), and so he struggled to come to terms with the fact that he was now living with a woman who, besides being his wife, was also an individual in her own right, with her own needs, passions and passing fancies.

The two of them were, in truth, ill-matched as long-term lovers, even though they were suited to each other in many other ways both as close friends and trusted colleagues, but neither was inclined to analyse the roots of their mutual problems, and the tension was allowed to worsen. They continued to work together, more often than not, in the same shows (and sometimes in the same double-act), but, backstage and behind the scenes, the extent of their mutual suspicion, resentment and animosity was well on its way to seeming spectacularly and perilously acute. 'How such a lot of noise could be made by such a tiny person,' Terry would recall with a shudder, 'was incredible,' whereas Pat, more than a little disingenuously, would later complain that many of her worst rages were provoked by her husband's apparent indifference to the future of their union.[71]

Their bitter but relatively trivial domestic battle reached a precarious truce in the autumn of 1939, when Britain declared war on Germany, and they seized on the chance to secure some work touring home and abroad in support of the troops. A brand new body called ENSA (the

Entertainments National Service Association) was in the process of being set up by the film producer Basil Dean in order to provide a more organised form of entertainment for Britain's military personnel, and among the first wave of amateur and professional performers to sign up were Terry Thomas and Pat Patlanski.

The pair's first ENSA engagement – a cabaret in northern France – followed soon after, but, far from the booking breathing new life into their ailing alliance, it merely confirmed its imminent demise. The truth was that Terry had 'wangled' the assignment for him and his wife because he knew that his latest mistress, a young singer called Marilyn Miller, was already ensconced in the company. Miller (the daughter of a well-known dancer of the time, also named Marilyn) had, he would recall with relish, 'long legs, deep bosoms, a beautiful classic face and a stunning complexion' (she could also, he noted almost as an after-thought, sing 'reasonably well').[72] Once he had arrived, however, the presence of Pat proved something of a problem, and so, rather callously, he quietly arranged for her to be dispatched back to Britain and placed in another touring company. Predictably, the timing and order of subsequent shows became increasingly unpredictable, owing (Terry later confessed) to the fact that 'Marilyn and I were "rehearsing new numbers" upstairs in my room'.[73]

For a while, the relationship was on the verge of being blissful, with the pair of them dividing their off-stage time between lengthy sessions locked together in bed (a testimony, he would claim, both to the beauty of his lover and 'the endurance of the chap with the gift of the gap'[74]) and many bitter-sweet hours spent sipping champagne outside local cafés, as the night skies often flashed and fizzed with the violent lights that revealed glimpses of the brutal dog-fights high above. They thus made the most of each other while they could, but they knew deep down that the union was unlikely to last: no one was sure where the whole world was heading, let alone where each love was leading, and so each day was treated as something special, and every memory considered a treasure.

The relative calm and quiet that characterised the so-called 'Phoney War', they accepted, was destined not to go on, and, by the arrival of the spring of 1940, it became painfully obvious that it was not going to go on any further: 'Hitler marched through and round the Maginot Line,' Terry would recall, 'and in no time was doing his mad gig opposite the white cliffs of Dover.'[75] The two lovers returned promptly to London, went sadly their separate ways, and then continued working for ENSA.

Terry Thomas kept himself busy working on his new solo act, while also attending to his various duties as the newly appointed head of the cabaret section of ENSA at its London base at the Theatre Royal in Drury Lane. He soon acquired a reputation as a very polished and popular performer, as well as a surprisingly firm and feisty organiser ('Look,' he would bark at Sir Seymour Hicks, his far more experienced opposite number at ENSA's drama division, whenever the latter attempted to challenge him over any particular issue, 'there's no point in farting at thunder!'[76]), and it seemed that he was at last starting to settle inside his very own safe and fairly secure little niche. Then, in 1942, he received a rather abrupt and unwelcome surprise: 'a cunningly worded invitation to join the Army'.[77]

Fearing that it would seem somewhat 'rude and ungrateful to refuse', even though he felt that he was already gainfully engaged in the war effort with ENSA, he accepted the invitation 'with dignity, if not enthusiasm', and prepared to report for duty.[78] It was time for the rule-breaker to follow some rules.

CHAPTER TWO

I Say!

My job is to make people laugh,
not put the world right.

THE SECOND WORLD WAR started for Terry Thomas in the north of England, when, on 23 April 1942,[1] he was instructed to join the Royal Corps of Signals at its training depot at Ossett in West Yorkshire. Arriving in a large silver-coloured hire car, and laden with masses of personal luggage (containing everything from a wide range of 'fine raiment' to a large collection of costumes, scripts, wigs and false noses), he swanned into the guardroom with a fancy Spanish guitar under his arm and the faint smell of vintage Pol Roger champagne on his breath. This war, for him, was destined not only to be against Germany; it was bound to be against his own so-called superiors, too.

'What's your *number*?' barked the tall, square-jawed, squinty-eyed sergeant-major, who could see that he had a 'theatrical type' on his hands. Terry Thomas smiled benignly, revealing the crafty old gap-toothed grin, and answered brightly: 'Kensington 0736.' The sergeant-major stifled a sudden gasp of indignation, thrust out his chest, stuck out his chin, and stuffed a slip of paper into this troublesome young wag's hand. 'You ain't Terry Thomas any more,' he crowed. 'You are now just an effing number!' What happened next, however, shook up the sergeant-major far more than he could ever bear to admit. 'Yes mate,' grinned Thomas with a charmingly defiant but vaguely unnerving sort of semi-growl: 'Number One!'[2]

What followed, as a result of this initial show of insolence, was an 'awful' five weeks for Terry Thomas.[3] He was made to run several times more often than anyone else every day, over distances that grew longer and at a pace that grew faster, and was rarely given more than the minimum amount of time to recover. He gasped, coughed and retched, and the sergeant-major stood by and smiled. Predictably, his feet (traumatised by such a brusque transition from light suede shoes to heavy leather boots) were a cause of agony from dawn until dusk, and he felt 'stiff inside as well as out'. He also started suffering from a chronically nervous stomach: 'A duodenal ulcer was prodded into activity.'[4]

For once, however, the sergeant-major's bullying tactics backfired when it came to humbling an unorthodox spirit. 'The Army brought out in me my two strongest characteristics,' he would recall: 'I hated to be under-estimated and I was extremely competitive.'[5] Far from appearing close to being crushed, therefore, he began to give every impression of being 'frightfully keen'.[6] He worked hard, hid the pain, 'saluted almost everything that moved' and did his very best to stand out and impress (and, just to show his sergeant-major that the performer inside the soldier would never, ever be cowed, he hired Ossett Town Hall and staged a Sunday night concert).[7] His efforts paid off: at the end of the preliminary training period, he was awarded the Senior Soldier Flash 'A' for being the best recruit, and promoted to the rank of corporal.

He was duly posted to a base of (in his words) 'Cromwellian austerity' at Huddersfield, where he was assigned linesman duties (which mainly involved climbing up and down, and sometimes perching on the tops of, telegraph poles twenty feet high – a daunting task for someone who felt dizzy 'at no greater height than a cocktail bar stool'[8]), and – ever the fan of higher status and better costumes – he began to set his heart on earning a commission.[9] By the time, however, that he had endured two further postings elsewhere in West Yorkshire (first to Dewsbury, where it nearly always seemed to snow, and then on to Shepley, where it nearly always seemed either to snow or rain), his hopes had been dashed by a significant decline in his health. In addition to the physical problems that had persisted since his first few traumatic weeks of training, his hearing difficulties (caused initially by that injudicious water stunt during his days as an extra on movie sets) were now deemed to be in genuine danger of growing worse. 'You don't stand a hope in hell of getting a commission,' an Army doctor told him, and, following a meeting of the medical board, it was decided that he should be down-graded from A1 to B1 at the start of 1943.[10]

He was not too disappointed by this news because, shortly before the decision was made, he had been offered a place in one of the newly formed services-sponsored touring revues called, collectively, *Stars in Battledress*. Drawing on the best talents to be found among the whole of Britain's armed forces (rather than being limited, as the original concert parties had been, to whatever was on offer in a local division), *Stars in Battledress* therefore carried a considerable cachet and promised one or two rather pleasant little perks for any potential member, and so the invitation held huge appeal.

Captain George Black, one of the officers in charge of the tour's 'Central Pool of Artistes', had been in the audience for a Sunday concert at the Astoria Cinema in York when Terry Thomas strolled on to the stage and performed one of his tried and tested sketches (focussing, on this occasion, on a range of improbable treatments for a soldier's aching feet: 'everything from Epsom Salts and vinegar to methylated spirits and a mustard poultice'[11]). Black (whose impresario father, George Black Snr, had been responsible at the end of the 1920s for turning the London Palladium into a profitable theatre, as well as for founding the endur-ingly popular Crazy Gang comedy troupe) was a shrewd judge of nascent talent, and so, more or less immediately, he saw something in this droll young dandy that made him eager to sign the man up. The military downgrading, therefore, merely made it even easier for Terry Thomas to re-embrace the world of entertainment, and so he accepted Black's offer with undisguised relish.

His first official contribution to the troupe took place about a month into 1943 in London at an Army show based at Olympia. It took the form of a routine (inspired by the plight of a well-known newsreader of the time called Bruce Belfrage, who, one evening shortly after the start of the London Blitz, had been obliged to stay on air, while being showered in plaster and soot, straight after Broadcasting House had been bombed[12]) that he had devised a couple of years or so earlier, on an ENSA tour, while sitting in a run-down Norwich pub 'drinking the worst beer I had ever tasted in my life'.[13] Entitled 'Technical Hitch', the sketch (which featured him as a similarly harassed BBC announcer) began with him rushing on to the stage, shouting at someone in the wings to 'pay off the taxi', and then searching desperately for the missing records that were due to be played next on air. After being beaten by the red light, he proceeded, somewhat breathlessly, to introduce himself to the listening audience as 'their old friend', Freddie Featherstonehaugh-Bumleigh (which, he pointed out, should be pronounced 'Freddie Feston-Hay'), and then announced that the first 'simply spiffing' gramophone record he was set to play was of Al Jolson singing 'Sonny Boy' – which, in the absence of the actual recording, he had no choice but to sing himself while waving his jazz hands hopefully at the microphone. At the end of this spirited impersonation, he mouthed hysterically at his pianist, '*Where are the records?*' When his equally hysterical pianist mouthed back words to the effect that he had no idea where any of the wretched records were, and suggested, *sotto voce*, that Freddie 'should go and get stuffed', he twitched, grimaced, and then launched into further, and increasingly mannered, impersonations of Britain's clipped crooner Noël Coward, the African-American bass-baritone Paul Robeson, the Peruvian songbird Yma Sumac, the Austrian tenor Richard Tauber and – positively the last straw – the entire Luton Girls Choir. Finally, after one more frantic search for the missing discs, he signalled the breaking down of the turntable by making squeaking noises and clicking his thumb against his front teeth. 'I'm sorry,' he announced apologetically. 'We seem to have a technical hitch.'[14]

Even though it lasted an epic twenty-six minutes, the routine (brightened by all kinds of topical references, lively slapstick sequences, sophisticated one-liners and the odd 'racy' allusion) appears to have struck those who saw it as refreshingly novel and well-observed.[15] 'The audience lapped it up,' he later claimed, 'and I was "made" overnight.'[16]

He then joined a number of other performers – including the violinist Eugene Pini, the tenor John Duncan and a 'light classical' string sextet – for a *Stars in Battledress* national tour, overseen by the Cockney stand-up comic Charlie Chester. The venues were generally large and long-established, the shows (compared to the run-of-the-mill divisional concert parties) were fairly rich and well-presented, and the captive military audiences (grateful for the distraction) were noisily enthusiastic. Working on a regular basis in front of these live and attentive audiences, Terry Thomas soon improved as a crowd-pleasing performer and compère, not only by making the most of his 'turn' as the all-purpose pompous-ass character 'Corporal Stevens', but also by tightening up and refining his 'Technical Hitch' routine to such an extent that, by the end of the tour, it was running for a far more disciplined twelve-and-a-half minutes.

He never looked back, and spent the rest of the war as one of the most prominent and influential members of *Stars in Battledress*, taking his own unit (as a newly promoted sergeant[17]) all over Britain and most parts of occupied Europe. He also managed – like a number of other canny performers – to sneak away every now and then to make an unbilled appearance, quite illegally, at various clubs on the West End cabaret circuit (where a more sophisticated style of material could be attempted, and a better quality of brandy imbibed).

Making the most of the unofficial licence he now enjoyed as a 'special' sort of soldier, he seized on every opportunity to erase any trace of regimentation from his appearance: growing his hair a little longer than would normally have been allowed, re-adopting his old cigarette holder and persuading the wardrobe department to help him create his very own bespoke form of battledress. Even his commanding officer, Lieutenant-Colonel Basil Brown, was secretly impressed by such striking sartorial impudence: 'Terry managed to get hold of one of those leather jackets issued to drivers,' Brown recalled. 'He also got a great big fur collar which he had put on it and a service cap which he succeeded in pulling back so that it looked like an officer's in peacetime. He looked very smooth and wherever he went he was saluted by the troops, left, right and centre.'[18]

It was not as though he was in any way oblivious to the plight of the 'proper' soldiers; on the contrary, like the rest of his fellow performers, he took the task of being a military 'cheerer-upper' very seriously indeed – particularly when it came to lifting the spirits of those young men who were far from home and unsure of their future. It was just that he had no time for what he called 'Army "bull"', and his artful irreverence was his way of keeping the worst of it at bay.[19]

After D-Day, he took another *Stars in Battledress* show to Europe, travelling through France and Belgium as they were liberated, and reaching Germany in May 1945. He was, by this stage, back in more or less full 'TT' mode: wearing a 'wonderful uniform' that had been specially made for him by one of Winston Churchill's favourite tailors, waving around a new malacca cane and dispensing Wodehousian phrases as if they were freshly cut flowers, he did his best to remind everyone that colourful eccentricity was no longer expressly forbidden. His attitude also matched the mood of the military's rank-and-file, because, for all of his quaint Edwardian airs and graces, he, like them, was clearly keen to see the end of the pointless deference. His targets, in his comedy, were the kind of parade ground bullies, bumptious bureaucrats and bemedalled buffoons who had made so many ordinary soldiers' lives a misery over the course of the past few years, and so the sight of each punctured pretension set in motion another large wave of laughs.

It did not matter when he appeared (sometimes it would be early in the day and sometimes unusually late at night) or where (a conventional theatre, a pungent-smelling shed, a hastily assembled stage somewhere out in the open air, the top of a dusty hillock or a ledge on the back of a truck); he kept on growing in confidence, expertise and enthusiasm as each new test was passed. 'I picked up an enormous amount of experience,' he would say of these days in *SIB*, 'because, in the open market, one wouldn't be working fifty-two weeks a year, doing shows in all kinds of circumstances. If you can be funny at eight in the morning you can be funny anywhere.'[20]

Colleagues were particularly impressed, and somewhat intimidated, by how driven and determined he seemed to be when it came to conjuring up comedy: 'The only time old Terry is really serious,' said one co-performer at the time, 'is when he is putting on a show. I thought working with him would be a lark, but in the theatre he is worse than any sergeant-major.'[21] They were merely the first in a very long line of people to be unnerved: as frivolous and carefree as he often aspired to appear, Terry Thomas would always be, when at work, as tough, as testy and as meticulous as any other unrepentant perfectionist. He really did want to put on the most memorable show that was possible.

When the time finally came for him to return to England, he was dispatched to join the staff of the Central Pool of Artistes (now re-christened 'Combined Services Entertainment'[22]) at its elegant London HQ on Upper Grosvenor Street, W1. It was here that he started to witness what soon came to seem like an endless succession of his fellow young and up-and-coming entertainers – including Benny Hill, Bryan Forbes, Ian Carmichael, Frankie Howerd, Norman Vaughan, Kenneth Connor, Janet Brown, Arthur Haynes, Michael Denison, Peter Sellers, Reg Varney, Terry Scott, Billy Dainty, Bill Pertwee, Wilfrid Hyde-White, Spike Milligan, Graham Stark, Peter Ustinov and the budding actor Ivan Owen (who would later find success, if not quite fame, for himself as the unseen co-creator, voice and manipulator of an eighteen-inch puppet fox – called Basil Brush – whom he modelled on none other than his old friend T-T[23]) – passing through on their way back to find work in the post-war civilian world.

Thomas, now tired and somewhat unwell after his hectic year on tour abroad, suddenly felt that he was in danger of being left behind, and so, with a mounting sense of panic, he started to seek a quick means of release. 'I'd told thousands of troops all over Europe that they'd see me in a West End show after the war,' he would recall, 'and I wanted to keep my promise.'[24] Fortunately for him, however, one of his colleagues intervened before he could be tempted into doing something rash. 'Why on earth do you want to get out?' a sympathetic entertainments officer exclaimed. 'I can tell you a way to stay in and be out at the same time.' Thomas was intrigued. 'How?' he asked. 'Go up to your colonel,' explained the officer, 'and ask him for twenty-eight days' compassionate leave. At the end of it, you report back and he gives you another twenty-eight. You can get in some variety dates and you'll be getting Army pay as well.' Thomas's eyes sprang open wide and the gap-toothed grin flew back into view: 'Goodness gracious me! Well, thank you very much. Cheers!'[25]

Thrilled to have been alerted to such a lucrative loophole, he lost no time in making the most of it, getting in contact again with his old captain, George Black (who was now back in civilian life and working alongside his brother, Alfred, for their father's Stoll Moss Theatres Group), and putting his name forward for any bookings that might be available on the variety circuit. Black was delighted to have Thomas back on his roster, and found him work more or less immediately at some of the best theatres and clubs in the country. Accompanied by his pianist, the recently demobbed Harry Sutcliffe, Thomas duly reprised all of his old Army routines (with 'Technical Hitch', of course, as his *pièce de résistance*), and also began to develop one or two new ones as he moved from one venue to the next. Interrupted only once a month by the need to travel back to London to 'wangle more leave' from HQ ('What a wheeze!'), the nationwide tour provided him with invaluable experience, as well as plenty of priceless exposure, and set him up very nicely indeed for his imminent return to civilian life.[26]

Another potentially influential old friend whom he re-encountered during this period was the producer Philip Hindin (one of whose later claims to fame would be adapting the American show *Call My Bluff* for the BBC). The two of them had known each other since the mid-1930s, when TT was doing crowd work as an extra at movie studios and Hindin was working for the casting office Wielands. When Hindin bumped into the performer again just after the war, he was delighted to resume his friendship with someone whom he regarded not only as 'a real nice guy' but also a serious prospect for a successful career in show business:

> He reminded me that just prior to our joining up I had booked him ten link-up broadcasts for Radio Luxembourg at £5 a time and that he'd never paid me commission! He offered me a fiver which I refused. I said he was going to be a big star and I wanted to be able to walk down Charing Cross Road and get a laugh out of telling the pros that 'Terry-Thomas still owes me a fiver!'[27]

At the start of 1946, while Thomas was still officially attached to the armed services, he came to an arrangement with Jack Adams – of the theatrical agency Archie Parnell and Company in Soho's Golden Square – to represent him as a professional performer, and Adams was soon alerting a wide range of potential employers to the likely appeal of his new client.[28] Early in March, Thomas himself – aiming his sights high as usual – wrote to Eric Spear, an eminent BBC producer, with a proposal for him to star in a radio show all of his own (and Spear, in turn, was sufficiently intrigued by his audacity to consider helping him shape a sample script).[29] By the middle of March, the perpetually-on-leave Sergeant Terry Thomas let it be known (mainly by those who did not yet know him) that he would from now on be managed by the newly established International Artistes organisation in High Holborn (run by a famously redoubtable young woman called Phyllis Rounce), as well as being assisted by Jack Adams at the Archie Parnell agency. He was clearly champing at the bit.

Relief came at last on 1 April 1946, when he was formally demobbed and was free to 'come out' as a professional entertainer. Appalled at both the style and the standard of the demob suit that he had been given (an ill-fitting double-breasted, dark blue, twill-weave woollen item churned out cheaply by Britain's so-called 'tailor of taste', Montague Burton), he promptly sold it for £10 and went shopping for a few new colourful waistcoats. Back came the cigarette holder, the clove carnation, the silk ties, the white gloves, the fancy jackets and the suede shoes. He was ready to resume the bright life of 'TT'.

He could not do so immediately as far as his living arrangements were concerned, because both he and his semi-estranged wife Pat (who was currently on tour – with her latest lover in tow – in another concert party-style revue) had been made homeless by a German bomb during the war. He therefore decided, for the short term, to make the best of a bad situation, and converted a derelict wooden barn behind one of the large houses in London's Old Brompton Road. Dubbing it 'Ye Cowshed', he crammed it full of exotic souvenirs from his *Stars in Battledress* tours, placed a couple of flower displays outside and swanned on regardless. He then found a suitable centre of daytime operations: Daddy Allen's Club – a modest first-floor bar and restaurant above a shop in Great Windmill Street. One of the most appealing things about Daddy Allen's was its ideal position for meeting prospective collaborators or employers from either nearby Archer Street (where the Musicians' Union had its HQ) or the Windmill Theatre itself; among other positive features was the fact that the club had a licence to sell alcohol throughout the afternoon, served roast lamb with two veg for the tiny sum of one shilling and ninepence, and employed a young waitress called Jenny Bell whom T-T described admiringly as having 'knockers like Bentley head lamps'.[30] It was here that he could stand at the bar, have a few drinks and swap gossip and tips with the likes of such other budding entertainers as Harry Secombe, Tony Hancock, Peter Sellers, Michael Bentine, Jimmy Edwards and Spike Milligan, as well as up-and-coming writers such as Frank Muir, Denis Norden and Eric Sykes. The networking duly commenced in earnest.

His agents began knocking on doors at the BBC. Jack Adams wrote to the bookings department on 26 April, pointing out what Thomas could do, what shows he would suit and at what venues he could be seen. On 30 April, one of Adams' colleagues, L.M. Barry, followed up this letter with an enthusiastic recommendation of their client to any prospective producer, describing him as 'one of the best of the new post war Acts that I have seen and should be terrific for broadcasting'.[31] The agency also bombarded the offices of all the major impresarios, inviting them to take in one of Thomas's forthcoming appearances on tour. Such hustling ended up paying off, because a fair number of prominent movers and shakers did take the trouble to have a look at the performer for themselves, but the first one to act on his interest turned out to be none other than George Black, who signed Thomas up for a role in a new production that he and his brother were planning for the West End.

Entitled *Piccadilly Hayride*, it was to be the first major theatrical production overseen by George and Alfred Black following the recent death of their father, and it was designed as a showcase for the prodigious comic talents of Sid Field. Probably the most original and inspired British comic actor of the immediate post-war period, Field drew on a repertory of peculiar characters (including a cockney spiv called 'Slasher Green'; an effeminate, velvet-coated portrait photographer; a pompous professor of music; and a camply dim-witted novice golfer) to amuse his broad audience. Having shot belatedly to national fame in 1943 as the star of the revue *Strike a New Note* ('No comic', wrote J.B. Priestley, 'can ever have had greater immediate success, going up like a rocket that exploded its gold and silver in the darkness of wartime London'[32]), and earning the admiration even of the most competitive of his local rivals (Arthur Askey would recall fondly that, when an extra matinée was added to the run, 'every pro in London booked seats to see this wonderful new comedian'[33]), Field was now being fêted by the likes of Cary Grant, Bob Hope, Jack Benny, William Powell, Groucho Marx, Danny Kaye, Stan Laurel and Charlie Chaplin, as well as celebrated by the critics as Britain's new 'clown prince'.[34] He was, in short, *the* big comedy star of the moment, and Terry Thomas – who was already a firm admirer – could not have been more thrilled to be made part of his cast.

Opening at the Prince of Wales Theatre on 11 October 1946, the twice-nightly show was an immense success right from the start (so much so that the management took the unheard-of step of shutting down the booking office for several days to allow the staff to deal with the exceptional rush of advance bookings), and it would go on to run for no fewer than 778 performances (attracting more than a million paying customers and taking over £350,000 at the box office – thus winning praise in theatrical circles for being the West End's biggest money-spinner in years). Thomas's role was primarily that of compère, which made him, in effect, the second comic lead. Apart from providing brief but witty introductions for such supporting acts as the French-born ventriloquist Robert Lamouret and his 'talking' puppet duck Dudule, Thomas also performed an updated version of his 'Technical Hitch' routine, and, most memorably, appeared alongside Sid Field in an opening sketch that purported to be about a day in the life of King John. Playing the part of the effete cook Lambert Simnel, he was first seen carrying a cup of tea on a silver tray into the apartment of the king (played by Field in the style of Slasher Green):

SIMNEL: [*Enters stage left*] Good morning.
KING: Mornin' Brighteyes – how are yer?
SIMNEL: Nicely thanks.
KING: Where's me tea?
SIMNEL: [*Pointing to tray*] Thy tray is *ici*.
KING: [*Suspiciously*] How do you mean, 'It's easy'?

SIMNEL: No, no, I said '*ici*'. It's all right – I've gone all French. [*He gives a high-pitched falsetto laugh*]

KING: [*Irritably*] Shut up doin' that first thing in the morning!

SIMNEL: What do you want for breakfast?

KING: I'll 'ave some kippers.

SIMNEL: Kippers? Good gracious, you have them *every* morning – you'll turn into one, one day!

KING: Well? It don't matter to *yew*, dew it? Don't stand there lookin' at me as if you've never seen me before. Git out and get me breakfast worked in 'ere or I'll break your wickets!

SIMNEL: You are beastly! [*Crossing to a door on the right*] You are unkind! Sometimes I think you take *pleasure* in upsetting me! I *know* you think I'm ugly!

KING: *GIT AHT OF IT!*[35]

The playful, quick-witted and comically elegant Field dazzled Thomas as this sketch progressed: 'Sometimes it took me five minutes to compose myself enough to say my line because Sid made me laugh so much,' he would recall. 'He never stopped ad-libbing. You had no idea what he would come out with. One night he looked at me and said, "You iron!" This was a cockney rhyming slang abbreviation for "iron hoof". In other words – he was calling me a poof!'[36] Field made Thomas 'corpse' so often in another sketch, in which he was meant to spring up in the stalls in the middle of a Slasher Green spot and start heckling the character, that it started ruining the running time and ended up being dropped from the show.

It was by raising his game in order to survive on the same stage as this clever, inventive and – mercifully – generous performer that Thomas was assisted to come of age as a comedy actor: '[Sid] was easy to get on with; a marvellous person to have around, very friendly and warm. Even though he was the star of the show, he seemed not to mind that the newspapers gave such a lot of coverage to me [as well as to him]. I even had a two-page article in *Punch*.'[37] In truth, Sid Field was on such fine form that nothing – and no one – could have shaken his own sense of personal and professional satisfaction, but there was no doubt either that the huge success of *Piccadilly Hayride* also helped to make Terry Thomas, within a matter of a handful of days, into a genuine show-business 'name'. A mere three weeks into the show's run, for example, the newspapers – several of which had already been predicting a wide range of positive things for him – revealed that he had been added to the bill of the forthcoming Royal Variety Performance. Thomas, contemplating taking his first bow before the King and Queen on the stage of the London Palladium, was ecstatic: 'I'd arrived.'[38]

Now on a basic wage of £200 a week (more than £18,000 by today's values), supplemented by the payments he was earning from a string of lucrative one-off cabaret engagements (he would go out on a lorry with a piano and a pianist and play at various clubs, private parties and Masonic functions in and around the West End), he felt that the time was right to start living in the high style to which he had always longed to become accustomed. He therefore found a smarter place to live (an elegant, upmarket property at 11 Queen's Gate Mews, a short stroll away from the Royal Albert Hall in South Kensington[39]), hired a housekeeper, Doris Cooper (the sister of Gladys, the well-known actor), to fuss over his food and furniture, iron his morning newspaper and 'ensure that I would always be immaculate', and a secretary, Joan Haigh (who was later replaced by the much longer-serving Helene Moody), to keep an eye on his increasingly busy schedule. He also bought the first of his many much-loved sporty 'spin-arounds' – a smart new bull-nosed Morris motor car ('open, of course, with a wonderful little dicky-seat and a Hotchkiss engine') and 'borrowed' a butler/chauffeur called Harrup ('an extraordinary fellow who out-Jeeved Jeeves') from a well-to-do friend named Geoffrey Marriott.[40] Then, of course, there was a large wardrobe to restock.

He bought most of his formal clothes from Cyril Castle and his riding gear from Huntsman – both of them based in Savile Row. Mr Castle made him twenty-four suits to be worn on a rotating basis, and every special requirement was incorporated into each of his designs: a breast pocket seven inches deep to accommodate a cigarette holder; an extra-tight, straight-cut lapel buttonhole guaranteed to hold a fresh flower snugly in place throughout the day (pins were simply out of the question); various shades of coloured silk coat linings; gold or silver side-grips (in addition to brace buttons) on the trouser waistbands; and carefully weighted stays at the trouser cuffs to protect them from rubbing against the heel of either shoe.[41] Ever the perfectionist with an obsessive attention to detail, he even went so far as to start ordering a range of tailor-made underpants.[42]

Ties, too, were always very important to Terry Thomas, who could often, he admitted, be 'terribly temperamental' about them.[43] Masses of the things, therefore, started tumbling in from Jermyn Street: silk ones, woollen ones, plain ones, patterned ones, patriotic red-white-and-blue ones and the odd 'jocular' one – the more, and the more varied, the merrier as far as he was concerned. Then there were the waistcoats, which he liked to design as well as purchase off the better class of peg. He had the most *chi-chi* of them specially made for him by a firm called Wings in Piccadilly at a cost of around £25 a throw (about £700 in today's prices), and, in 1952, he would even help establish the Waistcoat Club to promote such products as essential items for a gent to wear.[44] 'I had waistcoats made of silk, satin, suede, bearskin, velvet [and] wool,' he would recall fondly, 'and there was even one made of white mink.'[45] His all-time favourite among the more than a hundred he would accumulate would be the one he had made out of soft black velvet decorated with coloured flowers embroidered in silk, but he was also very proud of his little black moiré number that boasted some eye-catching gold fern embroidery, because it caught the eye of King George VI (one of his old role models) when he performed at a Christmas party for the royal household at Windsor Castle.

His addiction to cigarette holders had begun back at the moment, soon after he took up smoking as a teenager, when he decided that he had 'classic hands': 'I have always hated nicotine-stained fingers,' he would explain; 'a holder prevents your fingernails looking like nutmeg.'[46] He had given up his dozen-a-day smoking habit in 1945 (after experiencing certain niggling health problems during the war), but decided to hang on to the old holders as an elegant personal prop. Now that he had a public image to promote, however, he wanted something a little more distinctive, and he found it – 'the most irresistible holder' – in the window of Dunhill's: 'It was slightly outré because it was made of lacquered, black whangee (a type of bamboo) with a gold band twisting neatly round it,' he said. Acknowledging that, at seven inches in length, it was over-long by most people's standards, he admitted: 'I would go for walks near my home while smoking with it, just to get my eye in. It wanted a bit of nerve to use a holder of that shape and size in real life.'[47]

The finishing touch to the Terry Thomas look was always a fresh clove carnation every day, which he bought from a florist in Old Brompton Road. 'The carnation had to be clove,' he insisted. 'Wherever I went, a clove carnation adorned me. Even if I only slipped out to the pub, I always dressed as if I was going to a stage or a cabaret floor.'[48] When quizzed about his extraordinary image and extravagant tastes, he would inform reporters: 'I am a dandy. Or rather, a *dam*-dy. I don't dress conventionally and I'm damned if I ever will.'[49]

Such an ostentatiously devil-may-care attitude certainly did help to get him noticed, but, as an unintended consequence, it would also help get him into a spot of trouble on a number of unhappy occasions. Early in 1960, for example, he came off stage after giving a midnight charity performance at the Odeon cinema in Liverpool and discovered that someone had stolen his most expensive custom-made cigarette holder – a spectacularly flashy little item (valued at £2000 at the time) decorated with forty-two diamonds and a gold spiral band – from a table inside his dressing room. The police soon tracked down two of the diamonds in the possession of a twenty-eight-year-old local man named Alan David Williams, later described in court as an 'unemployed salesman' and 'variety artist'. They found the other forty, along with gold parts of the holder, hidden inside a roll of carpet at the Queen's Drive home of a twenty-year-old unemployed comedian called James Joseph Tarbuck – a young man who, ironically enough, was destined for great fame and a fair-sized fortune from the mid-1960s onwards as the mop-topped, smart suited and booted, 'boom-boom'-ing stand-up comic Jimmy Tarbuck, one of the resident hosts of *Sunday Night at the London Palladium*.

Tarbuck was charged with theft and Williams with being an accessory after the fact, and both were committed for trial at Liverpool Magistrates' Court in April 1960. It transpired at the trial that the desperately ambitious Tarbuck had sought out T-T on several occasions both before and during the course of the midnight charity concert, asking him for the chance to make an appearance and perform some of his own material. The star, however, had replied to each of these repeated requests by 'pointing out to him that we had too many artistes already [and therefore] it would be madness to put anybody else on'.[50] Feeling hugely frustrated (and depressed by the fact that he was beginning to slip deeper into debt), Tarbuck responded to the perceived snub by slipping into Terry-Thomas's unoccupied dressing room and making off with the cigarette holder in what the defence claimed was 'a moment of pique rather than dishonest intent'.[51] After keeping it hidden at home for a week, he proceeded to break it up and then sold a couple of the diamonds to Williams for £3 in order to ease one or two of his most pressing financial problems.

Once in court, both young men pleaded guilty and were duly sentenced (Tarbuck was placed on probation for two years and Williams was given a twelve-month conditional discharge), but Terry-Thomas was left feeling angry and somewhat demeaned – not so much by the theft (which he later dismissed as a 'silly jape' by a 'completely and utterly unknown' comedian), but more as a consequence of having had to endure what he considered to be the envious, resentful and cynically sniping remarks of certain barristers who were acting on behalf of the defence. Mr Harry Livermore, in particular, had infuriated the star by accusing him repeatedly of inflating the value of the cigarette holder in order to create a 'publicity stunt'. 'How could you say such a thing?' shrieked an outraged T-T. 'Of course it is not. If it had been a publicity stunt surely it would have been easier to have had it made from gilt and glass.'[52] The performer eventually got the better of the barrister, tweaking a few raw nerves of his own – such as when, in response to the accusation that he had been 'silly and overtrusting' to have left such a highly prized possession unattended, he looked Livermore coldly in the eye and observed, 'You have your collar on the wrong way round,' thus provoking the visibly rattled barrister to bark back, 'You will not insult me.

I have no aspirations to be a clergyman, if you want to know!'[53] – but he remained resentful of all the supposed condescension he had encountered in the courtroom. As for the expensive cigarette holders: he was waving another one around as he left the building and passed by the waiting reporters, thus making sure that he was seen to live up to his motto – 'I shall not be cowed'.

It was a heady, hectic and very lucrative time for him back in the late 1940s, and he certainly made the most of it ('Money is solid applause,' he remarked. 'I like it'[54]). For all of the hedonistic aspects of his image, however, he did little, in reality, other than work: on top of his formidable West End theatre and cabaret workload, he also started broadcasting on a regular basis on the radio (appearing as a guest star on such popular BBC programmes as *Variety Bandbox*, *Workers' Playtime*, *Happidrome* and *The Carroll Levis Show*), and he continued to find it hard to turn down the odd additional booking (provided the price was right) on the provincial variety circuit. By the time that *Piccadilly Hayride* finally came to the end of its sixteen-month run, on 17 January 1948, he was well-known, well-liked, widely sought-after – and absolutely shattered.

Suffering from 'a resurrected stomach ulcer and a bad case of nervous exhaustion', he staggered off to see a specialist in Harley Street, who, after examining him, recommended a month of rest and recuperation at Champneys 'nature cure' health farm in Tring. Run in those days by its founder, an eccentric Latvian naturopath by the name of Stanley Lief, Champneys – the first stately home health retreat in Britain – sounded tolerable to Thomas (whose friend, the novelist and playwright Algernon Blackwood, had often sung its praises) until he actually got there. Lief startled him straight away by announcing that, far from being pampered with regular massages, manicures, pedicures, rounds of smoked salmon sandwiches and tall flutes of chilled champagne, he would be expected to survive each day on little more than three oranges, a small portion of watercress and plenty of water. Thomas startled Lief by admitting rather sweetly that, fond as he was of watercress, oranges and water, he was much, much fonder of 'steaks, chops, liver and kidneys, bacon and sausages, chicken, and duck, and partridge, and pheasant, and grouse, and veal, and pork'.[55] He added that his plan was to take a brisk walk out every morning through the surrounding fields, carrying a brand new Boss & Co shotgun, and make it a rule 'to stay out until I had shot a rabbit'.[56]

One of Lief's assistants hurried Thomas off to his small and rather Spartan-looking room before he could cause any further offence, handed him an orange and a jug of water, and ordered him to start 'cleansing' himself internally. The next few days were, as a consequence, 'unbearable', and he doubted that he would last beyond the first week. Then, as luck would have it, 'salvation' came in the somewhat bulbous form of Sir Bernard Docker (the flamboyant chairman of the Daimler Motor Company) and his similarly 'larger than life' wife, Lady Norah, who were also staying and suffering at Champneys. After comparing notes on their respective hunger pangs, the threesome readily agreed to become committed co-conspirators: 'While taking our recommended afternoon walks in the fresh air,' Thomas later admitted, 'we used to slip away in the famous gold-plated Daimler for the odd clandestine scone.'[57]

It could have been down to Lief, or it could have been down to the cheats, but, for one reason or another, Thomas returned to London feeling fit and fully refreshed. Eager to make up for lost time, he went straight back to work, touring the halls, acting as compère at the London Palladium and making his breakthrough on radio in October 1948, at the age of thirty-seven, as the star of his first series on the BBC's Home Service, the variety showcase *To Town with Terry*. This was the project that first made people within the BBC realise just what a talented, determined and, on occasion, difficult and outspoken performer Terry Thomas could be.

Featuring a fairly familiar mixture of sketches, solo routines, musical interludes and a range of popular and topical star guests, the show – which was scheduled to go out on the air every Tuesday evening at 7 p.m. for forty-five minutes – was intended to serve as a suitably flexible context for the man whom the BBC was now billing as one of its bright new stars,[58] but Terry Thomas was far from being immediately impressed. While the first intended set of guests (which included the very popular singers Anne Shelton and Vera Lynn, and, as unexpected 'straight men', the British Movietone News narrator Lionel Gamlin and the greatly respected BBC broadcaster Richard Dimbleby) was deemed to be broadly acceptable, the star was decidedly uneasy about the range of names proposed for subsequent editions. The choices struck him as having far more to do with availability and low rates of pay than with suitability or high quality. He was similarly unhappy about the limited amount of time that was being put aside for the preparation of each new script and its subsequent rehearsal. Acting like the strong and strict organiser he had been back in his old *Stars in Battledress* days, he started questioning most of his producer's ideas, made all kinds of technical and artistic suggestions and demanded a greater degree of commitment from the rest of the team. This was *his* show, he reasoned, and how it fared would affect *his* reputation, so he was determined to make it as good as it could possibly be.

The debut edition, which was broadcast on 12 October, was deemed a great success by the BBC's powers-that-be (who were happy to see it set off on a lengthy run), but Terry Thomas struggled to think about anything other than all of the real and imagined faults. He criticised others and he criticised himself. Lists were written, memos distributed and editorial sessions commenced. The basic message to all was: 'We must do better'. Not long after the series had started its run, therefore, he demanded a meeting with the Corporation's Head of Variety, Michael Standing, to discuss possible ways to 'tighten-up' the format, improve the quality and, ideally, boost the budget of his new show. Although it was not the sort of thing that a 'mere' artiste was supposed to do, he marched off to the executive's office in the BBC's Aeolian Hall in Bond Street and, over a cup of tea and a spongy bun, made his opinions eminently clear:

> I had quite a row with him. I remember banging his desk violently when he said that he didn't see anything *wrong* with the programme. That goaded me into saying something that I believe has a great deal of truth in it. 'You only think this programme is good because it isn't bad! That is the BBC's attitude, but it isn't mine, I can't afford it. For that matter, it isn't any artist's. No artist can afford to do anything that isn't really jolly good. But I suppose the BBC can

afford to put out mediocre stuff; in any case, it is generally agreed that they constantly do!'[59]

Comedy, he insisted, was no joke: it was a serious business. He was adamant that his work on the wireless was going to be of the kind of high quality that would render it genuinely memorable. A standard, he said, had to be set.

To his credit, he proceeded to lead by example, straining each day and each week to come up with a funnier, livelier and more varied kind of show, and, although there were plenty of grunts and grumbles in the background along the way, the rest of the team followed suit. 'You peg away,' he would say, 'and you must keep pegging away with complete faith that you will succeed until, suddenly, you find that you're getting somewhere.'[60] The result would be a six-month-long series that went somewhere, building up a large audience and receiving a fair amount of critical praise. Although there would never be anything particularly novel about the programme, it would at least improve steadily enough and develop into a relatively polished and entertaining affair, and its star (who would audibly grow in confidence as the series progressed) stood out as a performer of real promise. The effort (and the arguments) would come to seem to have been worth it: he helped *To Town with Terry*, and it, in turn, went on to help his career move smartly along.

It was also at this propitious stage that Terry Thomas made one final, small but significant revision to his on-stage identity: to coincide with the launch of his own show, he inserted a hyphen between the 'Terry' and the 'Thomas' in his name. He would later claim that it was not for 'snob' reasons that he decided to make the change, but rather 'to tie the two names together': 'They didn't mean much apart,' he argued; 'together they made a trade name.'[61] A letter from his management to the BBC (dated 28 April 1948), however, provided a supplementary explanation:

Would you be kind enough to notify all concerned that Terry-Thomas has instructed us that a hyphen shall be inserted between his two names. The reason is, I understand, that he hopes to discourage people from addressing him as 'Mr Thomas,' to which he has apparently a strong objection!! There is no Christian name before it.[62]

He did it, therefore, both for snobbish and pragmatic reasons, but, most of all, he did it because it felt *right*. From this moment on, he believed that he truly was Terry-Thomas: the metropolitan toff, dandy and artiste known to all, affectionately and indubitably, as 'T-T'.

CHAPTER THREE

T-T on TV

How do you view!

IT WAS ON a Wednesday evening in the autumn of 1949 that comedy first made its mark on British television. A dapper, rather raffish-looking man walked up so close to the camera that his face filled the whole of the screen, grinned the broadest of gap-toothed grins, and asked the viewers at home: 'How do you *view*? Are you *frightfully* well? You *are*? Oh, good *show*!' The man was Terry-Thomas, and what followed was not just the first edition of his debut series on the small screen – it was also the start of the first *bona fide* comedy series on British television. It all began with T-T.

Not many people at the time regarded the occasion as particularly auspicious, however, because not many people, in those days, had access to a set. Fewer than 127,000 people (about 2.5 per cent of the UK population) owned a combined radio and TV licence in 1949, and the vast majority of them were concentrated in London and parts of the Midlands (where the limited signal, at that stage, was strongest).[1] Even among those who did own a set, the experience of watching a solitary black-and-white channel – on a flickering little nine-inch screen – was probably low on their list of thrills once the initial novelty had worn off. In short, Britain was still predominantly a radio nation, but, although it might not have seemed like it to many at the time, such tastes were already beginning (albeit at a pedestrian pace) to change.

Sports fans had been greatly impressed the previous summer by BBC TV's live coverage of the London Olympics, and several more high-profile outside broadcasts would draw new viewers in over the course of the next few years (culminating, of course, with the crowd-pulling coverage of the Coronation of 1953). Slowly but surely, the schedules were growing more varied and attentive, building up a broad audience block by block: children were already being offered regular glimpses of the galumphing string-puppet, Muffin the Mule; Philip Harben, the TV cook, was showing viewers what they could do with a few eggs, some flour, a little milk and a few more eggs (he was terribly fond of eggs); Fred Streeter, the TV gardener, was advising viewers as to what they should stick in their soil; and an increasing number of concerts, plays, cabaret shows, talks and documentaries were now reaching the screen on a weekly basis.[2] It was a rather good time, therefore, for someone like Terry-Thomas to attempt to stamp his own signature upon the screen.

He had already made a name for himself on radio. *To Town with Terry*, his first headlining series during 1948–9, had confirmed his reputation as one of 'Britain's leading drolls' (as the *Radio Times* put it at the time[3]), without adding anything truly new to a tried-and-tested format. Limited to sound without vision, he had seemed somewhat subdued, like a peacock stuck in the dark, and the show simply offered variety lovers more of the same – albeit of above-average quality – instead of a little of something different. The series performed well enough in terms of ratings, but not quite well enough to satisfy the big ambitions of its self-confessed 'perfectionist' star (who had found some of the 'BBC boys' frustratingly 'amateur and lazy'[4]).

He was far from disheartened, and would try again in the near future with other radio shows, but, when the chance arrived to shape a series in a newer medium with fewer constricting conventions, he seized it without hesitation. Television had intrigued him ever since he first appeared on it, for a fee of thirty guineas, back in the autumn of 1947.[5] It had only been an isolated six-minute spot, but it led to further – very successful – appearances the following year on a high-profile variety showcase called *Stars in Your Eyes* (produced by Michael Mills, a man with an exceptionally sharp eye for spotting fresh comedy talent).

Seeing something in the performer that suggested he might, with the right kind and degree of expert assistance, develop into the sort of star who could 'carry' a show of his own, Mills began campaigning within the BBC on behalf of Terry-Thomas. The initial response from his colleagues had not been particularly favourable. Cecil Madden, who was responsible for planning and organising television's output at the time, wrote to Mills on 15 February 1949: 'Every time I have seen him here [at Alexandra Palace] he has always done substantially the same act, and we feel that if we undertook a series [like radio's *To Town with Terry*] all the work would fall on the producer and none on Terry.'[6] Mills, however, was a very determined – and stubborn – character (his affectionate nickname among colleagues was 'Dark Satanic Mills'[7]), and so he persisted, insisting that, with 'careful handling' and some decent scripts, Terry-Thomas 'could do a very good series for us'.[8] His budding protégé, in turn, did what he could to show all the sceptical executives how serious he actually was, studying every aspect of the BBC's output, familiarising himself with the medium's special methods and mores, and teaching himself one or two new tricks: 'for the first time in my life,' he would reflect, 'I really did my homework.'[9] Madden and some of the others remained unconvinced – particularly after they heard rumours from some of their old friends in radio about how the performer was capable of being 'difficult' – but, none the less, they allowed Mills to push on with his plans. Terry-Thomas was given his chance (with a fee of seventy-five guineas per show[10]) to make a new series for television.

What appealed most to the performer about television at that time was the fact that there were no real 'rules' about what a comedy show should be like. The genre, as such, did not yet exist, and so he had been placed in the exciting position of being one of the medium's pioneers. In radio, he had been obliged to fit in with a venerable comic tradition that could already boast such influential shows as *Band Waggon*, *Workers' Playtime*, *Garrison Theatre*, *ITMA*, *Hi Gang!*, *Merry-Go-Round*, *Ignorance Is Bliss*, *The Happidrome*, *Take It From Here* and *Variety Bandbox*, but now, in television, he had the licence to begin a distinctive comic tradition all of his own.

He knew that it was going to be a challenge. A television studio, in those days, was not the easiest place in which to create. The trio of cameras were large and cumbersome things mounted on big bicycle wheels, and the picture that each cameraman saw through his viewfinder arrived upside-down and inverted. Any adjustments to the camera's picture had to be made by another operator from a tiny room alongside the studio, and no particular picture could go out on air before the producer in the control gallery had nominated it out loud, the vision mixer had switched it to a preview screen, the senior engineer had given his seal of technical approval and, at last, the vision mixer had pressed the right button.

In addition to all of these built-in hindrances to any fast-witted and improvising spirit, the dazzle and heat from the arc-lights, as a critic of the time acknowledged, 'were intense enough to shrivel Muffin's hair off and cook Harben's omelette before he could slide it from bowl to pan'.[11] Another potentially troublesome factor was that the 'blocking-out' and timing of each sequence had to be scrupulously precise, as, of course, all of the shows had to go out 'live' and uncorrected (the only option if a performer forgot something and 'dried' was for the 'Cut Key Operator' to shut off the sound and shout out the next line while the puzzled viewers at home banged the top of their sets and fiddled with the volume). The studio camaraderie, however, was considerable, and, crucially, no one had been there long enough yet to have grown overly 'orthodox', obdurate and cynical: 'Nobody ever said to you, "You can't possibly do that",' recalled one producer from that era. 'They said, "Have a try and we'll see what we can do".'[12]

After coining the 'smashing' title of *How Do You View?* for his debut series (which he declared would be 'just the jolly hammer'[13]), Terry-Thomas could not wait to see what he could do. Ever since his days in a cramped little office at Smithfield Market, he had been jotting down ideas for sketches, shows, formats and characters into a battered black order book, and now he was eager to discuss them all with a proper creative team. The man who was to be his first producer/director, Walton Anderson (who had been based at Alexandra Palace since the final few years of the BBC's pre-war TV service), went to see him at his flat in Queen's Gate Mews, and the two of them began exchanging suggestions as to what the new show could, and should, seek to achieve.

Anderson – with whom Terry-Thomas would later claim diplomatically that he 'got on very well socially'[14] – envisioned a relatively conven-

tional, sketch-based format, 'topped-and-tailed' by a couple of inimitable T-T monologues. His star, on the other hand, made it clear that *he*
envisioned something far more unorthodox, with a fluid running order
from one show to the next, plenty of technical experiments and a general
readiness to utilise whatever seemed likely to surprise and intrigue the
audience. Most important of all, he envisioned something that was more
than just a radio show with pictures. 'Everybody has a seat in the front
row of the stalls,' he stressed of the new viewing experience. 'We have
got to act accordingly. TV isn't like films, radio or the stage. It has bits of
all three in it, of course. But it is something demanding a new approach.
Something new.'[15] Anderson, sensing that he was going to have to be the
one who made most of the technical leaps into the dark, said what BBC
producers always said – 'we'll see what we can do' – and then set off to
plan the first programme.

Eventually, after a few wrong turns and false steps (and more than a
few heated 'artistic differences of opinion' – such as when the star wrote
to his producer declaring haughtily, 'I have found in my experience
that, where the presentation of Terry-Thomas is concerned, my judg-
ment is better than anybody else's'[16]), a provisional framework was put in
place. The on-screen Terry-Thomas, it was agreed, would be a glamorous, mischievous and discreetly cash-strapped man-about-town who
would be able to talk directly to the viewing audience via the camera
lens, as though they were with him in his smart-looking bachelor pad,
and link together an unpredictable sequence of sketches, songs and
monologues (most of which, in the absence of a proper scriptwriter,
would have to be drawn and adapted from his existing stage act). It was
only a starting point, as far as the performer was concerned, but he felt
fairly optimistic about how far – and in what kinds of directions – it
could be developed once he had acquired a little more experience and
authority.

One thing upon which he insisted right from the start was the intimate, tone-setting introduction, and he rehearsed it over and over again
in front of the large studio mirrors. 'How do you *view*?' he used to say,
testing out every conceivable intonation and facial expression before
arriving on what he felt was the perfect version to introduce the on-screen

'T-T' to his viewing audience. Once this was mastered, he was ready. The initial series could begin.

The first three of the four, fortnightly, twenty-minute shows attracted above-average audiences and received uniformly favourable reviews from the few critics who were around in those days to write about it, but Terry-Thomas was still far from happy with what he regarded as the relatively unimaginative and pedestrian style of the production. He was greatly relieved, therefore, when Walton Anderson (who had suddenly become conveniently indisposed) was replaced by Bill Ward for the final programme. Aged thirty-three, Ward – 'a young, extremely beefy, breezy chap' from the West Country – was one of the most experienced (or least inexperienced) programme-makers in Britain, having been among the BBC's first crop of television technicians in the 1930s, and he had acquired a deserved reputation over the years for being the fastest-cutting director in the business. He was just the kind of open-minded, dynamic and decisive character that the project had always required.

Ward marched on to the studio floor, looked around, scratched his prematurely balding head and then asked his star performer: 'What do you think of this set?' His star performer replied: 'Terrible!' Ward nodded in agreement: 'Let's change it!' With that, he took off his jacket and threw it in a chair, rolled up his shirtsleeves and started work. 'I realised that this was the sort of chap I wanted,' Terry-Thomas would recall, 'a man after my own heart.'[17] Ward felt exactly the same: 'We got on like a house on fire – we hit it off straight away.'[18] Little could be done to change the last show of the series (apart from making it a little faster-paced), but, as soon as it was over, the two men started talking to each other in earnest about where they hoped to go from here.

While Terry-Thomas was excited to be able to pick the brains of someone as technically adept as Bill Ward, his producer, similarly, could not quite believe his luck to find himself directing a comic performer as gifted as T-T. He would later reflect on the star's remarkable sense of timing – 'His *pauses* were marvellous' – as well as his hugely appealing combination of disciplined professionalism with an inextinguishable instinct for playfulness: 'Terry had a very strong sense of comedy, and he also had an individual and personal sense of humour. I don't think Arthur Askey [for example] ever had a sense of humour. He had a sense of *comedy*, yes, but not a sense of humour. You couldn't pull Arthur's leg – he wouldn't have understood what you were doing. But you could pull Terry's leg – and he'd do it to you in return!'[19] Both the performer and his producer, therefore, now felt greatly inspired by the partnership they were forming.

The first major action taken by Ward, once a second series had been confirmed, was to enlist the services of a professional scriptwriter to help Terry-Thomas craft enough comic material to sustain another run. Ward's choice was Sid Colin, a budding young writer who had begun his career as a guitarist and singer with the popular British dance band, Ambrose and the Squadronaires (one of whose most famous songs, 'If I Only Had Wings', had been co-written by Colin and his fellow band member Ronnie Aldrich as an unofficial anthem for the RAF), before turning his attention to comedy. Although, like most of his recently demobbed contemporaries in the post-war period, Colin had no real track record to speak of (outside of wartime Gang Shows) as a script-writer, he was quick-witted, disciplined and bursting with ideas. Terry-Thomas thought that his early efforts were 'splendid', and so (after the star had taken his wife, Pat, to Kingston, Jamaica, for a short celebratory break[20]) their creative collaboration began.

Each basic script took a week to prepare. Then, at ten o'clock sharp the following morning, Bill Ward and Sid Colin would go over to see T-T at his home in Queen's Gate Mews for a three-hour session to read everything through and discuss possible changes. Everything had to be planned with the maximum amount of care and forethought. 'There was no method of recording the live show,' Bill Ward would recall:

Videotape didn't exist in those days, so [Terry] had to rely upon trusted friends who would be honest with him, and rely on Sid and myself. And I think one of the real plusses was that we *were* honest with one another. We never deceived each other. If it was a bad script we'd tell Sid so and Sid recognised that we were working to the same end, which was Terry's perfectionism. And Terry would ask about his performances, and we would tell him if he was good, if he was poor, if he was indifferent, and why. And similarly with the work that I did – they'd be honest about that, too. We worked as a very close team that had mutual respect.[21]

An intensive period of rehearsals followed, running for six full days. Then, in the hours leading up to each fortnightly broadcast, there would be a 'stagger-through' at 2 p.m., a band call at 4 p.m., another couple of run-throughs with the cast (during which T-T, in another radical and imaginative departure from the programme-making conventions of the time, sometimes studied the action with Bill Ward in the control booth while a stand-in went through his scenes – thus allowing him in those pre-tape days to acquire a better sense of how a particular routine or performance would look[22]); and, in the evening, the actual programme was performed and transmitted. This was precisely the kind of high-quality production that Terry-Thomas had always craved.

The result was a second series (which began, with a longer show that now lasted half an hour, on 5 April 1950) that was far more accomplished, audacious and memorable than its promising but patchy predecessor. Everything was now controlled carefully and quietly within the TV studio: an ill-advised bid by some anxious executives to have the programme shot in front of a live audience – like a conventional variety show – was thwarted after one grudging attempt, because the team was adamant that it had no need for theatrical 'cues' for laughter and applause from the viewers at home. ('I think that if you have an audience in the studio you play to it,' reasoned Terry-Thomas. 'The viewer at home becomes just an old auntie watching the show from the side of the stage, instead of being the person the show should be directed straight at.')[23]

The emphasis instead was on giving people something to look at on the screen that they could not experience merely by sitting in front of a stage. Bill Ward ensured that the sets were bigger, better and more believable for a show that purported to take the viewer into the world of such a dandified figure as Terry-Thomas. He also used the cameras to contribute to the comedy instead of just showing it: close-ups captured sly winks and grins to the audience in their homes; cross-cuts, fade-ins and fade-outs helped set up some gags and delivered the visual punch-line to others; and short pre-filmed segments, which sometimes featured unprecedented technical tricks (such as the clip in which Terry-Thomas 'lost' his head, and another that saw the camera peer through the gap in his teeth), enriched the rest of the mix. The writer Sid Colin responded to such invention with the structure of his scripts, creating a decrepit Wodehousian butler for T-T to play off called Moulting (played by the splendid seventy-year-old character actor Herbert C. Walton), and then followed this, in collaboration with Terry-Thomas himself, with a reper-tory of other supporting characters – thus allowing the star of the show to step in and out of his own semi-private sitcom. Such elements com-bined to make *How Do You View?* – a full two decades before the arrival of *Monty Python* – seem like 'something completely different'.

Each episode began with a six- or seven-minute attempted mono-logue from T-T (an idea copied a couple of decades later for, among others, the prologue in *Up Pompeii!*) that was interrupted several times by queries from his butler and various other servants before being aban-doned by the frustrated star. A brief musical number was performed while he raced off and changed costume; then he returned to take part in a five-minute spoof current affairs interview. This was followed by another short musical number while he changed into his next costume; and the final ten minutes featured a sketch shared by T-T and a special guest performer. A summary of the basic structure, however, does not do justice to the novelty, at the time, of either the content or the execution. The show was live, fast-paced and full of unprecedented TV comedy conceits.

The show was the first on television, for example, to regularly use 'serious' figures ironically, starting with its deployment of Leslie Mitch-ell (the deep-voiced BBC and British Movietone News announcer) and then Brian Johnston (the similarly posh-sounding presenter, compère and cricket commentator) as poker-faced comedy stooges, and the first to parody other TV personalities, programmes and genres. It was also the first show to acknowledge the context in which it existed (editions would often feature the star being tracked by the camera over the cables and through the corridors and control rooms of both Alexandra Palace and, later on, BBC TV's new headquarters at Lime Grove), as well as the first to reflect on – and joke about – its own and other programmes' reception (the comic actor Victor Platt would appear every now and again as that strange new creature, the 'TV critic'). It was, in sum, the first show that really tried its best to be genuinely *televisual*, and thus set the high standard to which subsequent comedy shows could aspire. Even BBC TV's own Controller of Programmes at the time, the normally reserved Norman Collins, was moved to mark the conclusion of series two by writing a fan letter to its star: 'Some of your character sketches have been as funny as anything that I have seen,' he gushed. 'I shall look forward to the return of Terry-Thomas.'[24]

The praise that each successive season of shows received, far from making the programme-makers sit back and rest on their laurels, spurred them on to try for even greater technical heights. They knew that, in their own little light-hearted and playful way, they were in the process of making broadcasting history, and they were eager to push the show on.

Another young up-and-coming writer, Talbot 'Tolly' Rothwell (whose pun-studded style had already been heard on *To Town with Terry*), was added to the team for the third, nine-episode, series (which ran from 8 November 1950 to 28 February 1951). To further freshen things up, a new set of recurring characters was introduced: in addition to Moulting the butler, Terry-Thomas was now assisted by, among others, 'the girl with the tea', Rosie Lee (played by the very talented Avril Angers – whose catchphrase was, 'Would you like it now, or will you have it later?'), and a chauffeur (played by the amiable and artful Peter Butterworth) called Lockit – whose job was made so much easier than usual by the fact that the on-screen 'T-T' (although he regarded a chauffeur as an essential status symbol) did not actually own a car. The show had by this time built up such a devoted following that some viewers, feeling sorry for Lockit's perverse redundancy, actually began sending in spare parts: 'Eventually,' Terry-Thomas would recall fondly, 'there were so many we could have actually built ourselves a jalopy.'[25]

Car parts were not the only items that arrived at the studio from the show's most avid fans. Terry-Thomas started receiving a wide variety of neckties, tie pins, shirts, shirt studs, spats, handkerchiefs, cufflinks, cravats, cummerbunds and cigarette holders, and he was even given one of the late Enrico Caruso's favourite waistcoats (made in 1850 out of grey silk and decorated with diamond buttons) by the legendary tenor's widow, Dorothy. He was also far from displeased, when he opened his mail, to find that some of his female fans wished him to have one or two of their most intimate items of lingerie (a word that he would always make sound like a blissful sigh).

Another – more public – sign of how popular *How Do You View?* had become was the presence in the studio of Princess Elizabeth, who paid the show a visit during her first tour of Alexandra Palace at the start of 1951 (when she watched Terry-Thomas rehearse a cod news-piece in which he played a Beefeater being interviewed by Leslie Mitchell). More and more people in public life thus seemed eager to associate themselves with the show. Even BBC TV's own new Head of Light Entertainment, Ronald Waldman, was keen enough to get in on the act – quite literally – by appearing on screen in one sketch as a shifty-looking Bow Street runner (an unprecedented gesture, in those days, for an executive to make).

It was thus very evident within the industry just how important both the show and its star now were – not only for setting such a high standard for other programme-makers and performers to aim to emulate, but also for being such massive consumer attractions ('If television has made Terry-Thomas into a name,' one critic remarked, 'then equally Terry-Thomas has made television into an entertainment'[26]). Market research was indeed now suggesting that some people were actually buying television sets for the very first time in their lives chiefly to see what all the fuss was about the man they called 'T-T': 'Here's Terry-Thomas to help you sell more sets,' declared a full-page advertisement in a trade magazine for Baird televisions, urging the nation's electrical retailers to use images of the star in cinemas to lure more and more viewers to the small screen. A powerful magnet for the medium had thus been found. *How Do You View?* was why a growing number of people were viewing.

One of the youngest of such fans was a nine-year-old girl named Sarah Miles – a future co-star of T-T's – who would later recall how great a fortnightly highlight the programme actually was inside her family's home in Essex: 'I was a very big fan of Terry-Thomas, as indeed was the whole Miles family in the fifties. The days he was on TV in our youth were the very best days of the week for all four of us. Sometimes I laughed so much that Mummy would scold me for peeing on the sofa cushions. Yes, he was that funny to us.'[27]

Bill Ward, the two writers and Terry-Thomas himself all felt justifiably proud of what, together, they had achieved: 'In spite of the fact that props sometimes fell down, doors didn't open, or I would ad-lib and distract my colleagues,' the star would recall, 'we had found the most marvellous formula which couldn't go wrong.'[28] No other entertainment team working at that time in television could look forward to an immediate future that appeared so bold and so bright.

After the third series was over, Ronald Waldman held up *How Do You View?* as the shining example of what he wanted all future entertainment programmes to strive to be like. 'Our aim,' he declared, 'is now to try and bring the entertainment profession as a whole to believe, with us, that television does not mean the mere photographing of something that could be entertaining in a theatre or a cinema.' What was particularly thrilling about *How Do You View?*, he said, was the fact that it was 'doing something that could not be done in any other medium. In other words, it is television, and all our evidence proves that it is one of the most popular programmes in our entire output.'[29] The critic Wilfred Greatorex, writing in the *Radio Times*, agreed. Congratulating Terry-Thomas for striking such an exceptionally rich vein of visual humour, he said that the performer 'understood that the home-screen offers scope for subtle expression, fine-grain comedy that can be touched-off by the flicker of an eyebrow, the roll of an eye, a twitch of the mouth. It is the idea behind the "very close close-up" technique which nowadays brings his lively face full-scale on the screen.' It was this technical intelligence, wrote the critic, combined with the natural charm of the show's 'unique and inimitable' star, that made *How Do You View?* such an impressive piece of television.[30]

Feeling proud and protective after receiving so much high praise, Terry-Thomas was tempted to stop the show while it was still very clearly at the top. It was an interesting issue for him to consider: being responsible for the first real comedy series on British TV meant that neither he nor anyone else knew what the most appropriate, let alone the most likely, lifespan for a much-loved show could or should be. It was all still largely uncharted territory. The sanguine pioneer in him wanted to keep on pushing and probing the medium, but the anxious professional entertainer in him was afraid of waking up one day, saddened to find that he and his series had finally outstayed their welcome.

It was not a decision, therefore, that he was in any kind of hurry to make one way or another, but, while he sketched out some provisional plans for another series of *How Do You View?*, a few ideas for alternative – or perhaps merely additional – ventures were set in circulation. He had already been exploring a number of other possible projects in recent months, including a radio situation comedy scripted by Sid Colin called *The Hammetts* (which would have co-starred Ethel Revnell and himself as a Cockney couple running a theatrical boarding house[31]), as well as a completely new television series entitled *It Strikes a Chord* and a number of ideas for movies, but his bosses at the BBC were quick to make it clear that they were loath to lose a show as popular and, in its own way, as prestigious as *How Do You View?*.

While his agent and the BBC tried to come up with a mutually satis-factory solution, Terry-Thomas toured Britain and then travelled to the east coast of America, testing the waters with a few cabaret engagements and studying what was currently making an impact on the US TV net-works. When he returned home, in the summer of 1951, he was not much clearer in his own mind as to what he should seek to do next. He bided his time by agreeing to do a few guest spots on other people's radio and television shows, and he mulled over a fairly wide range of other offers, but nothing new and sufficiently exciting seemed to materialise. Eventually, therefore, he agreed to make a return to television – for an increased fee of 140 guineas per appearance[32] – with a fourth series of *How Do You View?*.

If he and Bill Ward still harboured any serious misgivings about con-tinuing, they hid them well at the start of the new run. Both were bullish to the press about the show's prospects, stressing that, for all of the famil-iar ingredients that remained from the previous series, there would still be more than enough in the latest one to surprise and delight their large and loyal following.[33] One change that was certainly noticeable as far as the cast was concerned was the absence of Avril Angers (whose 'Rosie Lee' character was now deemed to be too old-fashioned and 'ITMA-ish') and the sudden presence of the much younger Diana Dors (whom Bill Ward had brought in to give the show a greater degree of sex appeal) as an improbable atomic scientist (among other things) called 'Cuddles'. Even though Terry-Thomas – ever the breast man – had been disappointed initially by the young starlet's 'modest mammaries', he warmed very quickly indeed to her 'fabulous figure', and proceeded to take great pleasure in playing opposite her in a succession of mildly risqué spoofs and sketches.[34] Other pre-publicised innovations included a regular 'home movies' section (in which Terry-Thomas, alluding perhaps to his own emerging cinematic interests and ambitions, portrayed such characters as the Italian neo-realist film director 'Terryto-Thosselini' and mocked a variety of post-war cinema styles), several parodies of celebrated American personalities and, somewhat jarringly, a fortnightly spot for a puppeteering song-and-dance man named Sam Williams.

Neither the viewers nor the critics seemed disappointed by what they witnessed when the first show of the series (which by this stage was based in Studio G at Lime Grove) went out at 8.45 p.m. on 19 September 1951, but, behind the scenes, the strain was beginning to tell. Being a pioneer had seemed exhilarating to Terry-Thomas in the beginning, but now, after trying so many new things and taking on so many fresh risks, the weight of expectation was increasingly hard for him to bear ('Once again,' he would observe before preparing for another programme, 'I shall find myself in the unenviable position of trying to be all things to all men'[35]). Other popular comedians were starting to follow in his footsteps with derivative series of their own – Eric Barker's began in 1951, while Arthur Askey, Tommy Cooper and Frankie Howerd would all launch their respective starring vehicles the following year – but Terry-Thomas was the only one who felt honour bound to appear not simply as funny as ever but also just as innovative.

Tensions duly increased between the various members of the production team as the series continued its run. The star began to clash, for example, with his two writers: just after the decision had been taken to extend the running time of *How Do You View?* from thirty to forty minutes, Sid Colin started assisting Eric Sykes on weekly scripts for the very popular radio show *Educating Archie*, and Talbot Rothwell (who would eventually find fame as the principal writer of the *Carry On* movies before moving on, like Sid Colin, to supply the scripts for Frankie Howerd in *Up Pompeii!*) also started contributing material to other productions and performers. Terry-Thomas felt that they were spreading themselves far too thin – and showing a certain amount of disloyalty and ingratitude, in doing so, to the man who had given both of them their first break. He also grew less inclined to forgive the BBC's continuing failure to provide the show with a fixed slot in the schedules (one edition would start at 8.35 p.m., another at 8.30, the next at 9.00 and the one after that at 8.15), fearing that some viewers might tire of chasing the series up and down the listings while others would miss it completely.

Such fears were not confirmed by the subsequent viewing figures, which remained impressive, but (according to the BBC's own fledgling attempts at audience research) there was a slight dip in the show's popularity over the course of its latest run. The attempt to 'pep the show up no end' with the introduction of Diana Dors had certainly backfired spectacularly – 'We got sackfuls (and I'm not exaggerating) of letters from viewers (mostly women),' Terry-Thomas would recall, 'saying "Get rid of that girl!"'[36] – and some fans complained that a formula in near-perfect working order had been broken merely as an excuse to attempt a quick fix. There had still been a fair number of high points, but it was felt that too many of the new ideas had fallen flat, and a little of the old fun had faded away. It had all been, it was alleged, a bit too forced, a bit too frenetic, a bit too *busy*. Tired, upset and frustrated, Terry-Thomas could only agree, but, rather than allow such an important, influential and widely admired show to disappear for good with little more than a whimper, he vowed to take *How Do You View?* all the way back up to its rightful lofty level.

The fifth series, therefore, saw everyone involved work hard to regain much of the old discipline, focus and firm commitment to the collective cause. The emphasis this time around would be on stronger and more coherent scripts, more character-based comedy and fewer but better gimmicks. The team stopped worrying so much about being seen to be 'innovative' and concentrated instead on being seen to make people laugh. Diana Dors departed, the characters of Moulting and Lockit were retained and the versatile young impressionist Janet Brown (an old *Stars in Battledress* colleague of T-T's who was now married to Peter Butterworth) joined the cast as a dizzy secretary called Miss Happ. As the material improved and rehearsals progressed, the positive spirit returned.

Beginning on 2 April 1952, and running for six fortnightly episodes, the new *How Do You View?* reminded people of the old *How Do You View?*, and nobody felt inclined to complain about that. It was no longer the only show that did what it did, but it still did it better than most – if not all – of the rest, and its legion of long-standing fans were more than happy to have it back on such vibrant and sharp good form. At its heart, once again, was a rejuvenated star, keeping the comedy moving along with the deftest of playful touches. 'Terry-Thomas was the most sensible comedian I ever met,' Janet Brown would recall. 'He loved the show and wasn't afraid of letting this wonderful collection of characters get the laughs. He instinctively knew that the audience would say, "Oh, wasn't the Terry-Thomas show funny last night?", regardless of whether they laughed at me, Pete, H.C. Walton or Terry himself.'[37] (This was an admirable attitude he would never lose. Georgina Cookson, who appeared with him several years later in the movie *The Naked Truth*, would reveal: 'Terry was absolutely extraordinary to work with, because, unlike most comedians, he wasn't selfish. He'd say, "I think this scene would work better if *you* had better lines," and he'd swap the lines over and give me some of the best remarks – which was unheard of!'[38])

There were still some comedy elements that were undeniably ahead of their time – such as the surreal moment in each show when Lockit, the chauffeur with no motor, would enter clutching a steering wheel (or sometimes just sporting an indicator strapped to his arm), say in all seriousness to Terry-Thomas, 'Jump in, sir,' and the two of them would walk off together as if it was the most natural thing in the world for them to do. Most reviewers, however, while fully appreciative of such features, tended to celebrate instead the sheer professionalism of the cast and crew and the unforced charm of the central characters. The ground-breaking show now seemed more like a talented old friend, and the common wish was to see it continue.

Ironically, however, just as the future of the show once more looked all sweetness and light, the relationship between Terry-Thomas and the BBC suddenly turned all sour and dark. A newspaper article, which had appeared during the latter part of the series' run, hinted at the star's continuing dissatisfaction with his treatment by the Corporation, recalled his past frustrations with the quality of some of his writers' scripts and claimed that he was seriously considering quitting television completely in the near future. Terry-Thomas roundly dismissed the article's various speculations and allegations as the illegitimate mischief-making of the 'cheaper sort of journalist', but (in an era in which the paucity of journalistic stories about television bestowed an exaggerated significance upon any that did actually make it into print) a certain amount of the mud still stuck, and some executives at the BBC would never really trust him or his representatives ever again.

On 2 October 1952, after hearing that the star's agent had been pushing for some high-profile guest spots that might lead to discussions about another major television deal, Ronald Waldman – still furious about his star's supposed betrayal (but apparently strangely forgetful about his remarkable creative contribution) – wrote to his Controller of Programmes: 'For a large number of reasons I don't want Terry-Thomas to feel that he can have television as and when he likes it and, at the same time, have the ability to make pretty slanderous statements to the Press about the material that is given to him. . . . It would be a help, therefore, if the Service would be unable to find a fifteen-minute spot for him on his own.'[39] The BBC did manage to find a place for him at the end of the year among the large cast of its live *Christmas Party*, but then replaced him at the last minute with Arthur Askey after he was deemed to have downed a glass or two more than he should have done in the 'green room' backstage.[40]

That, in effect, was that as far as Terry-Thomas's long-term television career was concerned. He left with his still semi-estranged wife Pat[41] for her native Johannesburg on 13 November, so that he could star as 'The Honourable Idle Jack' in *Dick Whittington* and Pat could spend Christmas with her family (the trip proved a disaster, because the pantomime was 'so tatty and unrehearsed it was pathetic', he rowed for the umpteenth time with Pat and found Johannesburg to be 'even more depressing than Norwich or Finchley'⁴²). Returning home at the end of April 1953, he went through the motions in a summer season, launched a new but relatively run-of-the-mill variety series on radio called *Top of the Town*,⁴³ then coasted through a short-lived but lucrative revue at the London Palladium (with a cast that included George Formby and the Billy Cotton Band) called *Fun and the Fair*, and toured some of the bigger provincial theatres.⁴⁴ As far as television was concerned, there would still be the odd one-off special – such as the one-hour farewell outing for the *How Do You View?* team towards the end of 1953, a prestigious revue at Lime Grove (attended by the recently crowned Queen Elizabeth II) entitled *For Your Pleasure* (screened in October 1953), and a much-anticipated starring vehicle for himself and Max Miller, called *Around the Town*, transmitted during the week in 1955 when the BBC first went head-to-head with the newly formed ITV. At the start of 1956, there would even be a new six-part series (four years after the last one) called *Strictly T-T* (which promised *How Do You View?*-style 'fun and games' from the star's bachelor apartment in the fictional 'Holdergap-on-Tees', and also, incidentally, employed a young man named Michael Winner as a call boy). T-T's great pioneering days on TV, however, were long gone.

He seemed, for a while, to be somewhat unsure as to what he most wanted to do next, and was unimpressed by the majority of the offers that came his way. Apart from agreeing to release a delightfully silly novelty single (as 'Terry Thomas, Esq., and his Rock 'n' Roll Rotters') entitled 'A Sweet Old-Fashioned Boy' (which featured such typically T-T interjections as 'Oh, lovely – that's the *mostest*!' and 'See you later, *alma mater*!'⁴⁵), he sat back and allowed a little time to pass him by. 'Between you, me and the starting handle,' he would tell a reporter about how the past few months had gone, 'I've turned down nearly £20,000 worth of work.' Explaining that he wanted to avoid falling into

a dull routine of 'hack work' and 'guest spots in other people's programmes', he spoke admiringly of some of the actors he admired in
European cinema, such as the suavely independent Sacha Guitry and
the subtly witty Louis Jouvet (both of whom used their movie work more
to subsidise their other activities than to satiate all of their artistic desires),
and expressed the hope that, one day soon, he might start moving in the
same urbane direction.[46] As far as his immediate future was concerned,
however, he was more sure of what he wished to avoid than he was
about what he wanted to embrace.

There was always stand-up comedy in the music halls and the night
clubs, where, with his remarkable charm, he could get away with what,
at the time, were such 'saucy' stories as the following:

> A school teacher met the local vicar. And she said, 'You're the very
> man I wanted to meet. Do you think you could come to the school
> next week and talk to my girls about sex?' So he said, 'I should be
> delighted.' That evening, he wrote in his diary: 'Speak to girls at St.
> Margaret's about S . . . sailing.' He didn't want to put in sex, in case
> his wife saw it and mocked him. A fortnight later, the vicar's wife
> met the schoolmistress who remarked, 'I can't thank your husband
> enough for coming to talk to my girls.' And the vicar's wife said, 'He
> was delighted. But I can't understand why he chose that subject.
> He's only done it twice in his life. The first time it made him sick
> and the second time his hat blew off.'[47]

Conventional stand-up, however, no longer struck him as a truly
rewarding activity.

So-called 'serious' theatre, as opposed to mere revue, held some
appeal for him as a fresh challenge, but any bold dreams of venturing
very far in that particular direction were destined soon to be dashed. He
did appear in a rather creaky-looking revival of Gilbert Wakefield's pre-
war farce *Room for Two* – even shaving off his famous moustache and at
one point donning drag to play the leading role of the womanising
Hubert Crone – but, after opening in London at the Prince of Wales
Theatre at the end of February 1955, the production was dismissed by
the critics and neglected by the public, and it closed after little more

than a month. His only other serious attempt to 'cross over' into so-called legitimate theatre would meet with a similarly dispiriting fate five years later, in the summer of 1960, when, after enjoying a relatively successful provincial tour, he returned to the West End at the Duke of York's Theatre in *It's in the Bag* (Robin Maugham's anglicised adaptation of Claude Magnier's French farce, called *Oscar*, about, of all things, a wealthy but blackmailed soap manufacturer). Once again, the reviews were generally poor,[48] the audiences stayed away in their droves and Terry-Thomas was left feeling intensely frustrated. 'The odd thing about his career,' Richard Briers (who appeared alongside him for the first time in *It's in the Bag*) would reflect, 'was that, although he was totally successful all over the world, he couldn't ever fill a London theatre. It was extraordinary. He was so popular, so well-known and so talented, but London theatre always defeated him. He couldn't understand it. *I* couldn't understand it. But he was bloody livid about it – and Terry could get livid quite quickly!'[49]

In the mid-1950s, therefore, television remained, regardless of whether T-T wanted it to be or not, the best (as well as the most tried and tested) of his available professional options. He was thus tempted over to the commercial company Granada in the summer of 1956 in order to try his hand at being a regular panel member (alongside fellow comedians Tommy Trinder, Alfred Marks and 'Monsewer' Eddie Gray, or sometimes the comic magician David Nixon) on a new show called *My Wildest Dreams* (a variation on *What's My Line* in which members of the audience would challenge the performers to guess their secret ambition[50]). Although the programme somehow managed to survive for two long series, it none the less remained a cheap and unimaginative affair that never appealed to the critics (one of whom lamented the fact that the format 'seemed to prove that four comedians, each extremely funny in his own right, cancel out one another when they appear together'[51]). A tired and disillusioned Terry-Thomas (who had long been niggled by the foghorn-voiced Tommy Trinder's laboured attempts to dominate every episode) was greatly relieved when the project was finally over. 'The critics were right,' he moaned. 'It was a terrible show.'[52]

It did not really affect, however, his hard-won high standing in show business; the fond memories of earlier, far superior, efforts remained strong and sharp and vivid, and his many fans were hopeful that his next venture would prove to be much better and more worthwhile. They would not have long to wait, as things turned out. As several critics were already predicting,[53] Terry-Thomas was on the verge of a glamorous new career in movies, first in Britain and then abroad, and it would indeed not be long before he advanced from being merely one of the most popular comic actors in his own country to one of the most distinctive and widely recognised Englishmen in the world. Television had just been his first big step, and it was now time for him to move on.

The departure did, however, cause him a measure of sadness and personal regret, because he knew that the medium that now owed him and his old *How Do You View?* team so much would probably soon forget that it had ever owed them anything at all. Most of the earliest shows, having gone out live, had not been recorded, and so nearly all of the innovations, all of the bold experiments and all of the brave risks would only really live on in the minds of those who had witnessed them at the time.

He remained thoroughly proud, none the less, of his contribution to British television. He had done precisely what he had set out to do: he had changed the way that we viewed for good.

CHAPTER FOUR

Hollywood

I say, good show, sir – absolutely bang on!

AFTER HIS LONG run of television success, Terry-Thomas was becoming a little restless. He still had a role to play on radio, if he wanted it, but radio had never been a medium for which he had much of a real affinity (he fully agreed with the critic who had said: 'You have to see him as well as hear him in order thoroughly to appreciate his line in elegant idiocy'[1]). He was still in demand on the variety circuit, too, but, as he would soon come to observe: 'I find that I don't like Variety any more. I've grown up – it hasn't.'[2] Any special plaudits, of course, were always welcomed – he was absolutely delighted, for example, to top *Tailor and Cutter*'s list of the Ten Best Dressed Men of 1953 (eclipsing such ultra-smart luminaries as Sir Malcolm Sargent, John Mills, Douglas Fairbanks Jnr, Cecil Beaton, Terence Rattigan and the infant Prince Charles, who was cutting a dash that season in a 'baby bow-tie' and 'junior deerstalker'[3]) – but it was fresh challenges for his career that he really craved. This craving would soon draw him into the sphere of the movies.

The big screen now seemed like the best option for someone who was looking to test himself before a broader audience than the one that British television, at that time, could provide. Ever since his first days as an extra, he had dreamed of making a proper career for himself in his favourite medium, the cinema, and now, at last, he saw that his chance had probably come. The offers, which had been flowing in for some time, were starting to sound too tempting to turn down, and so he decided to take the plunge: 'It was the cinema for me, and me for cinema!'[4]

He had already dipped an impeccably pedicured toe into the American market – and then pulled it smartly back out again – a few years earlier. He had gone to New York in March 1951, between series of *How Do You View?*, ostensibly to perform the odd cabaret engagement but also to tout himself around for future Stateside projects. No sooner, however, had he checked in to his hotel suite, sat down and switched on the TV, than the visit had begun to seem doomed: 'Don't forget to watch next week, folks,' mumbled Ed Sullivan, the tall, broad and chronically confused-looking host of *The Toast of the Town*, on the tiny black-and-white screen. 'We have England's top television star, *Tommy Tucker!*'[5] It was par for the course for the bumbling Sullivan, who early on in the next decade would introduce Morecambe and Wise to America as 'Morrey, Camby and Wise',[6] but it was still quite a blow to the ego of Terry-Thomas. He went on to do well enough on the show itself, and received mainly (if only moderately) favourable reviews when he played a brief cabaret season in the elegant Wedgwood Room of the city's Waldorf-Astoria Hotel, but the experience, in general, was not particularly encouraging – and being mistaken for a floor-walker while shopping for ties in Macy's department store did nothing to brighten his mood.[7] He returned home after a three-month stay feeling somewhat deflated, and threw himself back into his work on domestic television at the BBC.

Hollywood, therefore, seemed beyond him for the foreseeable future, but steady success in the British film industry, on the other hand, now appeared well within his reach. In 1955, after sleepwalking through a number of instantly forgettable cinema shorts (such as 1948's *Copy Book Please* – a three-minute lesson from the Crown Film Unit about the best way to address a letter – and then 1951's *Cookery Nook* – a thirty-minute demonstration by Terry-Thomas, Michael Bentine and Philip Harben of how to cook and then clean a typical post-war gas oven) and several similarly evanescent feature-length efforts (including the 1947 Carroll Levis musical-thriller *The Brass Monkey*, Dicky Leeman's over-indulgent 'let's do the show right here' 1948 concert party romp *Date with a Dream* – which also featured a brief and somewhat unflattering contribution from T-T's wife, Pat Patlanski – and 1949's

Helter Skelter – a self-consciously zany *Hellzapoppin'*-style comedy, set mainly inside the BBC's Broadcasting House, in which the 'Technical Hitch' routine was reprised), Terry-Thomas was finally handed a worthwhile role in a movie of real significance.

Private's Progress was set to be the first in a series of movies made by the twin Boulting Brothers, John and Roy, that satirised various facets of Britain's post-war way of life and the pillar institutions of its Establishment. Terry-Thomas had been unimpressed when he first learned that he was wanted for what seemed like the relatively minor role of a heavy-drinking, pill-popping Army officer (he would have much preferred to have played a silly-ass sergeant-major), but, after being persuaded by his agent of the time, John Redway,[8] to re-read the script, he saw the bigger picture, and signed up to take part.[9]

Set in 1942, the film (which was released in March 1956) featured Ian Carmichael as Stanley Windrush, a naïve, upper-middle-class Oxbridge undergraduate called up into the Army and taken under the wing of a Cockney wideboy called Henry Cox (played by Richard Attenborough). Terry-Thomas appeared as Major Hitchcock, a lazy but basically decent sort of cove who has learnt to cope with the various crises that creep towards him by shrugging his shoulders, passing the buck and then downing the brandy. 'You're an absolute *shower!*' he shouts at his men through the opened window of his cosy office. 'No doubt you think *I'm* a shower, too,' he adds uncertainly. 'I wouldn't like to say, sir,' replies Private Cox. 'Well, *I* would,' he grumbles. 'I've got to be – to turn out *rotters* like you!'

The director, John Boulting, found Terry-Thomas very easy to advise once he had managed, against all the odds, to persuade the actor to do without one of his most iconic 'T-T' accessories. 'Terry was initially determined to hold his cigarette holder all the time as a prop,' his co-star Ian Carmichael would recall. 'He felt part of his life was being ripped away when the Boultings insisted he left the thing in the dressing room. But he gave a marvellous performance. I found him a very easy and very amusing man to work with. He was a total professional.'[10] One of his major influences at that time, as a movie actor, was Spencer Tracy, whose ability to use stillness and silence as well as – if not better than –

most other performers used movement and sounds encouraged T-T to supplement what dialogue he had with subtle little expressions that made the viewer curious about his thoughts. Nowhere was his expertise in front of the camera more evident than during the scene in which Major Hitchcock responds to the fact that there is 'a bit of a flap on' by sneaking off to watch a movie at the local cinema: as he settles into his seat, starts glancing around and spots several men from his own unit (who have obviously had the same devious idea as himself) scattered about the shadowy stalls, he registers his rich mixture of shock, anger, irritation and discomfort by doing very little apart from a very slight arch of his eyebrows and a subtle tensing of his lips. 'I just looked at the camera and kept my mind blank,' he later explained somewhat self-deprecatingly. 'In this way, the audience does the work. We shot it twice, for safety, then John said to me, pleased, "Thank you, dear boy". I was tickled pink when *Sight and Sound* nominated this scene as "the best close-up of the year".'[11]

Although he was barely on the screen for more than ten minutes in total, he still came close to stealing the show from the central characters. Whether he was wincing from a hangover while his sergeant-major stood close by and bellowed out his orders, or slipping a couple of headache tablets to one of his chastened men, or shouting '*Schnell*, you *stinkers!*' to some dilatory German prisoners, he was always eminently watchable, suggesting a depth and complexity within the melancholic major – a bounder now too bowed down to be bothered to bound any further – that left the audience wanting to find out more.

The Boulting Brothers were certainly far more than just satisfied with his efforts, because they promptly signed him up to a five-picture deal. They were by no means the only cinema team, however, who were now keen to work with Terry-Thomas: Frank Launder and Sidney Gilliat – the duo responsible for such popular home-grown movies as *The Rake's Progress* (1945), *London Belongs To Me* (1948), *The Belles Of St Trinian's* (1954) and *Geordie* (1955) – persuaded him to play the part of Charlie Boughtflower, a part-time philanderer and weekend bounder, in their darkly farcical comedy *The Green Man* (1956). The movie (which starred the wonderfully artful Alistair Sim as a freelance assassin whose plan to blow up yet another pompous government minister is hindered unwittingly by George Cole's hapless vacuum cleaner salesman) did not actually include much for Terry-Thomas to do, but what little time on screen he had he used exceptionally well.

Rolling up outside the country hotel in his smart open-topped sports car, he leaps out, gives his 'beautiful girl', Lily (played by Dora Bryan), a quick kiss and a hug, and then launches into a ramblingly neurotic account of how the 'mem-sahib' at home has been acting: 'She's been behaving very *mysteriously* just lately. You know: pools of silence broken only by the odd vitriolic ripple.' For all of his mischievous glee at having sneaked away to be with his mistress, it is clear that he cannot stop himself from worrying about his wife and the state of their shared domestic life: 'She keeps on making cryptic remarks and then going into a huddle with her mum,' he complains. 'Oh, I shouldn't take any notice of *her*,' says his mistress, who is anxious to have him start focusing on the fun to be had so much closer at hand. 'Yes, but you know what it is,' he replies. 'Undertones – always *undertones!*' When, due to a case of mistaken identity, he is warned that 'his' life is in danger, he jumps to the inevitable wrong conclusion: 'I can take a tip – I'll get my bag!' he gasps, before adding, 'Mark my words – her mother's behind this!'

He followed this deftly executed cameo with his second movie for the Boulting Brothers, the legal satire *Brothers in Law* (1956). Playing a seventeen-time offender by the name of Alfie Green (a Cockney spiv clearly modelled on Sid Field's very own 'Slasher Green'[12]), he educates a wet-behind-the-ears barrister in the ways of law and strategic argument, but ends up being angered when he is only charged with one count instead of his customary twelve ('Bloomin' insult!'). Relishing the rare chance to play against his famously dandified upper-crust type, Terry-Thomas took the role so seriously that, dabbling in a spot of Method acting, he slept in his character's clothes for a couple of weeks prior to the start of filming, and then rubbed the seams of his suit with a pumice stone to accentuate the scruffy effect. It was an admirably professional effort – especially as, once again, he would only end up on screen for a matter of a few minutes – and, once again, his fleeting presence stood out to good effect.

Behind the scenes, he had also learnt some invaluable lessons as a movie actor. His director, Roy Boulting, was a stickler for disciplined contributions from all of his cast, and so, adopting a quite deliberate 'cruel to be kind' policy, he pushed T-T extremely hard to get every single one of his lines and movements as precise as he possibly could – even making him go through as many as 107 takes for one brief sequence that was set in a crowded pub. Although a difficult and sometimes intimidating experience for him to endure, T-T ended up leaving the set confident that he had rid himself of some bad 'variety' habits and was now much better equipped to make the most of his time in front of a movie camera.

Lucky Jim – his next project – proved, however, to be more of a patchy affair. Adapted by the Boulting Brothers from the best-selling novel by Kingsley Amis about life in one of Britain's post-war redbrick universities, the movie was compromised both by the clumsiness of its screenplay and the mismatch between its cast and its characterisations. Thirty-seven-year-old Ian Carmichael was unconvincing as the twenty-seven-year-old assistant lecturer Jim Dixon, a nervously upwardly mobile Northerner from a lower-middle-class background; sometimes seeming like a slightly tetchy provincial rebel, and sometimes like a posh metropolitan clot (with an accent that shifted back and forth between Derby, Doncaster, Exeter and Esher), he never really came close to bringing Amis's angry young man to life – and he was not helped by a narrative that favoured farce and slapstick over satire and social commentary. Terry-Thomas was, if anything, even less convincing as Bertrand Welch, the bearded and bow-tied would-be novelist ('It isn't written yet – it's *ripening*') and psycho-babbling popinjay who stands to gain everything that Jim Dixon craves (*Films and Filming* lamented his 'surprisingly flat performance'[13]). Hugh Griffith, who played Bertrand's even more pompous academic father, was far from happy at having to play opposite a 'son' who, at forty-five, was actually ten months his senior (Roy Boulting had to stop him from appearing in front of the cameras with his face caked in 'youthful' make-up[14]).

Jean Anderson, who played Bertrand's stern-looking mother, would recall the somewhat chaotic nature of the production to the comedy historian Glyn Roberts:

My memory of filming with Terry is one of disgraceful hilarity! On the first day's filming it was sprung on us that I had to ride a 'phut-phut' bicycle and Terry a Vespa scooter with Hugh Griffith on the pillion. John Boulting [the director] said, 'I suppose you can ride this thing?' Terry said firmly, 'Yes, yes, of course.' He had to drive through a gate round a little centre flower bed to the front door. Well, this scooter turned into a bucking bronco! Hugh fell backwards from the saddle and Terry parted company with the scooter.

Take 2 – This time the scooter stayed earthbound and went straight into the camera, scattering the crew. We all thought it very funny. John Boulting didn't!!

The next – I had to ride this machine over a grass field, narrowly missing young lovers hidden in the grass, after one lesson from 'props'. When I was off (and the engine was working) I noticed I had no idea how to stop it! I don't know whether the lovers or I was the most frightened.

The film ended with a sequence that involved Terry and myself racing each other to a little station up a narrow country lane. It was a freezing morning and we were almost paralysed with cold, which didn't help, as neither of us could keep very straight and had terrible lurches towards each other when, of course, we 'corpsed'. Again, John Boulting was not amused.

We were then sent to thaw out in the station master's little cottage, where there was a fire and a bottle of gin! Fatal!!

We must have got the shot in the end as it was the climax of the film.[15]

Understandably, a rattled Kingsley Amis would later complain that Terry-Thomas had been 'totally miscast' as Bertrand ('the leading shit of the novel'), but added, by way of a spectacularly backhanded compliment, that 'the hash he made of the part was so comic that the result was a large net gain'.[16] Amis actually rather admired Terry-Thomas as a man, and was intrigued by the fact that, unlike so many of the other (essentially morose) comic performers he had encountered, the amiable T-T seemed 'just the same person in the flesh as on the screen'.[17]

On one memorable occasion, when they were up in Scotland together for the première of *Lucky Jim* at the Edinburgh Film Festival, Amis and several other members of the crew were persuaded to follow T-T's lead and abandon the smart but somewhat boring bar inside the North British Hotel and go out in search of some 'proper' old Edinburgh pubs. Choosing one quaint-looking hostelry at random, their entrance caused the regulars to fall silent and the atmosphere to turn frosty. As the most eye-catching of the English visitors 'possessed to the full that actor's hunger for winning round, winning over an audience against indifference or even hostility', he ignored the Celtic attempt to intimidate, proceeded to talk 'at the top of his voice and in his most Eaton Square accent', and soon, sure enough, 'he had every man in that pub round him in a laughing semi-circle'.[18] On and on he went, regaling his new audience with a succession of shaggy dog stories and rude jokes. 'Strict justice would have awarded him a medium-strength kick up the arse for this display,' Amis would come to reflect, 'but at the time you had to admire and enjoy.'[19]

Later on, back at the hotel bar, after most of the entourage had retired to bed feeling drunk and thoroughly exhausted, Terry-Thomas was still in full flow, entertaining Amis and one tired and emotional colleague with some even racier gags and anecdotes. The show only stopped when, right in the middle of his latest story, T-T suddenly interrupted himself to announce: 'I'm terribly sorry, chaps, I don't want to break up the party, but I've come over most frightfully *randy* just in the last couple of minutes' – and with that he was off into the night.[20]

Terry-Thomas had been going off into the night on a regular basis during the previous few months, because his troubled sixteen-year marriage to Pat Patlanski had at last ended up on the rocks. 'We were always at each other's throats, and being mutually unfaithful,' he later reflected, even though, as he also acknowledged, they had 'shared a lot of good times', too.[21] Once they had finally agreed to separate, towards the end of 1954, Pat moved into their other property, 'Ye Cowshed', leaving her forsaken husband in his Queen's Gate Mews flat, but rumours of their break-up did not reach the public realm until 1957, when a *Daily Mail* gossip columnist decided to share the news with the nation. Terry-Thomas then went on to lead a slightly more open form of his previously semi-covert bachelor life, coming over 'frightfully randy' on countless occasions in many kinds of contexts until he eventually met the young woman whom he would later describe ('physically speaking') as 'the greatest love of my life' – the Australian-born singer and actor Lorrae Desmond.[22]

Born Beryl Hunt in the town of Mittagong, in the Southern Highlands of New South Wales, in 1932, she had moved to London shortly before turning twenty and (armed with a couple of 'glam' dresses, a handwritten list of goals to achieve and a new name expressly for the stage) began trying to make her mark on the variety and cabaret circuits. By the mid-1950s, she was attracting a growing amount of attention as a recording artist, releasing such popular singles as 'I Can't Tell a Waltz from a Tango' (1954), and was also appearing occasionally as a guest on BBC radio shows. She came into contact with Terry-Thomas in 1954, when both she and he were appearing in the north of England during the summer season, and an instant rapport was formed (they even posed for some playful publicity shots one sunny afternoon on the beach at Southport) which soon evolved into an increasingly flirtatious friendship.

They first worked together a short while later, in 1955 on a Combined Services Entertainment tour of Kenya, and she joined him the following year as a regular on his new television series, *Strictly T-T*. It was not long before they became lovers, and the thoroughly smitten T-T began confiding to close friends that she was 'the sexiest person' he had ever met, as well as the most 'dedicated woman in bed'.[23] It was in bed, and *in flagrante delicto*, that the couple were caught one Sunday morning when the erstwhile 'Mrs T-T', Pat Patlanski (having secretly held on to her key to the on-off marital flat), decided to pay an unsolicited visit. Upon finding Ms Desmond in action directly above her estranged (and infuriatingly grateful-looking) horizontal husband, she grabbed a dog's lead from out of her handbag and started lashing out indiscriminately with the leather leash. 'With great presence of mind, considering that she was starkers, Lorrae did not let herself appear to be affected at all by this attack,' her lover would recall. 'She pulled the sheets up to her neck and started turning the pages of *The Observer*.'[24]

Eventually, after the furious Pat had exhausted herself with all of her frenzied flailing, she asked for a bottle of champagne and then shuffled back out of the door. According to Terry-Thomas, she would 'never stop reproaching herself' for her wild and violent (and patently hypocritical) reaction to his infidelity, and for many years after she would tell her friends that, if only she had not done that, 'we might have ridden our crisis, as we had others before, and got back together again'.[25] As it was, her husband would remain with Lorrae Desmond for the rest of the decade (even though, by his own admission,[26] he did not always stay faithful to her). 'I would have married her like a shot, and we often discussed it,' he later confessed, 'but Pat repeatedly refused to divorce me.'[27]

The lovers often worked together both in cabaret and on tour, and sometimes even managed to share vacations in such pleasant locations as Majorca, Positano and various parts of the South of France (where they spent some time with Pablo Picasso, who 'didn't think it a bit funny' when Terry-Thomas enquired of him if anyone had ever asked, 'Can I have a word in your eye?'[28]), but, whenever circumstances contrived to keep them apart, fights 'based on nothing' tended to break out in the middle of conversations 'conducted on long distance telephones'.[29] A succession of 'positively throbbing reconciliations' ensured that the relationship would survive such squabbles, but she had a promising career of her own to pursue, and he was making rapid progress in movies, so the crises seemed bound to continue.

His next trio of projects certainly took up the vast majority of his time. Moving at a near-breathless pace from one production to the next, he followed up *Lucky Jim* with *Blue Murder at St Trinian's*, *The Naked Truth* and *Happy is the Bride* (all of which were released close together, to favourable reviews and a positive box office, at the end of 1957). By far the best of these three, in terms both of the effectiveness of his own performance and the quality of the picture as a whole, was *The Naked Truth* – the first in a series of comedy collaborations with Peter Sellers.

These two actors would seem drawn to each other throughout the next few years, each one helping – largely just by sharing the screen – to highlight what was special about the other. They made, in many ways,

an improbable actorly pair – not just in terms of their off-stage personalities (T-T being the relatively confident extrovert and Sellers the neurotic introvert) and their on-set attitudes (Sellers liked to arrive word-
perfect and ready for the first – and, he hoped, only – take, whereas T-T
tended to take time to warm up and master his lines), but also in terms
of their respective on-screen aptitudes (Sellers excelled at exploiting the
rich colour of a particular character, while T-T was equally adept at
mining deep into a particular type). Together, however, they divided
their satirical labours between them and somehow seemed well-
matched. Within the same artful vision of contemporary Britain, Sellers
would provide insights into a range of awkward outsiders, and Terry-
Thomas would do much the same for a set of real or would-be insiders.
For the remainder of the 1950s and the start of the 1960s, the pair would
project something plausible, as well as amusing, about the kind of
clashes in class, taste, outlook and ambition that were niggling away at
their nation.

The Naked Truth, their first shared effort, turned out to be a thoroughly enjoyable and rather prescient little comedy about the attempt
by a scandal magazine editor called Nigel Dennis (played by the suavely
caddish Dennis Price) to blackmail his next four victims (Terry-Thomas
as a harmlessly lascivious peer named Lord Henry Mayley, Peter Sellers
as a hypocritical TV personality, Peggy Mount as a respected crime
writer hiding a shady past and Shirley Eaton as an attractive young
model with a psychotically jealous fiancé). Although somewhat compromised by having the licence only to hint at what the censors in those
days preferred movies not to disclose (such as the homosexuality of Peter
Sellers' character and the highly promiscuous past of the young model),
Michael Pertwee's screenplay still managed to accommodate plenty of
above-average comedy dialogue as well as encourage some excellent
ensemble acting. Apart from boasting a *tour de force* performance from
Sellers at his most charmingly smart and versatile, the movie also benefited from the splendid efforts of a supporting cast that included the
likes of Miles Malleson, Kenneth Griffith and a young Joan Sims at her
scene-stealing best.

It gets off to a fine start with the smarmy magazine editor's visit to the home of Lord Mayley, where he proceeds to present the priapic aristo-crat with a glossy-looking foreign publication:

MAYLEY: *'Scandalous'*? What's this?

DENNIS: Oh, it's one of those American scandal magazines. You know: the ghastly truth about people's private lives. Do borrow it if you wish.

MAYLEY: [*Sounding rather excited*] How very charming of you! [*He is already gazing gratefully at all the filth*] I shall thoroughly enjoy reading this. [*He flashes a nervous smile*] Rather *naughty*, I believe?

DENNIS: [*Impassively*] Ah, yes. [*Moving smartly on*] Well, now, let's get to business. I myself am running a modest little magazine in England entitled *The Naked Truth*.

MAYLEY: Rather a *vulgar* title, isn't it?

DENNIS: Oh, vulgar, perhaps, but terribly *apt*. [*He holds up a copy for Mayley to see. The front cover features a picture of the peer. Dennis starts turning the pages*] Here, on the inside, we have a short biography of your public life and works.

MAYLEY: Er, very nice.

DENNIS: While on the opposite page we have … the *real* works.

MAYLEY: [*Puzzled*] About me?

DENNIS: Oh, yes, indeed.

MAYLEY: Well, if it's about me, why is it titled: 'Guess Who'?

DENNIS: Because, as British law stands, the public mustn't be able positively to identify you, Lord Mayley, with the *naughty* hero of this article.

MAYLEY: 'Naughty'? [*He looks a little flustered, but tries to maintain a smile*] But I don't quite understand … if it's about *me* …

DENNIS: Have you a weak heart? Or high blood pressure?

MAYLEY: … No … ?

DENNIS: Well, ah, *read* it then – just to check the facts.

[*Dennis sits back and gloats until Mayley's startled eyes pop up over the top of the covers*]

MAYLEY: You can't print THIS! [*He leaps up from behind his desk*]
You *CAN'T* print this! It's *libel*!

DENNIS: It's the naked truth, old lord.

MAYLEY: But-but … no publisher would *dare*!

DENNIS: Oh, yes, *I* would. I've been into the legal aspects most
carefully. The fact that 'Mr X' was the centre of an 'amorous
incident' in Regents Park –

MAYLEY: [*Glancing nervously over his shoulder*] *Shhh! SHHH!*

DENNIS: – has no connection with Lord Mayley's magnificent gifts
for charities. Of course, by judicious word of mouth, I suppose
the public *might* be persuaded to *connect* the two …

MAYLEY: [*Shaken*] Y-You'll go to jail! I-I'll *sue* you!

DENNIS: Try it. You'd have to prove that 'Mr X' was you – and by
doing so you rather imply that the story's true, don't you? Dare
you risk that?

MAYLEY: But this is *England*! There *must* be a way …

DENNIS: There is: an immediate cash gift of £10,000 to The
Distressed Journalists' Association – of which I am the founder,
the treasurer and, so far, the only member – would I am sure
persuade the editor – myself – to suppress this particular issue
…

Mayley is then left alone with the cad's calling card and a new price
tag placed on his clandestine fun: 'Ten thousand pounds for a quarter of
an hour!'

The subsequent encounters between T-T's Lord Mayley and another
of the callous editor's victims, Peter Sellers' TV entertainer 'Wee' Sonny
MacGregor, are short and sharp and marked by a chilly sense of mutual
contempt. In the eyes of the snooty peer, MacGregor is clearly nothing
more than an unwelcome and worthless *arriviste*: 'I never did like you,'
he sneers. 'Not even on television.' In the eyes of the chippy small-screen
celebrity, Mayley is just an outdated and over-indulged social parasite:
'Make an ally out of *that* stupid idiot?' he exclaims to his dresser. 'No
thank you!' For much of the movie it thus appears clear that, although
both men now find themselves bound tightly together through black-

mail, they would still rather watch each other slip down deeper into the abyss than waste any time and effort trying to pull each other back up from the brink to safety:

MAYLEY: [*Poking his head around MacGregor's door*] I do think that you'll agree that we should help each other in times of trouble. Don't you?

MACGREGOR: [*Blankly*] Hmm. How much do you want?

MAYLEY: No, no! *I* want to help *you*! Mr MacGregor, if I mention the name 'Dennis', coupled with the fact that I know you're being … '*B'd*' … ?

MACGREGOR: '*B'd*'?

MAYLEY: Well – blackmailed! [*MacGregor attempts to shut the door in Mayley's face*] Look, may I come in?

MACGREGOR: [*Defensively*] Ha-ha! Wee Sonny MacGregor blackmailed? I think you're mistaken!

MAYLEY: [*Struggling to keep the door ajar*] Mr MacGregor, look, I know you're wondering why I'm here …

MACGREGOR: [*Calmly and coldly*] I *know* why you're here, friend. *You're* being '*B'd*' too!

MAYLEY: No, no, no – I'm a complete outsider!

MACGREGOR: I wouldn't say *that*!

Such exchanges worked well because, as Peter Sellers would later say of his acting relationship with T-T, 'we never try to outshine the other'.[30]

The real high spots, however, are the brief scenes that Terry-Thomas shares with his on-screen wife, Lady Mayley (played superbly crisply by Georgina Cookson), because the interaction between the two actors is so sure, so subtle and so sharp. Lord Mayley is the boyish scamp who thinks of himself as a manly rascal, whereas his wife is the wise and mature woman who is disinclined (most of the time) to disabuse him of his silly delusions. Addressing him with a level of sarcasm that is meant merely to ruffle his hair as it shoots just over his head (LORD MAYLEY: 'How do I look?' LADY MAYLEY: 'Very chick'. LORD MAYLEY: '"*Chick*"? I thought the word was "*chic*".' LADY MAYLEY: 'Yes, darling, it is, but not when applied to you.' LORD MAYLEY: 'Eh?'), she would rather let him go ahead and do the odd *slightly* naughty thing, and let him think that he was being *very* naughty, than provoke him into actually doing something really *bad*. When, for example, he sits with his head slumped over a steaming bowl of hot water after a late-night visit to his blackmailer's houseboat has ended up with an unplanned dip in the Thames ('I got caught in a storm'), his wife, with obvious relish, enters his room with more bad news to report:

LADY MAYLEY: Henry?

LORD MAYLEY: *Please* don't ask me any more questions about that storm!

LADY MAYLEY: An *orphan* of the storm has just arrived.

LORD MAYLEY: Eh? *What?*

LADY MAYLEY: Your *girl*.

LORD MAYLEY: Look, I keep *telling* you – I haven't *got* a girl! What's she like?

LADY MAYLEY: Oh, about forty.

LORD MAYLEY: *Forty?* I thought you said she was a *girl?*

LADY MAYLEY: I wasn't referring to her age.

LORD MAYLEY: Eh? *Oh!*

LADY MAYLEY: Poor Henry – it never rains but it pours, *hmmm?*

Poor Henry was one of the classic T-T characters – the kind of bounder who is never quite brave enough to stray very far, if at all, beyond any significant boundary – and few actors other than Terry-Thomas could have made him seem so endearingly believable. His timing, especially when showing the outward results of each desperate internal attempt to decipher his wife's ironic remarks, is sublime (arguably only Peter Sellers, Alec Guinness and Alistair Sim, during this fine era of British cinema, were as adept as T-T at 'showing' the slow registering of a potentially troublesome thought), and, as the review in *Films and Filming* underlined, 'not for one moment does he give us the impression that he is acting'.[31] He had really come of age as a movie performer, and a growing number of influential people within the business – on both sides of the Atlantic – were starting to sit up and take notice.

Someone who had already done so was the Budapest-born Hollywood producer, cinematographer and director George Pal, who signed him up, along with Peter Sellers, to play the pair of villains in his next big-budget movie for Metro-Goldwyn-Mayer: the comedy-musical *tom thumb*. It was the big international breakthrough for which both British actors had long been waiting, although, as Terry-Thomas would later acknowledge, it turned out to be a bigger break for him than it was for Sellers: 'My part was perfect, but Peter's was bloody awful. He wasn't difficult about it, but he knew it.'[32]

There was nothing glamorous about the actual making of the movie, which (although an American production featuring an American – Russ Tamblyn – as the leading man) was shot at Borehamwood rather than in Hollywood towards the end of 1957. Terry-Thomas was already suffering from various chills and ills before shooting had even begun (the result, he moaned, of spending too many hours in a freezing-cold lake near Guildford while filming the 'Thames' scene for *The Naked Truth*[33]), but he soon felt even worse once the cameras started rolling and his exertions brought on an unusually bad attack of lumbago. Pumped full of painkillers, he was obliged to spend much of the next eighty-five days running, jumping, crouching, riding a horse and fighting a duel in the extravagant and table-hurdling style of Douglas Fairbanks Snr. Not even the dubiously high doses of codeine prevented him from suffering 'very, very acutely' from all of his aches and pains, but, perversely, the physical discomfort suited a role that demanded a stylised 'crooked' look. 'Although it appears as if I'm doing a sinister, crablike walk,' he would later explain, 'that walk wasn't put on. It was caused by lumbago.'[34]

He almost failed to finish shooting the film, because he was arrested in London two days before Christmas[35] on the suspicion of being drunk and disorderly prior to driving, leaving him hoping that his American employers would take pity and come to the rescue. Having been persuaded by an old friend to attend a festive drinks party at the Trocadero, he reappeared into the cool evening air – after adding a couple of complementary glasses of Krug '47 champagne to the last few capsules of codeine – to find two truculent young policemen standing by his latest sports car ('my 4½-litre olive-green Jensen drophead coupé'), which a commissionaire had moved without warning to just around the corner in Great Windmill Street. Policemen had always acted like a red rag to a bull (or an uncowable cow) to a free spirit such as T-T (who had been known to point a toy machine gun at them through his car window and 'shoot' them with ping-pong balls if he felt they were acting too pompously in his presence[36]), and this latest pair did not disappoint. When, therefore, he responded in a seemingly offhand and slightly befuddled manner to the questions posed ('rather rudely, I thought') by the two constables, and then slithered into the car and attempted to ignore them and start up the engine, they pulled him back out and bundled him into a Black Maria bound for a police station in Savile Row.[37]

It was at this point, he later admitted, that he became very, very angry ('and when I get angry,' he explained, 'I just go completely and utterly off my nut'[38]). He strongly advised one constable not to be such 'a bloody fool', and told the other one brusquely: 'Be quiet – *I'm* in charge here!'[39] Once inside the station, the police summoned a doctor to conduct a routine test: the doctor – one James Gossip – duly arrived, placed some silver and copper coins amounting to the value of six shillings and ten-pence on the station desk and invited T-T to count them. The agitated star decided – 'very unwisely', he later acknowledged – to 'fool about', first offering to count the coins 'in Cockney' and then declaring ('in shockingly bad taste') that small change was 'just chicken-feed' and loudly counting out thirty-five pounds instead from a wad of notes in his wallet.[40] Unfortunately for T-T, in his haste to mock his accusers he had actually slammed down *six* five-pound notes, not seven, on the station desk, thus arousing the doctor's suspicion that he was indeed dealing with someone somewhat the worse for wear from drink. T-T was then asked to walk across the room to the door and back. 'How would you like me to walk?' he enquired sarcastically of 'the old trout' Dr Gossip. 'Like a villain, a hero, like a poor man, or like a rich man?' The rattled doctor then pronounced him 'under the influence of alcohol' – to which T-T responded by snapping, 'And the same to you!'[41] It had not gone at all well.

He appeared on remand at Bow Street Court on 16 January 1958, charged with 'driving a car while under the influence of drink to such an extent as to be incapable of having proper control over the vehicle'. Pleading 'Not Guilty', he elected to go to trial, and the case was eventually heard on the morning of Friday, 14 March. Peter Sellers was there in court, as were various other supporters and a legal team from the movie studio led by the redoubtable show-business lawyer Oscar Beuselinck. After having waited patiently out in the passage with what he would describe as 'some delightful whores', Terry-Thomas was called into the court room, where, after protesting that he was a motorist who was in possession of a twenty-seven-year unblemished record, he went on to explain, several times, that it had all been a terribly unfortunate misunderstanding due to his succession of 'misread jokes'.[42] The police doctor's responses proved not to be particularly helpful to either side, as, whenever he was asked to confirm or deny any of T-T's alleged remarks, his stock answer was a glumly non-committal: 'He may have done; he said such a lot.'[43] As for the two police constables, their respective accounts were found to contain a number of inconsistencies, which had the defendant struggling not to pipe up with a triumphant 'I told you so!' He escaped eventually without censure after MGM provided the court with a medical report, along with film stills, to support his claim that he had merely been the victim of an exceptionally arduous work schedule and some unusually powerful prescription drugs. Work on the movie went on without further incident.[44]

In spite of these illnesses and incidents, Terry-Thomas would always refer to *tom thumb* fondly as 'my second favourite film'.[45] It certainly enhanced his reputation as far as Hollywood's grandees were concerned, who came to think of him as their archetypal mischievous Englishman (and, as a consequence, took to identifying potential 'Terry-Thomas' roles in many of the latest scripts). Back in Britain, he was even nominated for a 'Best Actor' BAFTA, as well as being accorded the honour of a weekly comic strip ('The Adventures of Terry-Thomas', drawn by the well-regarded cartoonist George Wakefield) in the very popular *Film Fun*. Most important of all, he started to receive better offers for bigger roles in bigger and better movies.

The next three or four that he made in Britain, while mulling over some tempting long-term offers from the US, would be among the most memorable of his entire career. His old friends the Boulting Brothers started the sequence off by casting him as the star of their new satire about post-war British diplomacy, *Carlton-Browne of the F.O.* (1959). Described by Terry-Thomas as 'teak from the nostrils upwards' and 'a bit of a Charlie' (in other words, 'a certain type of Englishman … the Englishman who reads *The Times* and no other newspaper. A brolly carrier. A squash player. A bowler hat wearer'), Cadogan de Vere Carlton-Browne is the humble head of the Foreign Office's Miscellaneous Territories department (or 'The Dustbin', as his far more distinguished father prefers to call it) who ends up being dispatched to Gaillardia – an insignificant little semi-colony that is rumoured to have recently become the site of some covert Russian mining operations – in a final desperate bid to strengthen ancient British ties.[46]

It is apparent right from the start that no one rates poor Carlton-Browne very highly at all. Indeed, he only gets given the mission very grudgingly by a government still lazily reliant on a mixture of nepotism and the old boy network:

CARLTON-BROWNE: Had you anyone in mind, Minister?

FOREIGN SECRETARY: As Head of the Department, I suppose it'll have to be you.

CARLTON-BROWNE: Oh.

FOREIGN SECRETARY: Now, look, Carlton-Browne: we all remember your late father …

CARLTON-BROWNE: Oh, he's not 'late' yet, sir!

FOREIGN SECRETARY: [*Sounding puzzled*] Oh. I'm glad to hear it. A great ambassador, anyway. [*Adopts a grave expression*] But this could be of the utmost importance. If you have *any* doubt – any *doubt* at *all* – as to your … *capacity* …

CARLTON-BROWNE: Good heavens no, sir!

FOREIGN SECRETARY: [*Looking unconvinced*] Oh. Well, I hope you're right.

When the hapless 'CB' arrives, he finds the country divided into two rival camps, the one in the north ruled by a progressive new young king and the other in the south ruled by his reactionary great-uncle. While

CB tries to make sense of the chaotic situation, the duplicitous Prime Minister, Amphibulos (played by Peter Sellers), seizes the opportunity to play the various powers off against each other with a brand of self-serving diplomacy in which 'all our cards are under the table'. Eventually, after a clearly still clueless CB angers his superiors (following what he claims to have been 'an exhaustive investigation') by requesting further guidance instead of supplying it himself, he is well and truly ripe for manipulation by Amphibulos. Joining the Prime Minister on the beach for a spot of diplomacy in the sun, he pleads for help:

> CARLTON-BROWNE: I've got to tell my Minister *something* – he's making a big speech next week.
>
> AMPHIBULOS: Hmmm. [*Pats CB on the shoulder and starts 'idly' drawing a circle in the sand*] You know, I can remember the time when *one word* from Great Britain and there would have been a war [*Draws line through middle of circle*] between the two peoples to keep them apart.
>
> CARLTON-BROWNE: [*Suddenly looking alert*] I *say*! I think I've got it: *partition*!
>
> AMPHIBULOS: [*Acting surprised*] Partition? Why, that's *brilliant*! I would *never* have thought of that! Oh, congratulations!

CB's uncharacteristically bold proposal soon backfires, however, in spectacular fashion: when Great Britain finds that it has gone and claimed the 'wrong' side of the partition (with resources suitable for the construction of a hydrogen bomb situated on the other part of the island), the politicians hold anxious talks in London while revolution breaks out in Gaillardia. A suitably chastened Carlton-Browne, who has only recently returned to Whitehall, is ordered straight back abroad in a desperate bid to sort out the sorry mess.

After an abortive exercise in which the British troops surround their own headquarters, CB is captured by the king's counter-revolutionary forces. He discovers, however, that the king has arranged to marry a princess from the other half of the country, thus finally uniting north and south and ensuring a prolonged period of peace. An utterly bemused Carlton-Browne ends up being honoured not only by Gaillardia (with the 'Star of Elysium, Third Class') but also by his very own Great Britain (with a knighthood) for services in the cause of world peace and British diplomacy.

Although the movie was deemed controversial enough at the time to be withdrawn (on the strong recommendation of the Foreign Office) from the Moscow Film Festival (where it was feared that it would be regarded as Cold War propaganda), it was actually one of the Boulting Brothers' clumsiest exercises in political cynicism, petering out after a promising start into a plot that was overly simplistic and frustratingly pedestrian in pace. What redeemed the movie was the high quality of its two key performances. Peter Sellers took his screen acting on to another level with his subtle and restrained portrayal of the scheming Amphibulos (based in large part on a notoriously Machiavellian Italian entrepreneur and movie promoter of the time – and former colleague of the Boulting Brothers – called Filippo del Giudice[47]), while Terry-Thomas was equally sly and disciplined as the dutiful but dim-witted diplomat.[48] Whatever Britain's critics thought about the movie as a whole (and it would be fair to say that critical opinion was mixed), the vast majority were more than happy to celebrate this pair of lead performances,[49] and the same would be true of those who came to review the movie in the US (where it was retitled unhelpfully *The Man in the Cocked Hat*). The *New York Times*, in particular, was fulsome in its praise: 'There should be no doubt now that Terry-Thomas is a comic of first rank,' wrote A.H. Weiler. 'His stint as the foggy, slack-jawed bumbler Carlton-Browne is an artistic achievement.'[50]

Mario Zampi's slight but thoroughly delightful crime farce *Too Many Crooks* – which came out in Britain during the same period in the first half of 1959 – saw Terry-Thomas back in the far more familiar role of the vulnerable English bounder (called on this occasion William 'Billy' Gordon), and, once again, his mastery was never in doubt. From start to finish, his comic technique was elegantly precise, allowing him to go from the *louche* and leering rascal of the early scenes (eyeing up each shapely female form like a hot and hungry child looks at an ice-cream) to the increasingly edgy and bemused victim of the latter ones (when the women in his life just treat him like a tiresome teenager) without ever seeming forced or fabricated.

He begins by boasting in his office about the new sculpture of himself while flirting quite shamelessly with a young female journalist:

GORDON: Tell me … has anyone ever done *your* bust?
JOURNALIST: No.
GORDON: [*Gazing admiringly at her breasts*] Pity!

Then, once she has departed, he gets down to more of his bounderish business:

GORDON: [*Greeting his next visitor*] Guten Tag.
SWARTHY MAN: Bonjour.
GORDON: Oh, you're *French*!
SWARTHY MAN: No. I am Finnish.
GORDON: Oh. Then why do you speak French?
SWARTHY MAN: Finnish is too difficult.
GORDON: Er, you're right. I had a Finnish girl once. She was *very* difficult. Ha ha! Er … [*Looks at the man's violin case*] Well, glad to see you've got the 'violin'.
SWARTHY MAN: Da! With no strings attached! [*Opens up case to reveal a sample machine gun inside*]
GORDON: *Mmmm* … Very useful … [*Inspects gun*] Bad finish … [*Looks up*] How many?
SWARTHY MAN: Two thousand five hundred!
GORDON: When?
SWARTHY MAN: Next week!
GORDON: How much?
SWARTHY MAN: Fifty thousand pounds!
GORDON: *Hah!* Five!
SWARTHY MAN: *Hah!* Forty!
GORDON: Fifteen!
SWARTHY MAN: Thirty-five!
GORDON: Twenty!
SWARTHY MAN: Thirty!

GORDON: Twenty-*five*!

SWARTHY MAN: Twenty-five!

GORDON: Done! Just a minute – I hope they *work*!

SWARTHY MAN: Why?

GORDON: Because the last consignment your boss sent me of rifles *didn't* work! I had complaints!

SWARTHY MAN: Hah, er, surely you are joking? But ... I do not understand ... *Complaints?* From whom?

GORDON: There were one or two survivors.

Later, upon finding that his wife (whom, deep down, he really needs and perhaps, in his own immature way, still loves) has been kidnapped and threatened with being cut up into little pieces, but sensing that the perpetrators are a bunch of incompetent amateurs, he tries to bluff his way out of a blackmail attempt:

KIDNAPPER: I take it you have brought the money?

GORDON: No.

KIDNAPPER: Splendid. *Splendid.* Then we need only ... *What* did you say?!?

GORDON: No. Non. Nein. Nyet. In fact: *Nuts!* Not a sausage. Cut her up, old boy. This is a chance I've been waiting for for years!

KIDNAPPER: [*Appalled*] You-you're bluffing! Well ... y-you think I am ...

GORDON: Well, *I'm* not – and I hope *you're* not! This is the answer to a bachelor's prayer!

KIDNAPPER: You can't *do* this to me! To her. She's a fine woman!

GORDON: Well – *you* have her!

KIDNAPPER: *I* don't want her!

GORDON: Well, you *took* her, old man! Don't blame *me*!

KIDNAPPER: But ... It-it's disgusting! It-it's immoral! We-we'll cut her into pieces! Tiny *little* pieces!

GORDON: Well, naturally, you'll want to make a good job of it, won't you? Well, you really must excuse me – I've got a date. Rather a promising one, actually ...

Later on, when he has been led to believe that his wife really has been murdered, and he appears to be the prime suspect, he flees to his mother's house, where, upon finding that his wife is still alive, he faints down on to the settee. 'Oh,' his mother tut-tuts. 'I said he was drunk when he came in!'

He followed this pleasant concoction with two of the most notable (and most enduringly popular) British comedies of the period: the Boulting Brothers' *I'm All Right, Jack* (1959) and Robert Hamer's *School for Scoundrels* (1960). Together, they would mark the peak of his pre-Hollywood movie career.

I'm All Right, Jack revisited the class-ridden community of characters who had previously been seen in *Private's Progress*, but this time, instead of showing what had held them together in wartime, it focussed on what was now driving them apart during the peace: a series of increasingly bitter disputes between management and unions, and the growing threat to the economy (and society) posed by organised strikes. It was an undeniably topical theme: in the ten years prior to 1955 in Britain, there had been an average of 1791 strikes per year, involving 545,000 workers and at the loss of 2,073,000 days of labour; in the ten years that would follow 1955, the average annual number would rise to 2521, involving 1,116,000 workers and resulting in 3,889,000 days lost. A sort of 'industrial cold war' was thus breaking out all over Britain.[51]

'Both John and I felt at the time,' Roy Boulting later reflected, '[that] the idea that one particular part of society should be held guilty and responsible for the failures of society at large, and that some other area should be free of blame, was ridiculous. We felt that all areas of society shared some common blame, and this is what we had to address ourselves to.'[52] In the little Britain depicted by *I'm All Right, Jack*, therefore, the bosses were corrupt (especially Bertie Tracepurcel – played by Dennis Price – who would happily transfer his shares elsewhere and then see his company go under in order to make a quick but criminal profit) and the union leaders were hypocritical clots (especially the archetypal 'bolshy' shop steward Fred Kite – played by Peter Sellers – who waffles on pompously but ultimately incoherently about things that will 'je-opardise' or 'reverberate back to the detriment of the workers', looks up reverentially at his library of unread books by Lenin and dreams of one day making it over to dear old Mother Russia to enjoy 'all them cornfields and bally in the evening'). Caught together in the middle, feeling impotent and confused, are supposedly insignificant little men like Stanley Windrush (Ian Carmichael) and Major Hitchcock (Terry-Thomas) – the former a management misfit-turned-workforce misfit and the latter a put-upon personnel manager, but both of them mere cogs in a system that is no less unjust now than it was before.

Although Peter Sellers stole the show with his brilliant portrayal of Kite, Terry-Thomas was also impressive as the half-hearted Hitchcock (whom the workers have nicknamed 'Everybody's Auntie'). Picking up where he left off at the end of *Private's Progress*, he is once again almost as believable as he is funny, sitting behind his desk and shaking his head slowly in disbelief at the countless things that contrive on a daily basis to prevent him from leading the quiet life that he craves. Lamenting the number of men nowadays (just like in the old days) 'who can break out into a muck sweat merely by standing still', he exclaims once again: 'They're an absolute *shower*! A positive *SHOWER*!' What pains him so is not just the fact that he knows that neither the workers nor the bosses are capable of doing their jobs properly, but also that he knows that *he* is not capable of doing *his* job properly, either.

The few scenes that he shares with Fred Kite provide one with some of the most memorable moments in the movie. Whereas Kite responds robotically to the internal prompts from his off-the-peg ideology, Hitchcock is powered by an almost manic brand of pragmatism, chattering his way into another legal loophole as he bids to make the latest 'bit of a flap' go away. 'That was a near one,' he gasps after Kite and his fellow labour aristocrats have departed. 'What a *shower*!' Alone in his office, he settles back in his sofa, puffs on a Slim Panatella and starts reading some of the suggestions sent in from members of his disaffected workforce: 'Dirty beast!' he mutters after looking at one of them, then folds it up and pops it into his pocket, leaving the audience curious to find out more. Later on, after the respective machinations of the higher-ups and the lower-downs over the role of the hapless Windrush have combined to oblige him, once again, to swallow his pride and slum it with some of the 'shower', he ends up with the despised Kite in his bolshy bolthole ('charming little place'), darning socks like a surrogate wife while listening to the lonely union leader ramble on about what inexplicable creatures women are:

HITCHCOCK: There you are [*Hands a sock back to Kite*] – not exactly invisible mending but it'll keep the draught out.

KITE: Hmm, takes you time to find out who your friends are, don't it? 'Cause, I've been betrayed.

HITCHCOCK: We've all been betrayed, old chap.

KITE: Hmm, d'you think she'll come back?

HITCHCOCK: *Mine* didn't. Thank God!

KITE: I dunno, I dun-*no* … I mean, I always gave her the best I could provide … she's always fit and well … I mean, it ain't as if she was overworked … You see I – [*Has a thought*] 'Ere: that's it! That's *it*! – 'Overworked'!

HITCHCOCK: Really?

KITE: Yeah! 'Ill health brought on by overwork'!

HITCHCOCK: I thought you said she was in tip-top condition?

KITE: No, no, not *her* – *Windrush*! That is how we get rid of him! He resigns on account of ill health brought on by overwork!

HITCHCOCK: Kite, that's absolutely *bang* on! 'Ill health brought on by trying to work the new schedules'!

KITE: Yeah!

HITCHCOCK: Ha *ha*! [*Raises his glass*] The best of British luck!

The critical success of *I'm All Right, Jack* (there were BAFTAs for 'Best Screenplay' for Frank Harvey, John Boulting and Alan Hackney, and 'Best Actor' for Peter Sellers) was complemented by its impressive returns at the box office: it was the biggest money-maker of the year in Britain, eclipsing all of what Hollywood, Europe and the rest of the home-grown cinema had to offer audiences in the UK. It went on to do exceptionally well in America, taking more money during its initial run at New York's Guild Theatre, for example, than any previous movie in that cinema's history, and averaging about £4000 per week by the end of the third month following its release.[53] Bosley Crowther, the influential movie critic of the *New York Times*, included *I'm All Right, Jack* in his list of the top ten releases of the year (alongside the likes of *Psycho*, *Elmer Gantry* and *The Apartment*), hailing it as 'the liveliest satirizing of labor and management that has ever been put on the screen',[54] while Stanley Kauffman at *The New Republic* praised not only the 'mimetically accomplished' performance of Peter Sellers but also the 'finesse' and 'extraordinary skill' of Terry-Thomas.[55]

School for Scoundrels, which followed soon after, served as yet another international showcase for the special talents of its star, Terry-Thomas. Subtitled *How to Win Without Actually Cheating!*, the movie was adapted by Patricia Moyes, the producer Hal E. Chester and the uncredited Peter Ustinov and Frank Tarloff from Stephen Potter's popular *Gamesmanship*, *Oneupmanship* and *Lifemanship* trilogy of satirical self-help books. After warning the audience that 'He who is not one up is one down', the movie went on to chart the progress of the impressionable Everyman Henry Palfrey (Ian Carmichael) as he is coached in each one of the dark and crafty arts of oneupmanship by Stephen Potter's on-screen representative, Alistair Sim. Terry-Thomas appeared as Raymond Delauney, a fully fledged bounder, shameless womaniser and downright ruthless oneupper.

The actual making of the movie was plagued by a variety of problems. The director, Robert Hamer, was a recovering alcoholic who promptly fell off the wagon in spectacular fashion during the latter part of the production; he was sacked on the spot (Hal E. Chester and the uncredited Cyril Frankel then stepped in to finish the film) and would never work in the industry again. One of the actors, the splendid but somewhat eccentric Alistair Sim, decided for some unexplained reason that he would not, on this particular occasion, pick up any props – thus causing his colleagues all kinds of last-minute on-set confusions: ('When I got to the Yeovil school in one of the early scenes and he gave me tea and a muffin,' Ian Carmichael would recall, 'it was all put in front of him, as he was the host. The director said, "Hand the muffins to Ian." And he said, "No, no, no, let him help himself. I don't want to handle anything." So there was I, the guest, having to help myself to the muffins and pour my own tea practically!'[56]). Finally, the producer, a volatile little American, irritated most of the cast (including Terry-Thomas) with his seemingly endless cack-handed attempts to make the dialogue sound more 'appropriate' for the US market. What eventually reached the screen, however, showed no signs of such behind-the-scenes strife, breezing through its allotted running time of ninety-four minutes as if the action had been slotted together on the spot.

All of the standout scenes – save for a couple of deft little cameos from Peter Jones and Dennis Price as a pair of oneupping car salesmen – were driven on by Terry-Thomas. The first (largely improvised[57]) tennis match between Delauney and Palfrey, for example, was an instant classic, with the fabulously unscrupulous Delauney – his left hand resting snugly in his pocket, and his right one stroking each serve effortlessly back over the net – using every crafty trick in the book to humiliate his hapless opponent (*'Hard cheese!'*). The meeting in the club restaurant, when Delauney proceeds to flirt outrageously with Palfrey's fragrant young girlfriend, was another unalloyed delight:

DELAUNEY: Oh, hell-*o*, hell-*oh*, hell-*ohhh*! Where did you find *this* lovely creature?

PALFREY: Oh, we met quite by accident as a matter of fact. I was trying to catch a bus, and April was –

DELAUNEY: Well, do the decent thing, old chap – fellow club members and all that sort of thing …

PALFREY: Er, yes, of course. Um, Mr Raymond Delauney – Miss April Smith.

DELAUNEY: What a *romantic* name! Oh to be in England, now that April's here! [*He grins and kisses her hand*] How do you *doooo*?

APRIL: How do *you* do?

DELAUNEY: Ah, have you two chaps finished dinner already?

APRIL: We haven't even *started* – we can't get a table.

DELAUNEY:Oh, fiddle-de-diddle! [*Calling out to the maître d'*] Skinner – my guests!

SKINNER: Certainly, sir.

DELAUNEY: [*Taking April's arm and walking her ahead of Palfrey*]

> Now tell me, you *lovely* creature – [*Turning back*] Oh, Palfrey
> … look after Skinner, there's a good chap!

T-T was equally good in the later scenes, when the newly tutored Palfrey begins to turn the tables on his tormentor:

PALFREY: What on earth was that?

DELAUNEY: [*Leaps out of his car and scurries round to inspect the back*] Oh!

PALFREY: Can I help, old man?

DELAUNEY: It's the exhaust!

PALFREY: Oh, *bad* luck! D'you know, it must have happened when you bashed into that brick wall.

DELAUNEY: Er, have you got a piece of *string*?

Most British critics applauded the movie's combination of an 'Ealing-rompy' tone with a 'refreshingly astringent' theme,[58] and, as the producer had hoped, it was welcomed warmly in most parts of the United States, where Terry-Thomas was now widely considered to be ripe for Hollywood stardom. Terry-Thomas considered himself ripe for Hollywood stardom, too. After coasting through a further trio of British comedies – the uneven but still very enjoyable crime farce *Make Mine Mink* (1960),[59] the instantly forgettable dog's dinner of a domestic satire *His and Hers* and the rather underrated light comic thriller *A Matter of WHO* (both released in 1961) – he therefore decided, a decade after his last attempt, to make his move across the Atlantic.

No one this time (not even Ed Sullivan) mistook him for England's 'Tommy Tucker'. This time, he arrived to be recognised and revered as the movie world's very own Terry-Thomas: 'In films such as *Private's Progress, School for Scoundrels* and *I'm All Right, Jack*,' observed the *New York Times* admiringly, 'his comedy style has won international acclaim.'[60] This time, it was clear, Terry-Thomas really did mean serious (funny) business.

There were guest spots on television and radio shows, newspaper profiles and magazine interviews, plenty of public appearances and innumerable mentions in the showbiz and society columns, as well as the offer of a major role (that of the stuffy company president 'J.B. Biggley') in a forthcoming big-budget Broadway comedy-musical entitled *How to Succeed in Business Without Really Trying* (he declined the invitation, after some careful thought, and the role was passed on to Rudy Vallee[61]). There was also an extended stay in Hollywood, where he was drawn immediately into the celebrity inner circle, and introduced to such long-established luminaries as Groucho Marx, Jack Benny, Cary Grant, Jimmy Stewart, Bob Hope, Bing Crosby and Frank Sinatra. He was particularly pleased to meet many of the most glamorous and shapely women in show business, and, entirely predictably, he proceeded to conduct a covert comparative study of prominent 'A-list' breasts (he found Marilyn Monroe's somewhat disappointing, but was fairly impressed by Jayne Mansfield's: 'They weren't flabby,' he panted, 'indeed, they were well-shaped and firm'[62]).

He loved the movie capital at the beginning of his time there. 'Hollywood had everything for me,' he would later reflect. 'I liked it and fitted into the scene.'[63] Rejoicing in the fact that he was so many miles away now – both literally and symbolically – from the drabness of fusty old Finchley, he was dazzled, amused and intrigued by all of the usual things that seemed larger, smarter or stranger than real life in LA: the big studios and the stately mansions; the grand hotels, sumptuous restaurants and discreetly decadent night clubs; the fussily manicured lawns and custom-designed swimming pools; and all of the impossibly bright and exotic banana trees, bougainvillea bushes, plumeria and flaming hibiscus that distracted the eye from the prosaic sand and stone.

It did not take long, however, for much of the novelty to start to pall. Having just turned fifty, Terry-Thomas was simply too set in his ways to think that a place like Hollywood could ever come to feel like a genuine second home.

The first seeds of his disenchantment were sown soon after he returned to Los Angeles, following a brief spell back in Britain, to make his debut in a Hollywood movie for 20th Century-Fox. The director Frank Tashlin (a former animator turned maker of cartoon-like live action movies, whose previous credits included *The Girl Can't Help It*, *Will Success*

Spoil Rock Hunter? and *Cinderfella*) had cast him[64] in an elaborate slap-stick farce called *Bachelor Flat* (1962). Terry-Thomas was to play Profes-sor Bruce Patterson, a British-born archaeologist based at a Southern California college, whose fiancée (Celeste Holm) leaves for an extended trip abroad after forgetting to mention that she already has a teenage daughter (Tuesday Weld) – who duly shows up unaware that her mother is now engaged. Before he had a chance to start work on the project, however, he found himself 'hijacked' by an exasperating little man by the name of Mitchell Gertz.

Gertz met Terry-Thomas at Los Angeles International Airport, announced that he was the star's new agent and dragged his 'client' off to his capacious but somewhat aesthetically neglected apartment for dinner. Ignoring his guest's protests that he already had an agent back in England, was really not very hungry at the moment and would much prefer to check in at his designated five-star hotel, Gertz proceeded to fry eight massive steaks while babbling on about percentages and profits. Terry-Thomas nibbled politely at a corner of one huge slab of beef, while Gertz gobbled up no fewer than six whole steaks in quick succes-sion. 'Mr Gertz,' exclaimed his wide-eyed guest, 'If you go on like this, you'll be dead in a very short space of time.' The hyperactive Gertz brushed such claims aside with a wave of the hand and a loud belch, invited Terry-Thomas to punch him hard in the centre of his stomach and repeated his assertion that, from this point on, he would be repre-senting the star in Hollywood.[65]

The following morning in the hotel, Terry-Thomas awoke with the hope that it had all been a silly dream, but then the telephone rang: it was Gertz again, babbling away, between munches on a succession of cream cheese and smoked salmon bagels, about percentages and profits. Silly though it might still have seemed, it was now clear, alas, that it was most definitely not a dream. He subsequently discovered, after making a number of anxious calls, that Mitchell Gertz was indeed a Los Angeles-based theatrical agent – his major claim to fame being the fact that, back in 1950, he had snapped up the rights to the character of Zorro and then, in 1952, struck a distribution deal with the Disney Corporation for a TV series based on the original pulp magazine stories – but the actor was still completely in the dark as to why, and how, this man had come to appoint himself the new agent of Terry-Thomas.

Once he was on the set at the studios of 20th Century-Fox, he sought out the casting director to explain how uncomfortable he was at being pestered by this rum little fellow called Gertz, and how distressed he was at the thought of such a man poking his nose into confidential contractual and financial affairs. The casting director nodded sympathetically and called the head of the studio, Spyros Skouras, to report the news that 'Mr Terry-Thomas' was not happy about Mitchell Gertz. 'You had better do something about it,' barked the studio head. One week later, after both the set and the hotel had been rendered reassuringly Gertz-free zones, the boss called the casting director back: 'When I told you to get rid of Mitchell Gertz,' he exclaimed, 'I didn't expect you to use such violent tactics. Mitchell Gertz has just died!' It turned out – much to Terry-Thomas's bitter-sweet relief – that Gertz had been brusquely dispatched to the other side by one too many steaks rather than at the hands of a studio-hired Mafia hitman, and work on the movie proceeded without any further incidents.[66]

It was this kind of intrusively bizarre behaviour, however, that would bother the star more and more (and he would never rely on agents again – not even back in Britain – preferring to represent himself in most of his future contractual negotiations).[67] He took a strong dislike to the various fads and fashions of Hollywood's rich and famous, such as the obsessively diet-conscious rationing of food while happily guzzling glass after glass of wine or whisky – 'everybody except me was sloshed'. Other aspects of LA life were equally anathema: the suspicion – bordering on paranoia – shown towards anyone who had the temerity to want to walk rather than travel everywhere by car ('The police patrol would want to know where one was going and where one had come from'); the rudeness of drivers on those occasions when he gave in and called a cab ('At the slightest sign, I gave the chap a lecture. We didn't have to endure that sort of thing in Europe and I didn't see any point in allowing people to be rude to me for no reason at all'); the aggressive pretentiousness of waiters at the poshest kind of places to dine ('I tried to discourage them by being more phoney than they were. I sniffed the wine, rubbed it on the palm of my hand, then *listened* to it'); and the expats who had allowed themselves to be 'Americanized' ('I hated Americanisms in speech. How they got on my nerves!').[68]

More seriously, he was rattled almost from the start by the movie colony's slavish adherence to a class system of its own making. 'Hollywood had its pecking order,' he later complained:

> People who were professionally in a different stratum of society did not get invited to certain parties. I disregarded that snobby rule and invited everyone I liked to my modest shindigs, irrespective of their jobs. I asked some cameramen, for example, and some little-known actors. To my astonishment, someone told me I was considered a bit of a freak to be so generous to people who were not in my class.[69]

He kept such common irritations at bay – most of the time – by surrounding himself with token reminders of the calmer, cooler, saner community that he hoped still remained back home in Britain. In the summer of 1962, for example, he bought and imported a £9500 Bentley Continental from England, and had two metal plates bearing the Union Flag fitted on either side ('a small touch of patriotism that appealed to me'[70]). He also chose his friends unusually carefully when staying in LA, preferring as a rule to socialise with his fellow 'unAmericanized' expats – such as James Mason and his 'incredibly Mayfair' wife, Pamela (who had brought their own English chef over to cook for them in Beverly Hills); Michael Wilding, whom he had known since the pair of them had been humble extras at Pinewood and Shepperton during the early 1930s; and two veterans from the pre-war era of the so-called 'Hollywood Raj',[71] Gladys Cooper (with whom he liked to gossip about their mutual friends and acquaintances on the West End stage) and Sir C. Aubrey Smith (with whom he liked to chat at great length about cricket).

There were also a few 'honorary' Britons, such as the anglicised Russian, George Sanders (who enjoyed swapping anecdotes with T-T about their formative experiences in English cabaret and revue), and the anglophile American, Edward Everett Horton (a camply fastidious, Ivy League-educated New Yorker, now living a high old life of luxury on his estate at Amestoy Avenue in Encino, who insisted on taking his dinner guests off to a nearby restaurant for their dessert in order to give his butler sufficient time to warm the post-prandial brandy). Out of anthropological curiosity, he also spent time with the odd distinctive American, such as Dean Martin (whose style of living 'was opulent without being ostentatious') and Liberace (whose style of living was opulent *and* ostentatious).[72]

If Hollywood had wanted Terry-Thomas primarily for some Peter Sellers-like chameleon quality, it might well have resented his reluctance to 'go native' and immerse himself entirely in its notoriously insular culture. Fortunately, however, it wanted him for the very thing that he was most intent upon preserving: his Englishness, his bow-tied Britishness, his un-American otherness. It also helped immensely, of course, that he was so exceptionally good at playing comedy, and the very favourable reaction that his contribution to *Bachelor Flat* attracted certainly served to underline his very special value.

The movie itself might have been as hollow and evanescent as a bubble of coloured gum, but T-T's performance – energetic, eloquent and technically very assured – remained vivid in the memory as a superior piece of light comic character acting. Coping remarkably well with a plot that obliged him to race from one room to another *sans* trousers, shy away from a succession of wildly flirtatious floozies, pursue a young Marilyn Monroe lookalike while in a semi-dressed and highly intoxicated state, clutch two white breakfast bowls to his chest while calling out for a couple more quarts of milk and do battle with a cute little dachshund dog over a gigantic dinosaur bone, he somehow managed to stay seeming surprisingly real and believable. He also possessed enough charm to use his Englishness more as a means of gently teasing the Americans than – as had long been the line of least resistance in a US-made movie – for mocking his own compatriots. It made for a refreshingly ironic and relatively self-effacing style of Hollywood comedy, and certainly highlighted the potentially broad international, as well as domestic, appeal of T-T to other American producers.

He was back in Los Angeles straight after shooting *Operation Snatch* (1962) – a slight wartime comedy about the British military's defence of the Barbary Ape colony – in Gibraltar, and *Kill or Cure* (1962) – a fairly entertaining little comedy-thriller, in which he co-starred with Eric Sykes, about a spate of murders at a country health farm[73] – at Borehamwood, and commenced work for George Pal on his big-budget MGM biopic *The Wonderful World of the Brothers Grimm* (the first high-profile movie to be filmed via Hollywood's latest technical gimmick: three-camera 'Cinerama'). Playing the arrogant but cowardly knight in the movie's third and final fairy-tale interlude, he shared his scenes with the rubber-faced American comic Buddy Hackett (who played his servant) and a jewel-encrusted, fire-breathing, stop-motion animated dragon. There was no real chance for satisfying acting; none the less, participation in such a prominent project brought with it plenty of invaluable publicity, and underlined his new status as one of Hollywood's favourite 'foreign' stars.

He seemed to be everywhere in America during 1963. He kept popping up on network TV, appearing as a 'special guest star' on programmes that ranged from the popular crime series *Burke's Law* to *The Judy Garland Show*. He could also be seen in cinemas – not just in the movies that he had most recently completed (which included a cameo role in Dick Lester's *The Mouse on the Moon*[74]) but also in a trio of short, self-produced travelogues: *Terry-Thomas in Tuscany*, *Terry-Thomas in the South of France* and *Terry-Thomas in Northern Ireland*.[75] As if that was not enough exposure, a record album was released. *Strictly T-T* (which had first been available in England in 1958) featured new versions of songs and sketches that originated from his BBC television shows.[76] It was followed a few months later by another: *Terry-Thomas Discovers America* featured such new material as the topical 'Booking The Beatles' routine ('I'm not quite sure *what* they look like – all I can picture is four stunted *plum* trees!'), an unlikely but deftly done satirical song about Hollywood's upmarket funeral homes called 'You Haven't Lived' ('You arrive in, like a drive-in/But you don't go out the same way/You haven't lived/No, you haven't lived/Until you've died in LA'), an anglicised version of the popular Allan Sherman comic song 'Hello Muddah, Hello Faddah' (renamed 'Hello Mater, Hello Pater') and a Noël Coward-style reflection on the Boston Tea Party called 'It Could Have Been So Pleasant':

We've lost Kenya, India, Ghana, Ceylon,
Rhodesia, Malaysia, Pakistan – gone!
You started a trend
Oh, where will it end?
It could have been,
It SHOULD have been,
So ruddy, bloody, PLEASANT! [77]

Whatever the medium, the message was the same: it was time for Terry-Thomas.

It came as no surprise therefore when, in November, he was among those stars appearing in the most extravagant, spectacular and strenuously hyped movie comedy of the year: Stanley Kramer's *It's a Mad, Mad, Mad, Mad World*. Featuring a massive cast that included such stellar names as Spencer Tracy, Milton Berle, Sid Caesar, Ethel Merman, Phil Silvers, Buddy Hackett, Jonathan Winters, Mickey Rooney and (in the briefest of cameos) Buster Keaton, this sprawling three-hour saga (remade in 2001 as *Rat Race*, whose asinine shallowness would make the moral complexity of the original seem almost Chekhovian by comparison) about the search by at least a dozen greedy people for some buried treasure was more like a succession of starry sketches than a seamlessly coherent story, but it had more than its fair share of memorable moments.

Terry-Thomas played Lieutenant-Colonel J. Algernon Hawthorne, a visiting British botanist who becomes embroiled in the hunt for money on his way back from collecting some specimens of spiky desert flora ('Say, where did you get that *funny* accent – are you from Harvard?' booms Ethel Merman's foghorn-voiced American battleaxe. '*Harvard?*' Hawthorne exclaims. 'Oh, rather *not*! – I'm *ENGLISH*!'). His best scenes are shared with the henpecked Russell Finch (played by a refreshingly subdued Milton Berle), who, out of a mixture of mischief and fatigue, starts to niggle the amiable Englishman once the pair of them have 'mislaid' their two female travelling companions en route to Finch's 'nut' of a brother-in-law:

HAWTHORNE: Look, wherever *they* are, surely the most *sensible* thing is for the two of *us* to press *on*! I mean, for all *we* know,

your brother-in-law may be *out* or *away* somewhere, and even if
he *were* the first to be there he's *still* got to find the *money*,
hasn't he? Now I *earnestly* recommend that we *forget* your good
lady and press *on* with all possible dispatch! [*Gets back into car*]

FINCH: All right. [*Attempts, sarcastically, a posh English accent*]
'We'll press on with all possible dispatch.' [*Gets back in car*]

HAWTHORNE: [*Sticking his head back out of the vehicle*] And I
don't *really* think that personal *rancour* is going to help the
situation. If I may *say* so!

Finch, however, cannot quite bring himself to leave the matter alone,
and, before he knows it, he has triggered a fully fledged, fever-pitched,
transatlantic spat:

HAWTHORNE: I don't wish to quarrel with you, Finch, but,
speaking as a representative of Her Majesty's Armed Forces, I
take the most par-*tic*-ular exception to –

FINCH: [*Scowling while butting in*] Oh, d'you want me to tell *you*
somethin'?

HAWTHORNE: What?

FINCH: You want me to tell you somethin'? As far as I'm
concerned, the whole British race is practically finished. If it
hadn't been for Lend Lease, if we hadn't kept your whole
country afloat by giving you billions that you never even said
'Thank you' for, the whole phoney outfit would've been sunk
right under the Atlantic years ago. [*Hawthorne, looking ahead
with a pained but dignified expression, pulls on the brake*] Hey,
what are you stoppin' for?

HAWTHORNE: [*Clenching his teeth in barely suppressed anger*] Get
out of this machine.

FINCH: 'Get out'? I can't … You-you're crazy –

HAWTHORNE: It's *my* machine and I'll do as I *bloody* well please!
OUT!

FINCH: [*Sounding contrite*] Oh, I'm *awfully* sorry! Y-you know, I've
been very *edgy* today, and, if I've said anything about England,
I apologise.

HAWTHORNE: [*Allows the vehicle to move on again*] Glad to hear you say so! [*Cheering up*] I must say, if I had the *grievous* misfortune to be a citizen of *this* benighted country, I should be the most *hesitant* in offering any criticisms what*ever* of any other!

FINCH: Wait a minute – are you knocking this country? Are you saying something against *America?*

HAWTHORNE: *Against* it? I should be positively *astounded* to hear of anything that could be said *for* it! Well, the whole *bloody* place is the most *unspeakable* matriarchy in the whole *history* of civilisation! Look at yourself, and the way your wife and her *strumpet* of a mother push you through the hoop! As far as I can see, American men have been totally *emasculated!* They're like *slaves!* They die like *flies* from coronary thrombosis, while their women sit under *hairdryers* eating *chocolates* and arranging for every second Tuesday to be some sort of *Mothers' Day!* And this positively *infantile* preoccupation with *bosoms!!* [*Speeding up his rant*] In all my time in this wretched, godforsaken country, the one thing that has appalled me most of all is this *preposterous* preoccupation with *BOSOMS!!!* Don't you realise that they've become the dominant theme in American culture? In literature, advertising, in all fields of entertainment – it's *everything!* I'll wager you anything you like – if American women stopped wearing *BRASSIERES*, your whole national economy would *COLLAPSE* overnight!

It was a classic Terry-Thomas peroration, and, once again, it exemplified the way in which – in stark contrast to Hollywood's conventional use of its comical English figures – his stateside characterisations were usually far too feisty and independent to fit any patronising on-screen stereotype.[78] A very healthy measure of self-mockery was certainly there ('Have a care,' he cries after Finch's brother-in-law has picked him up and hurled him into a lake. 'That chap's run absolutely *amuck!*'), but so was a brightly defiant sliver of dignity.

It was much the same off the screen, as Terry-Thomas was the only 'foreigner' among the major stars in the cast, and, as he noted later, some of his American colleagues had been less than welcoming towards him at the start:

> When I first joined the company, Jonathan Winters was jealous of me and took against me, always referring to me as 'the rich Englishman'. It took a lot of pleading from producer Kramer to prevent him from reshaping my Bentley. Jonathan, who carried an axe as a prop, badly wanted to bash it through the bonnet of the car.[79]

Winters never really relaxed nor revised his aggressively negative attitude, but most of his fellow Americans soon warmed to the solitary Englishman. 'I found him a wonderful human being,' the director Stanley Kramer would say. 'Buried among fifty American comedians he could have won a popularity contest.'[80] Ethel Merman, in her own inimitable way, became another fairly good friend both on and off the set: 'She was always telling you what to do, and you'd do it!' he would recall. 'She was so colourful and I was so amused by her that I let her get away with it.'[81] Edie Adams (who played Sid Caesar's spouse) became a fan after witnessing him attempt to 'break the ice' with his entrance at the Palm Springs Hotel: 'He showed up, bounding over to us wearing this huge Mexican hat which must have been six feet across, said "Oh, how are you?" and promptly dived straight into the pool fully clothed!'[82]

He found the chronic competitiveness of the other comic actors 'exhausting and embarrassing'. Even during lunch, the likes of Sid Caesar, Phil Silvers, Milton Berle and Dick Shawn would battle to outdo each other ('And little Mickey Rooney, not to be left out, began methodically decorating his face with food. He hung slices of meat over his glasses. He stuffed carrots up his nostrils. And he rubbed salad cream into his hair. He just went on and on trying to steal the show. I caught Spencer Tracy watching my reaction and we raised eyebrows together'[83]) – but he was never in any danger of becoming intimidated by other egos ('he knew what he wanted for Terry-Thomas,' recalled one of his former colleagues, Nicholas Parsons, 'and pushed hard for it'[84]). He was also genuinely thrilled to spend some time with two of his biggest personal heroes, Spencer Tracy and Buster Keaton: 'They were the only two people who ever produced in me this awe of greatness. I just couldn't meet them without being affected.'[85]

One other positive thing that was beyond all doubt was that Terry-Thomas (like all of his co-stars) benefited greatly from being associated with such a strikingly big box-office hit. The movie might well have divided the critics – some of whom chose to dwell on the overblown nature of the production as a whole, while others preferred to focus on the effectiveness of some of the elements within – but the consumers were more than happy to queue up to see it, thus helping it to gross $60 million worldwide. It was an excellent way for T-T to end an exceptional year in his career.

The following year, 1964, would turn out to be similarly eventful, equally successful and even more enjoyable for Terry-Thomas. Basking in the immense commercial glory of *It's a Mad, Mad, Mad, Mad World*, he helped publicise the movie as it gradually made its way into various parts of Europe and Australasia during the latter half of the year,[86] and spent some of his spare time sifting through a gratifyingly large number of offers involving roles in other big-budget productions. He also started work (for £100,000 – about £3 million by today's rates – his highest fee to date) on the movie that he would later describe as his favourite big-screen project: *How To Murder Your Wife* (which would be released at the start of the following year).

Written by George Axelrod (*The Seven Year Itch, Bus Stop, Breakfast at Tiffany's*) and directed by Richard Quine (*The Solid Gold Cadillac, Bell Book and Candle, Paris – When It Sizzles*), the movie starred Jack Lemmon as Stanley Ford, a happily unmarried cartoonist, who wakes up the morning after a friend's boozy bachelor party to find that he is married to a beautiful young Italian (Virna Lisi) – much to the distress of himself and the utter horror of his stuffy English butler, Charles Firbank (Terry-Thomas). The rest of the story sees Stanley go to the brink of turning a misogynistic cartoon murder from fiction into fact in a desperate bid to return to what Firbank terms the 'masculine and perfect' atmosphere of his old bachelor apartment.

There were several reasons why Terry-Thomas would look back so fondly on this movie. One was the rapport that he enjoyed, both on screen and off, with Jack Lemmon – one of the most down-to-earth, thoughtful and gentlemanly of Hollywood stars. Lemmon had been a friend for several years prior to this project (they had socialised on innumerable occasions, and Lemmon had used T-T as one of his models when he created the character of the eccentric English toff, 'Lord X', for the 1963 Billy Wilder movie *Irma la Douce*), but the bond between them became even stronger during the course of their time together on the set, and Lemmon felt relaxed enough in his company to share a drink or two while playing jazz piano for him between takes. Another reason for the good memories was the presence of the southern Italian starlet Virna Lisi, whom Terry-Thomas found 'unusually beautiful and voluptuous' as well as a fine professional. He was very impressed by the fact that, even though she could barely speak any English when filming began, she ended up learning the language well enough to 'deliver her lines most attractively'.[87] Although he kept his distance whenever her burly husband, Franco Pesci (an intimidatingly well-connected Roman industrialist), was present on the set (he had shown the extent of his possessiveness early on after the sight of his wife popping out of a cake – wearing nothing but a whipped-cream bikini – caused him to drag her away to her dressing room), T-T formed a firm friendship with Lisi that would lead them to work together again in the near future.

The main reason, however, why he came to rate the movie as his favourite was the fact that, as he put it, 'I felt that I did a very good job.'[88] He did indeed. As a grateful Jack Lemmon would remark:

> Terry was a consummate professional. When he walked on set to start the rehearsals for a scene, he knew his lines, my lines, Virna Lisi's lines, and everybody else's lines – and I'm not sure but he probably also knew all the lines in the script being shot on the next stage. Like most really good professionals he was generous to his fellow actors. He worked with you, not at you. He was a gentleman, a delight to be with personally, let alone professionally, and above all as an actor he had one of the qualities that I admire so much – he made it look so simple. There are many actors who can say a

line and get a laugh if the line is funny. Terry could get the laugh with a line that was not funny to begin with.[89]

The role of Charles Firbank was by no means an easy one for a comic actor to play. On paper, the character was an incorrigible snob, a bitter misogynist and, in general, a downright nasty piece of work, better suited to valeting for Leopold or Loeb than buttling for Bertie Wooster. On the screen, however, Terry-Thomas somehow found a way to soften the old sociopath up, making him seem more like a vulnerable, anxious and unworldly little fusspot than a straightforwardly hateful hitman's hitman. In doing so, he brought some welcome light to what could otherwise have been an overly shady Sixties sex satire.

It helped that the director allowed the character to sometimes ignore the so-called 'fourth wall' and address the audience directly via the camera, taking them on a special tour of his master's townhouse ('The last stronghold of gracious living in a world gone mad – *mad*!'), giving them a conspiratorial wink when things looked likely to go well, casting them a worried glance whenever things seemed on the verge of going wrong, and generally showing them what a potentially sweet-natured but currently seriously misguided soul lurked beneath the surface of the starch and pinstripe. It was the skill and subtlety of the actor himself, however, that kept the tone suitably ironic, slowly and seemingly effortlessly showing more and more of the uppity butler's self-doubts as the action moved on towards the dénouement.

Whereas his earliest scenes contain some of his most sublime silent double-takes (his look of queasy disgust after being told, first of all, that there is a woman in his master's bedroom, and then that this woman is his master's new wife, and then – worst of all – that this woman cannot speak any English, is better and funnier than any single comic line in the entire screenplay), the later ones feature several of his most dextrous deliveries of dialogue (such as when, his voice quavering with a mixture of hurt, frustration and anger, he protests at having to share a kitchen with his master's mistress: 'Sir. Mr Ford. This woman is *mad*! Stark raving *MAD*! She is not only preparing a lasagne *soufflé*, but look at the spaghetti *sauce*: green *onions* browning in at least a *pound* of butter!'). It is a supremely assured, effective and show-stealing demonstration of clever comic acting, fully deserving of all the plaudits that it prompted.

The critic Raymond Durgnat, reviewing the movie for *Films and Filming*, was quick to single Terry-Thomas out for special praise, remarking that the role 'reveals T-T's real forte as sophisticated comedy (rather than farce)',[90] while Bosley Crowther declared in the *New York Times* that 'everyone should be amused by Terry-Thomas's picky playing',[91] and *Time* magazine enthused that T-T 'hyphenates the movie with tomfoolery, holding whole scenes together by letting his face fall apart like a piece of shattered Limoges'.[92] The actor himself, reflecting on Durgnat's observation about his special aptitude for sophisticated comedy, felt that he had first 'revealed' this fact as far back as 1949, when he started out on the small screen in Britain with *How Do You View?*, but he was happy, none the less, to hear it acknowledged once again in the context of his contribution to a big Hollywood movie. 'No artist,' he once said, 'can afford to do anything that isn't really jolly good,' and, looking back on what he had done so far in movies, he was gratified to find that much of it had indeed been really jolly good.[93]

He had achieved everything that he had hoped to achieve (and a little more) when he first made the decision to concentrate on movies instead of staying with television, radio or the stage. He had established himself in the industry on both sides of the Atlantic. He had contributed memorable performances to some of the most notable comedies of the past decade, and had earned the right to be considered for some of the best and most interesting comedy projects that were currently being planned. What he wanted to do now, as his mid-fifties drew near, was to stand back for a moment, smell the roses (and clove carnations) and enjoy what he had done. It was time for Terry-Thomas to have some fun.

CHAPTER FIVE

A Bit of Fun

We've made it – we're up amongst the nobs!

TERRY-THOMAS HAD ALWAYS been an extravagant sort of man. Back in the mid-1950s, he had joked about the profligacy for which he was already famous, claiming that he might soon start using five-pound notes merely to light up his cigarettes: 'It's all good, clean fun,' he insisted. 'By burning my money, I'd be having £5 worth of satisfying, albeit – on a time basis – expensive fun. It would be one glorious moment of abandon.'[1] By the early 1960s, with his profile so high and his finances unprecedentedly healthy, he was ripe for a far more seriously sybaritic style of life: 'During my Hollywood period,' he would later admit, '"burning money", or rather, squandering it, became the norm rather than just "one glorious moment of abandon".'[2] The Finchley boy had now landed firmly in fantasy land.

It was a period in which he preferred to work in order to live rather than live in order to work. He funded his fun by accepting more and more well-paid but relatively undemanding guest spots in other stars' movies (when a reporter asked him why he was popping up in so many small roles, he replied blithely: 'I haven't the time to play big roles'[3]), and, on an increasingly regular basis, he topped up the coffers by appearing in all kinds of lucrative and long-running commercials ('I could earn £10,000 a day'[4]). He fronted advertising campaigns for ice-cream in Australia; shaving soap in Italy; Fruit of the Loom underwear, Maxwell House instant coffee, soft drinks and Sears in America; Gordon's gin in five different countries; and Grundig tape recorders, Benson & Hedges cigars, Van Heusen shirts, Lyons tea and Haig whisky in Britain. He also overcame his distaste for mass-produced chocolates long enough to be photographed 'filling the gap between meals' by taking a modest bite out of a Mars bar ('I spat out what I'd bitten into a basin') and indulged his taste for vermouth by shooting several endorsements of the drink in some of the most picturesque parts of Italy ('Now that *was* an arduous assignment'[5]).

Some of his earnings from advertising went straight into stocks and shares ('I have always had a fairly good feeling as to what should be done on the stock market,' he later said, 'and it normally came off'[6]), and some was invested in property – he even acted on the advice of his chauffeur of the time ('a chap called Bray') and bought a modest little grocer's shop in Munster Road on the outskirts of Putney which went on to perform 'very well'.[7] Most of it, however, went on getting up to mischief and having plenty of 'larks'.

He went to Spain, for example, met an attractive young woman, enjoyed some pleasantly saucy evenings with her out under the stars, and then allowed her to persuade him to smuggle back into Britain her new pet dog under a blanket in his car ('I was shaking with apprehension'[8]). He went up to Garstang in Lancashire to take a look at a supposedly very promising young horse – which, after it had done its best to kick him up and over into nearby Preston, he decided to go ahead and buy.[9] Always an avid admirer of fast and elegant motor vehicles (he was good friends with the racing drivers Mike Hawthorn and Stirling Moss), he drove himself around the English countryside in an extremely smart new AC sports car until he 'completely wrecked' it, stripping all the gears and then abandoning it 'somewhere on Exmoor'.[10] He crashed another of his vehicles through the window of a shoe shop at Williton in Somerset – after which he threw some shoes playfully at the local policemen, who just laughed and said, 'Blimey, it's Terry-Thomas!' Then he paid for all the repairs and went gaily on his way.[11] He accompanied his fellow comedian Jimmy Edwards (the pair of them camply resplendent in the requisite full hunting pink) at meets of the Old Surrey, Burstow & West Kent Hunt, and went riding on his own along Rotten Row in Hyde Park.[12] He entertained England wicket-keeper Godfrey Evans, fast bowler Freddie Trueman and a couple of other cricketers in his dressing room after a stage show; when the champagne, brandy and beer had run out at 3 a.m., he took them off to spend a few more hours at a night club, followed by breakfast at his place, before sending them away to play the next day of their Test match.[13]

He often strolled into one of Spike Milligan's favourite lunchtime haunts – Fu Tong's restaurant on Kensington High Street – to sit down at the writer's table and tell another long and tall tale (such as the one about the war that ended with him being awarded the Brent Cross: 'Don't you mean the Victoria Cross?' asked one of Milligan's mates, happily playing along. 'No,' gasped T-T. 'I never go *that* way home!'[14]). He sometimes whiled away a free afternoon by sharing a bottle or two of wine with old friends or colleagues such as Ian Carmichael ('He introduced me to the joys of drinking Tavel Rosé – the full-bodied Rhone rosé – *al fresco* in summer sunshine and strawberries bathed in Marsala. He was very insistent on the verb – *"bathed"*, NOT "Marsala poured over them"'[15]), and enjoyed taking parties to the art deco pub that he owned in the middle of the moors on the way to South Molton in Devon.

He consented to pose for sculptors (the American Freda Brilliant produced a bust of him in 1951, and in the UK Ronald Moody, the husband of his secretary Helene, created another one in 1954) and portraitists (the artist and 'society osteopath' Stephen Ward – who would later become a tragic casualty of the Profumo scandal – sketched him in 1961). He also added to his massive collection of clothes (which, according to the most recent reports, already contained '80 suits, 22 dinner jackets and tail suits and 150 fancy waistcoats'[16]), sampled some of the finest vintage wines and spirits and relaxed every now and then at the nicest – and most indulgent – of England's country health farms (where he often took his shotgun and went out looking for rabbits). He did his very best, in other words, to do whatever it was that he wanted.

At a time when the majority of the American film industry was firmly in the grip of gimmicks and glossy nonsense, and the British film industry was going down fast and deep into the doldrums, he treated much that he was offered with the disrespect that it deserved. A token attempt at experimentation, a minor British-made movie called *The Wild Affair* (first released in 1963, but not widely seen until 1965) about a young female clerk's final twelve hours before her marriage, had seen him appear *sans* both his customary moustache and his 'natural built-in gimmick', the gap between his two front teeth (filled in with a specially made denture), but the departure was not judged a success, and the attempt was never repeated.[17] 'I was never a trophy hunter so it didn't worry me that the character I had become brought no awards,' he later reflected. 'Once I had cornered the market, in the Sixties, as Hollywood's favourite silly-ass Englishman, the work piled up. It didn't bother me that I had been type-cast. Perhaps it should have concerned me more. I was stereotyped, but then – I didn't fancy myself as a nun!'[18]

Part of him, it seems, did still harbour some small measure of regret that one or two meatier roles had not come his way. The writer, director and producer Sidney Gilliat, for example (who had worked with the star on both *The Green Man* and *Blue Murder at St Trinian's*), would recall glimpsing T-T express his resentment of the sight of others – most notably his old friend Peter Sellers – making the most of more obviously challenging parts:

> During the shooting of *I'm All Right, Jack*, I was waiting outside the studio set of Kite's house when Terry, who was waiting for his call, suddenly came up to me and, indicating Kite's house, announced, 'I can do anything that fellow can do,' meaning, of course, Peter Sellers. He went on to complain vehemently that nobody seemed to realise any more that he had given an extensive range of imitations and mimicries in numbers of radio programmes and in various venues. I realised as he went on that, of course, this was quite right, that he had done many of the same things as Peter and done them very well indeed. I asked him why he didn't bring that aspect forward more with film makers etc., and he replied that nobody seemed to want to know. He was obviously jealous of Sellers, who had had a similar passage into films, and that was understandable. I think the truth was probably that he had typed himself – or been typed – as the dubious gap-toothed characters in films like *Private's*

Progress and other pictures of that period; and everybody was happy about that except Terry.[19]

He was now, however, well on his way to becoming – more or less – resigned to his 'silly-ass Englishman' fate.

He had spent more than enough time in Hollywood studios to realise that the 'business men don't seem to be able to mind their own business',[20] and that making mainstream movies was getting to be more and more of a whip-cracked and soulless routine. One anecdote that he often liked to tell summed up what he thought of the now-dominant industrial attitude:

There's a fellow called Telfer who makes more pork pies than anybody else in the bloody *world*, old boy. So the Americans went and asked him how he did it – incentive schemes, graduated bonuses, productivity scales, vacation benefits, you know the kind of thing. 'No,' he kept saying, 'no, I never do anything like that, no, I just let 'em turn the bloody things out the best they can. Oh, there is just one thing – every so often I goes down to the yard and I bawls, 'Faster you fuckers!'[21]

Although increasingly nostalgic for the sort of more intimate and carefully made movies to which he had contributed back in Britain during the 1950s, he was sufficiently realistic to know what as a professional actor he now had to do. As he always told his cousin Richard Briers: 'If you have a half-decent chance to work, then for heaven's sake *take* it – and don't let it go.'[22] So he carried on going, however reluctantly, with the flow.

If the process of making a particular movie failed to engage him as a performer, he was good at finding other, less conventional, ways to keep himself pleasantly entertained. When, for example, he was stuck on the set of the very laboured Rock Hudson and Gina Lollobrigida romantic comedy *Strange Bedfellows* (1965), he sat back in his chair and watched with barely disguised amusement as the supposedly big and muscular Hudson failed repeatedly – much to his embarrassment and her irritation – to lift his leading lady off her feet for longer than a couple of seconds at a time ('I could only assume that La Lollo had her bra stuffed full of sand, or something'). He found it even more entertaining when four unseen technicians were then called on to support the now furious Lollobrigida via a series of hidden wooden planks in order to create the impression that Hudson was carrying her on his own up a flight of stairs: 'I rather hoped that something would go wrong,' he later confessed. 'The resulting mess would have been hilarious.'[23] When there was nothing on set that looked likely to keep him amused, he would often wander off, assemble the portable ping-pong table that he took with him to every assignment and challenge someone to a game or two of table tennis ('I spent half my life playing'[24]).

He adopted a similar attitude when compelled to promote these movies at various cities and studios around the globe. Sometimes, if he spied a decent-looking champagne bar, restaurant or night club nearby, he would slip off as soon as possible from the stuffy media junket and start a very T-T-style story-telling party. On other occasions, as the comedy writer and performer Barry Cryer would recall, the star would find a more striking way to extricate himself from all of the tiresome and stage-managed hype: 'He was sitting, after dinner, in one of the Edinburgh hotels, when he suddenly stood up and announced, "I'm terribly sorry, I must go. I have a prostitute waiting for me at reception". Someone met him at breakfast the next morning and asked, hesitantly, how his evening had gone. "Oh, that wasn't true – I went to bed and read a book. I was *bored*, you see".'[25]

It was not that he no longer cared. It was just that he had finally learned how to come to terms, more or less, with the limitations of his own power and influence on any particular movie project. As a self-confessed perfectionist – the kind of person for whom even 'stains on summer-weight suits or suede shoes would come pretty close to displeasing me more than anything else in the world'[26] – he knew that, if he allowed himself to care too much about too many aspects of a production, he would almost certainly be driven into a wild and pointless rage on a daily, or perhaps even an hourly, basis. He kept such anger at bay, therefore, by doing whatever he could do as well as he could possibly do it, and then indulged himself with some kind of pleasant and relaxing distraction.

Eric Sykes – who had been a good friend of T-T's ever since the pair of them appeared together in the revue called *Large As Life* at the London Palladium back in 1958[27] – witnessed this relatively discreet off-screen hedonism at first hand when working alongside him on the large-canvas international comedy (about a newspaper-sponsored London to Paris air race in 1910) entitled *Those Magnificent Men In Their Flying Machines* (1965). On one sultry and slow-moving afternoon, for example, just before the director Ken Annakin was due to shoot an extraordinarily elaborate scene involving several stars and more than a thousand costumed extras, Terry-Thomas brought the proceedings to an abrupt halt by announcing that he needed to 'have a few words with Eric' before going ahead with the action. 'Terry led me to the car park some two hundred yards away out of sight of the film set,' Sykes recalled:

> Then Terry opened the boot of his car, turned to me and said, 'What would you like to drink?' I couldn't believe it, his car boot was better stocked than some of the clubs in St James's Square. 'I'll have a gin and tonic,' I said. Terry poured out a generous measure in a cut glass tumbler and, nonchalantly, he asked, 'Lemon?' and when I nodded he sliced a lemon and in two minutes we were sitting comfortably in the little space by the bar in his boot. I suddenly remembered the large crowd relaxing, the director looking at his watch, and the lighting cameraman staring through a piece of smoked glass at the sun.
>
> 'Terry,' I said, 'what did you want to talk to me about?'
>
> Coolly, he replied, 'Nothing, old boy, I thought we could both do with a drink.'
>
> Is it any wonder I enjoyed working with him?[28]

Another co-star who relished sharing the set with him during the shooting, and then socialising with him once the scenes had been done, was Sarah Miles – an avid fan since the days of his TV shows – who played the movie's main love interest, Patricia Rawnsley:

> I got to know him a little on the set and found him utterly enchanting. It is very rare for me to discover that a personality I've worshipped

on the screen turns out to be more impressive in person; indeed, most times, they are a complete let down. But in Terry's case, I found him just as funny, stylish and delightful in the flesh as I did during all those hilarious TV series of my youth. I cannot give anyone higher praise than that. I am very pleased that during a tea-break one day I was able to pluck up sufficient courage to tell him what he meant to me and my family and how dreadfully jealous my brothers would be that I actually managed to play a scene with our childhood hero. For our hero he undoubtedly was.[29]

Even the one member of the production team who had most reason to take issue with T-T's relatively 'relaxed' attitude – director Ken Annakin – was happy, most of the time, to let the star move along in his own inimitable manner: 'Everyone in the studio was laughing whenever he came onto the stage. He really could not help but be funny in everything he did because he always seemed to be just that little bit over the top.'[30]

Those Magnificent Men ... was one of the projects that actually benefited from the star's playfully pragmatic strategy, because Terry-Thomas (as 'England's foremost aeroplanist', the scheming, cheating, moustache-twirling bounder Sir Percy Ware-Armitage) and Eric Sykes (as his permanently put-upon but quietly critical manservant, Courtney) formed a very effective on-screen double-act (which ended up inspiring a pair of cartoon alter egos – Dick Dastardly and Muttley – in the popular Hanna-Barbera/Warner Brothers series *Wacky Races*).[31] While Sir Percy busied himself with losing friends and failing to influence people ('Morning, madam,' he muttered as he passed a kilt-wearing Scotsman; 'I say there, Yankee chap,' he called out to someone he took to be vaguely American; 'Buzz *OFF!*' he barked at just about everyone else), poor Courtney was obliged to do most of his devious boss's dirty work ('You're not going to sabotage it, guv'nor?' asks Courtney of one of their rivals' machines. 'I certainly am not,' snorts Sir Percy. '*You* are!') while putting up with his boss's dirty ideas ('I've given the Frenchman the address of a *very* lovely young lady,' whispers Sir Percy conspiratorially. '*Cor-rr!* I bet she's a bit of all right, guv'nor!' sniggers Courtney. 'You should know,' replies Sir Percy matter-of-factly. 'She's your daughter!').

This was fun at its most productive, because – on the screen as well as on the set – it seemed unforced and delightfully apt. The movie duly pulled in huge audiences and, perhaps thanks especially to the scenes featuring Sir Percy and Courtney, it also received some warm reports from the critics. The *New York Times*, for example, singled out T-T as 'the crackiest, funniest fellow in the film',[32] while Sykes won his own fair share of praise as the sympathetic sidekick ('It had been such a great pleasure to make,' he would recall, 'and, of course, it was very nice to be part of such a smash hit'[33]), and several reviews hoped to see more in the near future of the partnership the two actors had formed.

Sure enough, Sykes went on to work with Terry-Thomas several times during this decade – first on some of his lucrative but well-made and award-winning cigar commercials, and then in another big budget all-star romp called *Monte Carlo or Bust!* (1969) – and, on each successive occasion, he found that his friend was nestling a little more snugly in the lap of luxury. 'When we were working together [on *Monte Carlo or Bust!*] at the De Laurentiis Studios in Rome, I think some people there probably mistook me for Terry's valet,' Sykes recalled:

Whereas I was staying in a nice but modest – and affordable – hotel, Terry had a suite in a very grand establishment just off the Via Veneto, where the staff all bowed at him whenever he appeared. Every morning, I'd take a taxi into the studio (which in itself was always quite an adventure!), but Terry would be driven through the gates in this white Rolls-Royce he'd hired for the entire eleven weeks that we were scheduled to be there – and the commissionaire always saluted him! Terry would be sitting there smiling and waving, going, 'Oh, hell-o! Good morning!' That was how Terry approached these things, and it was very entertaining. When, most weekends, we'd fly back home to England on Alitalia, Terry always boarded the aircraft with this little wicker basket of his, which usually contained some cold chicken, a pot of caviar, some salad, cheese, hand-made chocolates and a chilled bottle of Chablis or Pouilly Fuissé, and, of course, with that gap-toothed smile, he had no trouble at all charming one of the stewardesses into preparing a

special meal for him – 'I say, my dear, would you mind awfully …?'
I even remember, on one occasion, he actually produced from that
basket two fresh pork chops and the stewardess happily went off
and cooked them for him! He was a delightful man who had found
a way to live – and work – that suited him, so that was the sort of
thing that he did.[34]

A pleasant change of location represented another attractive factor
whenever the time came for Terry-Thomas to ponder which one of his
latest potential projects to choose next. Starting in the mid-1960s, he
began indulging his 'insatiable appetite for travelling' by making some
of his movies in places other than Buckinghamshire, Middlesex or Los
Angeles.[35] During the second half of the decade, he would go to Morocco
to film a cameo in the comedy thriller *Our Man in Marrakesh* (1966).
He also went to shoot the very camp spy spoof *Se tutte le donne del
mondo …* (1966) in Rome and Rio de Janeiro; the hugely successful
wartime farce *La Grand Vadrouille* (1966) in Paris and the Côte d'Or;
the kidnapping caper *Top Crack* (1967) in Rome; the knowingly quaint
science-fiction fantasy *Jules Verne's Rocket to the Moon* (1967) in and
around Dublin; the *Kind Hearts and Coronets*-style black comedy *Arriva
Dorellik* (1967) back in Rome; played multiple roles, very well, in the
above-average farce *Arabella* (also known as *Ragazza del Charleston*,
1967) alongside Virna Lisi in Ostia; took part in a trio of crime capers –
Sette volte sette (1968) in France, Italy, England and Germany,[36] *Danger:
Diabolik* (1968) and *Uno scacco tutto matto* (1968) both in Rome; and
sauntered through *Una su 13* (1969) – one of the many movie versions
of the classic Russian novel by Il'f and Petrov, *Dvenadtsat' stul'ev (The
Twelve Chairs*, 1929) – in various parts of Europe as well as, of all places,
Jermyn Street in London. Even when the material was nowhere near up
to being the movie equivalent of Jermyn Street standards, the change
still seemed as good as a rest to the jobbing T-T: 'In many of the foreign
productions,' he would recall, 'my work was done so quickly, I never
even knew the title of the films or met the stars. Many's the time I have
finished one picture on a Saturday and been flying somewhere on the
Sunday to start shooting on the Monday. I loved to work and I loved to

work fast. Rome one week, Paris the next, Brazil the week after. It was madness.'[37]

A second, largely unexpected but very welcome marriage helped supply a sort of method to this madness. He now had a new wife with whom he wanted to travel the world – and he also needed to earn enough money to keep her in the style to which he was more than happy to see her become accustomed.

Ironically, after waiting patiently for so many years for the chance to legalise their love, Lorrae Desmond was not the woman Terry-Thomas went on to marry. Shortly after his first wife, Pat, finally agreed – grudgingly – to a divorce on 1 February 1962 (on the grounds of his alleged desertion eight years earlier[38]), the relationship with Lorrae suddenly appeared, once the strain had at last been lifted of having to share a life that was lived in limbo, to have run out of steam. There was no acrimonious falling-out – just a sad sense of their mutual resignation to their respective separate fates: she returned to work in her native Australia and ended up marrying a surgeon based in Sydney, while he, upon hearing the news, sat alone in his London apartment and broke down and wept. It was actually the young woman who comforted him during this time, twenty-one-year-old Belinda Cunningham, who would go on to become his new wife.

A lieutenant-colonel's daughter from Lincolnshire, she had first encountered Terry-Thomas in the summer of 1960. She was working in Majorca for a holiday job – at the pretty little Pension Miravista in the north coast resort of Cala Ratjada – when he arrived there (shortly after his first really serious, but ultimately unsuccessful, attempt to persuade the stubborn Pat to end their marriage) for a brief rest between movie projects. Even though she was twenty-six years his junior, and unfamiliar with most of the work for which he was now so famous, she was drawn to him more or less right from the start because of his twinkling eyes, ready wit and worldly charm ('I just saw this wonderful character just bounding down and I thought, "Wow!"'[39]). He, in turn, took in the sight of her soft blonde hair, deep blue eyes and her 'infectious smile' and felt an immediate attraction – and it was not long, once he had also taken note of her impeccable manners and 'gentle-voiced upper-class accent' (prompting the internal exclamation: '*Posh!*'), before the initial attraction led to a far more serious kind of fascination: 'I went overboard for her.'[40] He ended up sneaking off to see her late at nights in her room – which he was obliged to reach by creeping carefully across an extremely fragile tiled roof (it was, he later explained, 'a frightfully energetic period of my life'[41]) – and, once their time together in Majorca was over, he left for his next movie engagement feeling 'quite dazzled' by his unexpected holiday romance. He soon started seeing Belinda on a regular basis – taking care to hide this fact from his other lover, Lorrae Desmond – and began considering the possibility that he just might, at long last, have found his true soul mate.[42]

He did not find it easy, however, to take the relationship on to the next level. Even after both Pat and Lorrae had departed from the scene, the union still faced strong opposition from Belinda's father, Geoffrey, who was appalled at the news that his young daughter was 'carrying on' with an actor – and a comedian to boot – who was almost as old as he was. In a bid to break up the relationship, therefore, he arranged for Belinda to go off to Singapore, where he had hurriedly pulled some strings to secure a job for her as the personal assistant to the naval chief of staff, but, in spite of such efforts, the bond between her and T-T remained unbroken. They continued to write to each other and called whenever they could, found ways to spend some time together in person, and, before Lieutenant-Colonel Cunningham could do anything more about it, the relationship was well and truly back on track.

Once Belinda had returned to London, she and T-T became a *bona fide* couple, and he started proposing to her on a regular basis. Although she assured him that she was more than happy to keep the relationship as it was for the time being, she admitted, during further questioning, that the arrival of a child would probably change her mind – and so (against some of the more cautious of his old friends' advice) he did what he could to make that happen, and enjoyed himself hugely while he waited for the desired result.

One evening in 1963, when Terry-Thomas was away in the Yucca Valley shooting a scene for *It's a Mad, Mad, Mad, Mad World*, he put in a transatlantic call to Belinda, who was staying back in London at his home at Queen's Gate Mews, and prepared to embark on the usual casual exchange of saucy chatter and wicked gossip. 'Hello Terry,' she began brightly. 'You'd better buy the house next door; we'll need the extra room.' When he asked her why, she replied: 'I'm preg!'[43] Thrilled and 'a bit staggered' by the news, he flew back to see her as soon as he possibly could, and the couple (she dressed in white, he in a grey suit, colourful silk waistcoat and grey suede shoes) married one warm August morning in a private ceremony at Halstead Register Office, near Colchester in Essex. Their first child – a boy – was born in London (at the Princess Beatrice Hospital) on the morning of 15 March the following year, while T-T was stranded on the other side of the Atlantic making, of all things, *How to Murder Your Wife* in Hollywood. The baby would be christened Timothy Hoar Stevens, but his parents soon took to calling him 'Tiger'.

Terry-Thomas could not quite believe his good fortune at this time in his life: he had reached his fifties without experiencing either the pleasure of a genuinely happy marriage or the privilege of having his own child, and now, when he least expected it, he had them both. It was for this reason, above all others, that he was in such an exceptionally fun-loving state of mind during the mid-1960s. Belinda and their son made him feel young and carefree once again. The bosses no longer mattered that much, and neither did the underwhelming nature of the movie projects, nor the other actors, the critics, the gossip columnists or the agents. He had a wife and he had a family. That was now what really mattered.

He was amused by the fact that his well-brought-up wife (who always called him 'Mac' after one of his favourite daily tipples, the whisky mac) had so little knowledge of, or interest in, the most glamorously superficial aspects of show business (when an eager-to-please producer threw a celebratory party for the newlyweds at the start of their first stay together in Hollywood, Mrs Terry-Thomas failed to recognise the vast majority of the internationally renowned stars to whom she was introduced). He also liked the way that, thanks to her own healthy disregard for pointless social pretensions, she helped to keep his own suede shoes planted firmly on the ground. 'Being an Army daughter from a posh family,' he remarked admiringly, 'she was not impressed by my monogrammed shirts, for instance, and never stopped ribbing me about them.'[44]

What he loved about her most of all in those early days of their marriage was her sheer unforced and unpredictable *joie de vivre*, which encouraged him – at a time when he had started to grow a little cautious – to take more notice of his desires than he did his fears. 'I was the surprised one,' he later said, in the manner of a biter bit, of this youthful kindred spirit; 'I hadn't realised I had married an eccentric.'[45] If, for example, Belinda felt like taking a dip in their pool while her husband was sharing a drink and a story or two with a few of their mutual friends, she would simply slip away, have her solitary swim, and then reappear stark naked and dripping wet in front of their assembled guests. 'Aren't you coming in?' she would enquire of everyone. 'It's lovely!' Similarly, if, when dining out with her husband in Beverly Hills at the home of Glenn Ford and his wife, she found that the quarter-bottle of the 1928 vintage Pommard that the four of them were trying to share was very much to her taste, she would not hesitate to startle the notoriously parsimonious star by suggesting that it might not be such a bad idea if he went a bit wild for once and uncorked an entire bottle – if not two. She even thought nothing of telling her new sister-in-law, Mary ('a person with very old-fashioned manners'[46]), a limerick that T-T had feared – wrongly as it turned out – was far too crude for other, more conventional, members of the old Stevens family back in Finchley:

> *There was a young fellow named Berkin,*
> *Who was always jerkin' his gherkin.*
> *His mother said, 'Berkin, stop jerkin' your gherkin.*
> *It was made for ferkin' – not jerkin'.*[47]

'She made me relax,' Terry-Thomas would reflect fondly, 'and taught me that it was ridiculous to worry – the quickest way to get ulcers.'[48]

The two of them were determined to enjoy the life that they now shared to the full – regardless of how much money it might end up costing them: 'one didn't hold back,' he later confessed. 'What with entertaining, living expenses, exorbitant rents, staff and transport, I got through an alarming amount of the stuff very quickly. I was earning it, so why not spend it?'[49] This was an era in celebrity culture that did not so much encourage as demand such a degree of carefree and conspicuous consumption by the newly named 'Beautiful People'.[50] Richard Burton was buying Elizabeth Taylor a succession of brazenly eye-catching items of jewellery (starting with the 33.19-carat Asscher-cut Krupp Diamond[51]); Peter Sellers was collecting all kinds of properties, gimmicky high-tech gadgets and a veritable fleet of fashionable motor cars (including no fewer than ten Mini Coopers); David Niven had acquired an elegant Swiss chalet close to the ski slopes at Chateau d'Oex and a magnificent Cap Ferrat villa called Lo Scoglietto just above the harbour at St Jean; Raymond Burr had purchased the small island of Naitauba in Fiji[52] while Marlon Brando had snapped up a 150-acre French Polynesian atoll called Tetiaroa;[53] and The Beatles tried to purchase their very own private island in Greece before electing to establish their own multi-media corporation – Apple – in Savile Row instead.[54]

The Terry-Thomases were far from being in – or even wanting to one day get into – the premier league of big show-business spenders, but they still did their bit to keep the cash registers ringing in the likes of Old Bond Street and Rodeo Drive. 'There were so many shops handy and easy to get at, filled with tantalizing goods,' Terry-Thomas would later recall with a slightly rueful smile. 'Whatever Belinda and I wanted, we bought. And we wanted the lot. We knew the fat cheques in the pipeline were endless.'[55]

By far the fattest of these cheques came from his contributions to the kind of big-budget 'blockbuster' Hollywood productions that boasted huge starry casts but forgot to include much that could pass for a plot ('I'd hate myself for ever if I turned them down,' he joked, 'especially if, for instance, Peter Sellers took them'[56]). In 1967, for example, he was among the colourful but familiar ingredients in no fewer than three of these over-egged puddings: *The Perils of Pauline* (an incredible mess of an attempt at a camp period comedy[57]), Gene Kelly's self-consciously *à la mode* sex satire *A Guide for the Married Man* and a very weak Jerry Lewis vehicle entitled *Don't Raise the Bridge, Lower the River*. He was only in *A Guide for the Married Man* for a solitary three-minute scene – about a husband who cheats on his wife in their own bedroom with a buxom blonde bimbette (played by Jayne Mansfield in a diaphanous pink negligée) – but that was long enough for him to be reminded of how tiresome such productions could be. Gene Kelly (whom the actor considered 'a very prudish director'[58]) tried to cut the only funny exchange in the whole sequence on the grounds that it was 'vulgar': as the husband hunts for his mistress's missing brassiere, she tells him not to worry, assuring him that, should his wife ever find it, she will just think it must be one of her own – a prediction that provokes her flustered lover to cast a glance at her more than generous 42DD breasts and then mutter, 'Don't be *ridiculous*!' Terry-Thomas protested about Kelly's decision to the producers, who upheld his complaint and put the dialogue back in, and the star moved on as swiftly as he could to his next well-paid engagement.

His patience was strained rather more whenever he was obliged to spend a far lengthier time on set – which was certainly the case when he appeared alongside Doris Day and Robert Morse in yet another movie about how Doris Day's character gets to preserve her virtue. This time it was a half-hearted 'Swinging Sixties' sex comedy entitled *Where Were You When the Lights Went Out?* (1968), and it represented a painfully laboured attempt to revivify an outdated format. Cast, quite perversely and pointlessly, as a sleazily epicene and temperamental Hungarian, T-T not only had to endure endless unsolicited advice from Day concerning how she thought he should play each scene, but also had to put up with her many sudden and aimless improvisations when each scene was being shot. There was no point in complaining to the producers on this particular occasion, he realised, because one of them was Marty Melcher – who happened to be the doting husband of Doris Day. 'When I managed to dart an interrogating, raised-eyebrowed look at the director, Hy Averbrook,' T-T recalled, 'he shrugged apologetically, and with his hand high made a scissor movement behind Doris's head. He meant he was indulging his producer's wife, but would cut out her surplus material later – including a large number of pauses, long, long pauses.'[59] He made it through to the project's conclusion by doing what he usually now did when faced with such an overly 'helpful' fellow performer – 'listen to them politely, then do it my own way, as if the conversation had never taken place'[60] – but the fact that he barely made any effort to remain in character, let alone maintain a consistent accent, showed how little he cared about the whole sorry affair.

He got away with this semi-detached attitude thanks, in part, to the fact (of which he was well aware) that his American employers could never quite work out when he was being genuinely rebellious and when he was merely being 'English'. Indeed, his cranked-up brand of 'Englishness', though still eminently useful to US movie-makers, seemed to grow more peculiar in their eyes by the day as the strikingly different Anglo-images of moodily stylish David Bailey working-class icons, psychedelic rock stars and hirsute peace-loving hippies flew into California from the other side of the Atlantic: Terry-Thomas had always been odd, but now he appeared odder than ever to his attentive American friends. As a 1965 profile of him in *Time* magazine had already suggested, the intriguingly foreign T-T struck quite a few people in Hollywood as the kind of nut who was far too tough for them to crack:

> ... it is often hard to tell whether he is spoofing the upper-crust Briton or simply being one. On his travels, like any Blimp setting off on safari, he packs his portmanteaus [sic] with sartorial accoutrements for every conceivable occasion: white flannels for tennis, plus fours for golf, blazer for cricket, bowler, boater and deerstalker, tweeds, pinstripes, tails. Everything but the old elephant gun. He claims that he needs all those togs for professional use, but offstage he is seldom seen wearing the wrong suit or the same one twice. In real life he is as wildly gallant and exaggeratedly debonair as any character he impersonates.[61]

Terry-Thomas was happy to take full advantage of the confusion his image seemed to create, rebelling in such a disarmingly artful way that, before the executives had a chance to spot the dissidence in what had been done, the star had already slipped away to a set elsewhere, leaving behind an impression of eccentric behaviour that was no more enlightening than the smile of a gap-toothed Cheshire cat.

It probably confused some of his Hollywood colleagues even more when he made the decision to seek a new base in a place outside of his beloved Britain. It was not that he was looking to escape: apart from the fact that he felt a few of his countrymen would never let him forget that he hailed from humble little Finchley – a suspicion that grew stronger after he discovered that certain 'toffs' had blackballed him for membership of the RAC ('Being turned down by the RAC,' he fumed, 'is worse than being turned down by a tart in Piccadilly'[62]) – he remained a great champion of all (or at least most) things English, and always insisted on having the Union Flag flying above his current American abode. Admittedly, he seemed suspicious of the country's latest wave of youthful irreverence, and the new satirical magazine *Private Eye* had caught him recently in an uncharacteristically over-sensitive and humourless mood by appearing – at least in his eyes – to suggest with one cartoon that, in private life, he was actually a 'dissipated, drunken and dissolute character' (he was so rattled by this, in fact, that he sued the publication for libel, and won an apology and a substantial sum of money for damages[63]). Far more typically, however, he remained a proud and passionate patriot who was determined to remain a British citizen: 'I'm not dodging tax like all these blighters running off to Guatemala and other ridiculous places,' he told reporters. 'I don't think their attitude is at all right.'[64]

He had, indeed, only recently spent a great deal of time, money and emotion on renovating his elegant home in Queen's Gate Mews (enlarging one of the rooms and adding a solarium and plant house on the roof),[65] and had also long craved a decent second home in the English countryside, but the problem at this stage was that neither he nor his wife could find any property that really appealed to them in the Home Counties. When, therefore, he reflected on the fact that most of his movie work now occurred outside of the British Isles, and he also noted that – being 'a bronchial person'[66] – his health had improved considerably since he had been obliged to spend so much of his time in warmer climes, he came to the conclusion that it would make more sense to find a house in a part of the world where he would not only be nearer to some of the relevant movie studios but would also no longer be 'working sixteen hours a day [just] to keep myself in throat pastilles'.[67]

He and his wife thus started house-hunting abroad, exploring 'everywhere from Honolulu to Australia and back again'. He was particularly

keen on the idea of setting up a home somewhere on a warm and welcoming island, so he made a point of visiting as many as he possibly
could between his various movie projects, but none of the locations
ended up meeting all of his and Belinda's specific requirements: 'Each
idyllic-seeming paradise would turn out to be too hot, too humid, too
inaccessible for easy commuting, too Americanized for my liking or just
not suitable full stop.'[68] Then, after so many hopes had been dashed, the
couple found, almost by accident, just the sort of place they had been
looking for: the small Spanish island of Ibiza.

It was the actor Denholm Elliott who nudged the pair of them in the
right direction towards the end of 1967. He met Terry-Thomas one day
in Bel Air (the two of them had been friends for some years, and had
worked together on Michael Winner's surprisingly watchable 1965
movie, *You Must Be Joking!*), and, over a glass or two of champagne,
told T-T all about the villa he and his wife Susan had just finished building in the hills outside the sleepy beach town of Santa Eulalia del Rio in
Ibiza.

Elliott rhapsodised about the clouds of pink and white almond
blossom that blanketed the island each spring; spoke fondly of the proud
old toothpaste-white farmhouses that nestled on warm red terraces
framed by twisted grey olive trees and bushy bunches of translucent
emerald figs; described how stunningly beautiful the nearby meadows
could look when they were full of clumps of purple comfrey, deep-blue
borage, blood-red poppies, scarlet and blue pimpernel, white and pale-
yellow marguerites and firm young trees of golden-globed fennel; and
enthused about the simple but delicious *tapas*, *tortilla* and *albondigas* to
be eaten and the heady *Hierbas* liqueurs to be drunk. He also explained
about what a rich, relaxed and friendly atmosphere was often generated
by all of the amiable old expats, visiting actors and artists, colourful Ibi-
zencos and assorted local oddballs who congregated from noon onwards
each day at the drinking hole called *El Caballo Negro* but better known
to its core clientele as 'Sandy's Bar' (run by a tall, fair-haired, fine-fea-
tured, quietly spoken and diplomatic Irishman named Sandy Pratt, who
not only mixed a mean Bloody Mary but also allowed his regular customers to use the location of his bar as their mailing address).[69]

Terry-Thomas was intrigued: although he had been to the island, briefly, once before, he had left without catching so much as a glimpse of the sun-kissed Mediterranean paradise with which his friend was now so obviously besotted. 'My first impression when I had got off the boat for a quick walk-around Ibiza town,' he recalled, 'was, true, there were lots of pretty girls about, but the streets stank,' and, as he had always made clear, 'muck, dust, grease and unpleasant smells all worry me to the point of distraction'.[70] Much had changed since then, Elliott assured him, adding that there was a much more attractive and authentic part of Ibiza to explore once one had ventured beyond the touristy towns and stepped into the still-untainted countryside. T-T agreed to see for himself, and so he and Belinda set off for the island en route to a television show he was due to make in Monaco with Princess Grace.[71]

The couple fell in love with Ibiza soon after they arrived. Gone, it seemed, was the 'dreadfully smelly' land full of 'contrived people' with 'lank hair' and 'tatty Bohemian clothes': in its place, just as Denholm Elliott had promised, there was a warmly inviting and largely unspoilt little world for the two of them to embrace, and they proceeded to do so with great pleasure. 'This time,' he would declare, 'I was mad about the sparkling Spanish island.'[72]

After searching for quite a while, however, neither he nor Belinda had found an available villa about which both of them were keen enough to go ahead and attempt to buy (their long list of specifications – which had included a good access road, mains water, electricity, a telephone connection and 'a wonderful view' – met with much scratching of heads and shrugging of shoulders in an area of Ibiza that in those days was relatively primitive), so they decided eventually to do what the Elliotts had done and build a custom-made home of their own. This led to a different kind of problem: once some of the locals discovered that the millionaire English movie star Terry-Thomas was in the market to buy some land, the prices duly rocketed. He turned down one pleasant but unexceptional plot, for example, when he was told that the price would be £32,000 (which was getting on for £400,000 by today's prices); soon after, he found out that it had been sold to someone else for a mere £8,000 (nearer to £96,000 now). He promptly went on his guard, and, as a result, the whole process took far longer than either he or Belinda had envisaged. Eventually, however, when out together horse riding in the countryside, they came across the right place on the north-eastern side of the island – half a hillside by the village of San Carlos in Santa Eulalia, six hundred feet above sea level at its lowest point, with a breathtaking panoramic view stretching out across pine, olive, fig, carob and almond trees to a distant bay at Cala Mastella – and the right price, under £20,000 – and they secured the basis of their home in the sun. All that they had to do now was to build it.

The only thing there that passed for accommodation, when they bought the land, was a run-down hilltop *finca* (a small farmhouse), but the couple felt, none the less, that their new property had plenty of the necessary potential. As Terry-Thomas had always been 'allergic' to architects, he decided, rather boldly, to design the house himself. He knew that, as he had several new movie projects looming on the horizon, he would have to supervise the building – and the builders – while shuttling back and forth between Ibiza and various studios and sets in Hollywood, Pinewood, Paris and Rome, but he was determined to see that his plans were realised. After moving with his wife and child into a temporary 'operational base' nearby – it was actually an elegant little villa (*Casa Cala Pada*) that he was renting from the writer and 'jolly good egg' Robin Maugham – he proceeded in a typically unconventional manner by moulding the shape of his dream home with a lump of flour-and-water dough. His team of builders would have to refer to the resulting bread maquette until it became overrun with mildew, and then use a papier-mâché replacement throughout the remainder of the construction period.

The aim was to create something that would seem broadly in keeping with the traditional Ibicencan style, with dark wooden floors, big open fireplaces, large arched windows, exposed beams and thick, caramel-coloured stone walls with soft rounded edges. Belinda stored any additional little details, gleaned from sightseeing trips and conversations with locals, in a scrapbook with a view to incorporating one or two of them at a later date. T-T was also quick to act on any tips from friends and colleagues, as Georgina Cookson – his co-star in *The Naked Truth* and then fellow Ibiza resident – would recall: 'He did the most extraordinary thing. He couldn't decide what colour tiles to have in his pool, and somebody told him that the most wonderful green ones were in the ladies' lavatory at Palma airport. So he flew to Palma and went into the ladies' lavatory … and didn't like them!'[73] The 'basic' design, once it was finally drafted, accommodated thirty rooms – including no fewer than five kitchens ('kitchens were very useful things to have about the place', reasoned T-T[74]), several capacious leisure areas (whose walls were to be adorned with bright and colourful murals) and one large circular dining room (with a giant plastic sunflower attached to its ceiling) – as well as a swimming pool, a tennis court, a 'trampoline area' and a separate, two-bedroomed, red stone guest-house that was situated nearby.

Predictably, however, little progress was made whenever the amateur architect was away, as by this time Belinda was pregnant with their second child and the builders – for whom the phrase *mañana* was proving to be predictably addictive – were often left largely unsupervised. It turned out to be a blessing in disguise, therefore, when he was forced to take a short unscheduled break from making movies after doing 'all sorts of unspeakable damage' to himself while attempting to water-ski around the bay. The workers, it turned out, were not the only ones who were in need of his assistance – Belinda did, too: increasingly tired and depressed, she had recently been advised by her local GP to spend as much time as possible in bed, but her spirits continued to suffer as her pregnancy progressed. Feeling increasingly concerned about her health, Terry-Thomas summoned no less a figure from Britain than the Queen's own surgeon-gynaecologist, Sir George Pinker, to assess her condition, and only after the very charming and courteous Pinker had reassured Belinda about the health both of her baby and herself did the supervision of the building commence once again in earnest.

By the close of the summer of 1968, the dream house – which ended up costing £100,000 (about £1.2 million by today's rates) to create – had become a reality, and Belinda had given birth to another son.[75] The new house acquired the title of *Can Talaias*, and the couple christened their new baby with the distinctly unusual name of Trumper (because, as Terry-Thomas tried his best to explain, the dictionary definition of 'a "trump" is "a courageous person of exceptional generosity; an excellent fellow"[76]) – although, after their elder son Tiger declared that the plump little baby in his mother's arms looked 'just like a cushion', the family would never again call Trumper by any name other than 'Cushan'.

What followed, once T-T, Belinda, Tiger and baby Cushan had settled in their new Ibicencan home, was a period of happy relaxation interrupted occasionally by some starry private parties ('When we have parties,' he would boast, 'we *really* have parties'[77]). Ibiza had not yet become the strobe-lit trance and dance centre for which it would later acquire notoriety, but it was already considered a popular fleshpot for the more arty and unconventional members of Britain's show-business set (styled by some here as 'the Raj on the Med'). The Terry-Thomases would share countless sun-drugged leisure hours with the likes of Denholm and Susan Elliott, Jon and Ingeborg Pertwee, Maggie Smith and Robert Stephens, Georgina Cookson and her husband, Robin Maugham and his various boyfriends, Leslie Phillips and Caroline Barrett, Laurence Olivier and Joan Plowright, Diana Rigg and her partner of the time David Warner, Maria Aitken and her husband of the time Nigel Davenport, Ursula Andress and her on-off escort of the time Jean-Paul Belmondo, John and Mary Mills, Annie Ross, Charles Kay, John Hurt, Irma Kurtz, Caroline Mortimer, Richard Todd, Ronald Fraser, Farley Granger, Sal Mineo, Nico, Terence Stamp, the young PR specialist and budding impresario Lord Sydney Ling and the Baron and Baroness van Pallandt (the Danish pop-singing duo better known to the public at the time as Nina and Frederick). They would also get to know such colourful characters as the infamous art forger and flamboyantly camp figure Elmyr de Hory, the novelist and faux Howard Hughes biographer Clifford Irving[78] and the pioneering sex-change model and chic London socialite April Ashley.[79]

Someone always seemed to be getting up to something, or getting over something, or someone, in that part of the island. Plenty of pot was puffed, innumerable drinks were downed, the odd pair of lovers swapped partners and Diana Rigg was renowned for going *au naturel* whenever she went out and about in her garden ('she rarely put anything on for my benefit,' said Terry-Thomas uncomplainingly, after admitting that he often made a point of passing by just to check[80]). Sandy's Bar guaranteed everyone some good old Celtic *craic* (which was monitored discreetly but highly reliably by the ever-popular Mr Pratt), and on the hillside above Cala Llonga Major Christopher 'Cuth' Adami's restaurant 'The Wild Asparagus' provided them with a more formal and very English alternative (notable events associated with the House of Windsor being marked by loyal toasts and the playing of the National Anthem), but more intimate forms of fun – and far more curious kinds of crises – tended to take place in and around the various private villas that were scattered about nearby.

On one typically sunny afternoon, for example, Terry-Thomas was startled when he spotted a nun with 'substantial hands' lounging on Denholm Elliott's roof with a chilled pint of beer – she turned out to be April Ashley in fancy dress, recovering from acting as hostess at the latest of Robin Maugham's exclusive 'drinky' lunches.[81] Denholm Elliott himself was by no means unfamiliar with the experience of intoxication, and once drove the Oliviers straight into a ditch after sampling a little too much of Nina and Frederick's deeply alcoholic chocolate mousse. On another occasion, the composer Lionel Bart was seen being escorted back to the airport by a nurse from the Red Cross after drinking so much wine and whisky to drown his sorrows (caused by a boyfriend whom he had caught *in flagrante* with a female member of staff) that most of his teeth had fallen out and his stomach had started to haemorrhage.[82]

'There was something about Ibiza that encouraged excess while somehow making us feel that we were immune to the consequences,' recalled Susan Elliott:

I remember Diana Rigg describing a supper party given by Robin Maugham: a glorious sunset, champagne on the terrace; the guests, totally relaxed and uninhibited, exchanging the most bizarre stories of sexual couplings. The chatter was accompanied by yowls from the undergrowth, where two cats were mating. As Diana listened, feline passion seemed to overwhelm the party conversation until all she heard was a piercing shriek. It was, she said, a cry for all Ibiza, a perfect representation of island and people.[83]

'It was one non-stop party,' agreed Leslie Phillips. 'Everywhere you went were arty people, all the names of the day.'[84] Indeed, so reliable did this region of Ibiza become for supplying snippets from the ongoing celebrity soap opera that several gossip columnists from the English daily tabloids took to turning up there every weekend, knowing that – while having themselves an eminently high old time – they would probably compile enough material to fill the majority of their next half-dozen dispatches.

There were times, inevitably, when the general air of informality encouraged the presence of uninvited guests, and quite a few 'exclusive' parties witnessed the sudden arrival of a bewildering array of gatecrashers. Terry-Thomas, for one, certainly 'had a lot of ding-dongs' because of such brusque intrusions, and on one occasion had to expel no fewer than three dozen strangers from a supper party he and Belinda were giving for twenty of their friends. 'I didn't hesitate if I saw intruders about to scoff my chicken, paella or apple crumble,' he later declared. 'I marched up to them, asked who they were, why they were there and then ordered them out.'[85] He was particularly suspicious of any 'grubby hippies' who were spotted being mellow in close proximity to his villa, but he was always civil to them so long as they 'smiled benignly' and stayed well away from his private parties.[86]

He was not even that keen on having his own employees venture inside his cosy Ibicencan nest. According to Jon Pertwee's wife, Ingeborg, it did not take long for an 'air of gentle neglect' to develop within the villa, because 'Terry could not bear to have servants around him': 'Staff were banished from the house during Terry's waking hours, and the maids had to sneak in at dawn, do the chores and disappear again before he got up. He once told [Jon and me], with real anguish in his voice, that when waking up late one morning he saw his gardener working outside and had told him to go away.'[87] Even in the sunniest of places, it seemed, there was always an 'absolute shower' hanging about nearby, but he was adamant that not one drop, or drip, would be allowed to rain down on his precious retreat.

Avril Angers, his old friend and former colleague from the days of

How Do You View?, was struck when she paid him a visit there how artfully he tried to maintain his preferred degree of privacy:

> He came and picked me up from the market square and took us along this little track through a forest and up a mountain, and I said, 'How do people find their way?' Because there was no road, just a bumpy track. And he said, 'Oh, the blue stones.' I said, 'What do you mean, "the blue stones"?' And then I looked out of the car, and every now and again on the way there was a stone painted blue – he'd been out there painting them blue so that [his friends] could follow them up to his place![88]

Such tactics, combined with the use of Sandy's Bar as a contact point where unexpected callers could be discreetly 'vetted', usually ensured that he was left in as much peace as he wanted.

As far as T-T was concerned, the pros of living in Ibiza far outweighed the cons. His health had certainly improved since he had been there: 'All my life I had suffered from bronchial trouble which had caused me thousands of sleepless, sweat-soaked nights with stomach-churning coughing attacks and a general feeling of doom,' he would recount. 'Once I was in Ibiza I was free of it. Once I got settled in my house, 600 ft up, the condition seemed to leave me and I began sleeping like a baby.'[89]

He was still an obsessive and pernickety perfectionist ('I don't mind eating off a tray,' he would seek to assure his far more easy-going companions, 'if the tray is perfectly laid and presented'[90]), and still exceptionally fastidious (insisting on – among other things – spotless bed-linen, always keeping two pairs of slippers in use at any one time so as to avoid the risk of 'old dog' smells, and changing his tailor-made underpants no fewer than three times every day[91]), but his general outlook on life had also improved since making the move to the Mediterranean. He was happier and more relaxed now that he was no longer obliged to spend so much time in the same place as boorish producers, spoilt stars, sycophantic star entourages and uncontrollable would-be agents ('Before every take people were screaming all sorts of things and getting frenetic,' he complained. 'I find that rather unnecessary'[92]), and could bask instead in the 'blissful, exultant aura' of an 'unblemished paradise' that was 'restful if one sought peace and unbelievably lively if one didn't'.[93]

He admitted that he still had 'all sorts of inhibitions', but added that 'I love to see my wife tear her clothes off and go rushing into the sea and not give a damn,' and looked forward to the day when he would pluck up the courage to become a streaker – 'but I would walk'.[94] He certainly felt sufficiently 'with-it' in the late 1960s to have his cream Mercedes Benz 'painted over with hundreds of miniscule terracotta, green, brown and yellow flowers to match my favourite Liberty print shirt'.[95]

Even his notoriously volatile relationship with his first wife Pat had evolved, in the years since their divorce, into a genuinely warm, equable and mutually respectful form of friendship. After taking custody of their beloved dog – a long-haired dachshund named Archie (whom she would always describe as her 'consolation prize'[96]) – Pat had left England and settled in a pretty little two-bedroomed cottage in Majorca, and the old wounds had started to heal. Although, as her ex-husband would acknowledge, 'she went on loving me very deeply', there was no animosity between the former Mrs Terry-Thomas and her younger successor: indeed, once the dust from the divorce had begun to settle, she and Belinda became increasingly close friends, and T-T took to calling his ex-wife on a regular basis for a chat, a bit of a gossip and the odd piece of wise advice. 'She was a clever old thing,' he later reflected, 'and a good listener.'[97]

He was most grateful of all for the time that he could now share with Belinda, Tiger and baby Cushan inside a home he regarded proudly as not so much a 'dream-house' as a 'dream-*palace*'.[98] There would be plenty of days ahead filled with carefree games of tennis, billiards and ping-pong, countless swims in the nearby cove, occasional drives and rides through the countryside and many long and lazy sessions together topping up their tans under the hazy sun. He was now having fun with his family, instead of just having fun on his own, and he loved every moment of it.

He still had to (or at least wanted to) work every now and again, however, and that necessitated spending certain periods of enforced absence from all of the dear old things in Ibiza. One of the most interesting of these engagements would take him back to Britain, and the BBC, to film his first series for television in twelve years: *The Old Campaigner*.

He had been lured back to the Corporation once before, in October 1963, only to leave abruptly again under something of a cloud. On the second morning of rehearsal for an edition of the popular pilot sitcom showcase *Comedy Playhouse* – an amusing tale about a crooked London lawyer, scripted by Marty Feldman, entitled 'Nicked at the Bottle' – he called his agent, declared that he had made a terrible mistake and promptly walked out on the production. According to his own version of events, which he first recounted publicly many years later, his agent was dispatched to the insalubrious-looking rehearsal room at the Blarney Club in Tottenham Court Road to explain why his client could not afford to spend 'a few unpleasant weeks mucking about in a rotten play', while T-T set off to lick his self-inflicted wounds at leisure somewhere in the South of France ('it was as simple,' he would claim, 'as that'[99]).

According to the angry memos preserved in the BBC's archive, however, the star behaved even more unprofessionally, in reality, than that. What actually happened, the bookings manager Holland Bennett informed his superiors shortly after the actor's abrupt departure, was that Terry-Thomas walked away without providing anyone with a meaningful explanation, and then, an hour or two later, his agent called to haggle over a variety of issues – such as the size of the fee and the order of billing – which had already been discussed and settled to the agent's apparent satisfaction. Later the same day, the doughty producer Michael Mills (whose relationship with the absent star stretched all the way back to his small-screen debut in 1948) marched over to T-T's London home in Queen's Gate Mews, rapped several times on the door without eliciting any reply, and marched back to Television Centre (where, over a stiff drink or two in the BBC bar, he no doubt bemoaned both his errant employee's bad form and his own bad luck). The following morning, Mills called another actor, George Cole, and promptly enlisted him as T-T's replacement.[100] The production thus went ahead as scheduled, but – without the pulling power of its original high-profile star – it would be denied the chance to develop into a series.[101] A suitably contrite Terry-

Thomas wrote belatedly to Michael Mills – two days after the show was recorded (but before any possible legal proceedings against him could commence) – in a bid to explain the reasoning behind his damaging actions:

> I must apologise for the abrupt way in which I left you last week, but as it was impracticable for me to continue, it seemed the best way to do it. I should be the first person to agree that I could be accused of lacking in good manners, but in 'using the secateurs' a lot of discussion was avoided, which apart from being very exhausting could not possibly have altered the situation.[102]

Mills, however, was far from satisfied with this apology, and serious discussions about whether or not to sue the star went on internally for more than a month before the decision was made to draw a line under the entire unhappy episode.[103]

Why had it all gone so horribly wrong? One factor might have been that Terry-Thomas only had memories of working regularly in television during the era of *How Do You View?*, when, as a pioneering programme-maker himself, he had often known as much as – and in some cases more than – many of his colleagues and superiors about the right way to bring a comedy project to the screen; perhaps overlooking how much better, more professional and (one would have thought most obviously) more experienced most television production teams had become during his prolonged absence, he could easily have returned to the TV environment with the same combative 'I'm right – you're wrong' attitude that had helped him protect and improve his own shows back in the 1950s. Then again, he might just have come back and found that so much had changed about the medium he once had mastered that he suddenly felt a little like a dinosaur, out of date and disorientated; perhaps he even lost his nerve. Another possibility, of course, is that word had just reached him of a better-paid project, in a better climate, elsewhere (the movie *How to Murder Your Wife*, which was filmed towards the end of the following year, could have been the one), and he had not wanted to risk being tied up in England with a subsequent full-length series. Whatever the true reason for the sharp exit, however, it was clear that he had handled the matter embarrassingly badly, and knew that he had let down an old and very influential friend in Michael Mills, as well as alienating several other powerful people behind the scenes.

Terry-Thomas was somewhat surprised and relieved, therefore, when four years later, in the summer of 1967, he found himself being welcomed back by the BBC – and Michael Mills – to appear in another edition of *Comedy Playhouse*. This time, however, he was genuinely keen on the project – a story called 'The Old Campaigner' that had been crafted with him expressly in mind by the very experienced screen-writer Michael Pertwee – and was convinced that it possessed the requisite 'legs' to run on into a series. Cast as the 'old campaigner' himself, James Franklin-Jones – a globetrotting salesman (known as 'FJ' to his colleagues) who jets around the world on behalf of Balsom Plastics while continuing his incorrigible quest for 'crumpet' – he was on his best behaviour throughout: braving without complaint a set of rehearsals that were held in an over-heated church hall at St Mary Abbotts in Kensington; regularly taking his fellow cast members (who included Derek Fowlds as FJ's young and naïve assistant, Clancy) for drinks at a few of his favourite old London watering-holes; and breezing through the recording session using every discreet little scene-stealing trick in the book.

The episode began with FJ's planned 'business' trip to Paris (which clearly has more to do with *cherchez la femme* than purveying the plastic) being disrupted by his immediate superior, who has just ordered him to take a junior executive, Clancy, with him to acquire a bit of 'experience' out in the field. 'Damn!' mutters FJ to himself as he contemplates the likely hindrance to his naughty antics. Resolving to try and make the best of a bad job, he lets Clancy think that the change of plan was his idea and promises him a jolly educational time: 'I've got an idea you might find it quite interesting ...' Once ensconced inside their Paris hotel, FJ gives his wife a quick, cursory call ('Missing you like *hell*, darling!') and then announces that, provided he can get through to the right couple of 'birds' in his little black book, he and Clancy just have time to squeeze in a quick '*cinq à sept* before din-dins'. Sensing, just about, what his boss appears to be suggesting, Clancy is shocked, protesting that he is completely devoted to his lovely fiancée, Isabel, back in London:

CLANCY: I just love *Isabel*!

FJ: Look: *I* love my *wife*! That's why I'm unfaithful to her when I'm *away*!

CLANCY: But-but ... why?

FJ: For one very good reason: health.

CLANCY: I'm sorry, sir, I've lost you.

FJ: You've got a watch, haven't you?

CLANCY: Er, yes.

FJ: Hasn't anybody told you that it deteriorates if you shove it away in a drawer and don't use it?

CLANCY: Well, not for one night!

FJ: We're not talking about *watches*!

CLANCY: But you brought them up!

FJ: Look, old boy: medical experts all agree that abstinence causes impotence, frustration and all sorts of other neurotic symptoms!

CLANCY: My father was a prisoner of war for three *years* – I never met a more normal man!

FJ: Yes, but, you see, it takes *time*! How old is he?

CLANCY: He's dead, actually.

FJ: Oh, sorry. How old was he when he died?

CLANCY: Forty-six.

FJ: Well –

CLANCY: *HE WAS RUN OVER BY A COMBINE HARVESTER!*

FJ: Well, there you are!

CLANCY: What do you mean, 'There you are'?

FJ: *Flabby reflexes!*

Promising his reluctant protégé a splendid night out on the tiles (and then under the covers), he picks up his black book and starts dialling. Much to his surprise, however, time has moved on, and so have his old flames: Simone has died ('What a *rotten* bit of luck – she was a real *swinger*, that girl!'), Frédérique has married ('Never mind – she's as common as dirt!') and Di has moved to Rome. Louise, however, is available – and she has a like-minded female friend. Unfortunately for FJ, however, Louise turns out to have aged rather badly, and her friend resembles a badly squashed version of the Marx Brothers' comic stooge, Margaret Dumont ('Devastation, old boy!' FJ whispers to Clancy. 'Dev-a*station*!'). He feigns a sudden injury to send them away, but then, after frantically arranging another double date, he slips over on the bathroom floor ('Bloody French soap!') and is rendered out of action. The following morning, he discovers that Clancy has enjoyed a night with a very attractive young hotel maid. 'If this ever gets back to the office,' he snarls enviously to Clancy, 'I'll *destroy* you!'

Recorded 'as-live' (with a few fluffed lines and the odd camera wobble), the programme moved along at a decent pace, and, thanks to the familiarity of the Terry-Thomas persona, it seemed to arrive ripe and ready for an extended run. Greatly impressed by the high quality of the script, the general effectiveness of the performances and both the critical and audience response, the BBC soon reached the same conclusion, and thus wasted no time in commissioning a series. 'This is a winner for us,' declared one executive via an internal memo, even though, as he noted nervously, 'Terry-Thomas costs money!' (He was right: T-T's agreed fee would turn out to be £1650 per episode – a massive sum, by the standards of the BBC, at the time.)[104]

The six-part series of *The Old Campaigner* – which ran from 6 December 1968 to 10 January 1969 – went ahead with one notable change to the regular cast – Jonathan Cecil (who at the age of twenty-eight was already a very effective *farceur* and crafty character actor) was brought in as a replacement for Derek Fowlds. The able and very amiable Fowlds was, understandably, sad to miss out on the series, because he had formed an instant rapport with T-T (who was one of his comedy idols) when they worked together on the pilot: 'I longed to have done [the series],' he recalled, 'because I would have loved to spend more time with him. It was such good fun and we had a ball.' He later learned that someone connected with the production had wanted a more overtly 'comic' and less sympathetically 'naturalistic' character for FJ to play against, so Fowlds' dryly amusing and very sensible straight man gave way to Cecil's more eccentric kind of sidekick, but the departing actor was pleased to receive a kind and supportive letter from the star expressing his sadness at not being able to continue their promising collaboration.

Fowlds, by way of a consolation prize, was hired soon after (in March 1969) to appear on BBC1 alongside T-T's new 'mini-me', the gap-toothed puppet Basil Brush: 'Often when I looked into Basil's foxy eyes,' Fowlds recalled fondly, 'I thought I was working with Terry again.'[105] Jonathan Cecil, meanwhile, was thrilled to have been given the chance to form his own comic partnership with the star, and was delighted to find him so welcoming:

> We got on terrifically well. He'd been one of my childhood heroes, so I was a little awestruck at first, but we soon became great friends. We shared the same sense of the preposterous. He loved one story I told him about the play I was appearing in at the time – called *Halfway Up the Tree* – directed by Sir John Gielgud and starring Robert Morley. I'd overheard Robert complaining to Gielgud about the ending. He said, 'I don't like the end of this play, John, darling. I don't understand it.' And Gielgud replied, 'Neither do I, but I think it's terribly good – it's very Chekhovian.' Terry was delighted to hear this, and so whenever he didn't care for the script or felt a line wasn't right, he'd turn to me and mutter, 'I say, Jonathan, this is rather *Chekhovian!*'[106]

It seems that Terry-Thomas had also wanted to find some kind of role in the show for his young second cousin, Richard Briers. Although, when he had first seen Briers in action on the stage in a far from captivating play, he responded to the query from Richard's father as to how long he thought the production would run by groaning, 'What's the time *now*?' (and he also advised the young man, without any obvious sign of irony, to 'lose all of those rather *frightful* vocal mannerisms'[107]), T-T had gone on to follow the progress of his relation with genuine interest. Quietly confident that the young man was 'destined for really big things',[108] he had helped, encouraged and advised him whenever he could. 'He used to ring me up about once a month and tell me a joke,' Briers would recall. 'He used to say, "Is that *you*, Ricardo …?" And then he'd launch into some funny story.'[109] T-T could also be relied on, when he felt it necessary, to deliver the odd urgent and bracing pep talk:

> There was one time when I was in this farce – *Cat Among the Pigeons* – and Terry came to see me, then he went backstage after one performance, and he said, 'What are you *doing*?' And I said, 'I know – I wasn't very good, was I?' He said, 'You're pretending you're not there!' So I said, 'Well, actually, funnily enough, my wife said that.' He said, 'Well, it's *true*. You've gone grey. You've lost all of your energy.' And that was obviously a big problem because I was actually playing the *lead*! He couldn't understand something like that: playing the lead and just appearing to throw it away. So he said, 'Ricardo … do you want to be a sodding *star* or not?' And I said, 'Well, yes, I do.' So he said, 'Well, then, in that case, you're going to have to bloody well pull yourself together and start SHINING!'[110]

After appearing with Briers, briefly, in the 1960 stage play *It's in the Bag* (which folded a mere ten days into its West End run) and then in the relatively minor movie *A Matter of WHO* the following year (which featured enough shared scenes to suggest there was the potential for a promising partnership), he had been hoping to find another, better project on which the pair of them could work. At long last, *The Old Campaigner* struck him as the one. By this stage, however, the RADA-trained Briers was a star in his own right as far as British television was concerned, having made his name first with the 1962 BBC legal comedy *Brothers-in-Law* (inspired, somewhat aptly, by the movie of the same name that had included T-T among its cast) and then with the BBC sitcom *Marriage Lines*, a very popular show about the ups and downs experienced by a young husband and wife, in which he had starred alongside Prunella Scales for five series between 1963 and 1966.

Curiously enough, although Terry-Thomas (or his ghostwriter) would later misremember this matter and claim in his memoirs that Briers was not only asked but also went on to appear with him in *The Old Campaigner*,[111] the family reunion, for some or other unknown reason, never actually happened. There is no record of Briers ever having been listed as part of the cast for any episode, and no mention in the BBC archives of his possible involvement. The recordings of the shows themselves have long since been wiped, but Richard Briers confirmed: 'To be perfectly honest, I can't even remember watching the show – no recall of that at all either in my or my wife's memory. I certainly wasn't ever *in* it, nor was I ever consulted about the possibility of taking part. I did one play with him and one film with him, but I didn't do a television show with him, I'm sure of that.'[112] When, therefore, Terry-Thomas began filming *The Old Campaigner*, his cousin was otherwise engaged on the stage, appearing at the Criterion Theatre in London in *The Real Inspector Hound*, and there were no further changes to the cast.

The series itself – which found new ways each week to frustrate the would-be promiscuous bounder – developed in an encouraging direction, with the comic partnership between T-T and Jonathan Cecil proving particularly propitious. Cecil would recall:

He was very generous – he liked to share the laughs out. He wasn't always frightfully good at learning his lines, so you were never entirely sure what he was going to say next, but he was tremendously funny. Some of the lines he came up with were funnier than anything in the script. I remember bumping into him in Regent Street one day in December – he suddenly loomed into view from out of the fog – and he just said, 'I've thought of a good line for our next episode: "There's a new restaurant we should go to. Excellent food, charming service – and the head waiter looks exactly like Vanessa Redgrave".' Then he disappeared back into the fog again![113]

Cecil was also greatly amused by his co-star's off-screen antics:

Terry could be comically perverse. Before recording each programme I used to sip a small glass of port. 'Oh, surely you're not drinking before the recording?' Terry said to me – his own hip flask being much in evidence. Another time Terry went out night-clubbing and certainly looked it at rehearsal the next day. Seeing me arrive virtuously alert he greeted me with, 'I say, you look as if you've had a night out on the tiles!'[114]

The pair were clearly relaxed in each other's company, with a strong sense of mutual trust as comedy actors, and their already sure rapport looked set to continue to progress.

The sad thing was that the show would fail to return for another series. It fared well enough in the ratings but seemed to get overlooked, in the crowded schedules of the festive season, by the most influential reviewers,[115] and so (with the likely size of T-T's fee also proving a problem) the hoped-for second run was never commissioned. 'I think some people,' speculated Jonathan Cecil, 'were making noises to the effect that, as Terry was in his late fifties, it was a bit distasteful for him to be chasing after young girls. That, of course, was ridiculous. He was playing the part that millions knew and laughed at. The audience *expected* him to behave like that and would have been very disappointed if he hadn't. We were looking forward to doing another series but in the end it just didn't happen – a great pity, really.'[116]

Terry-Thomas soon shook off the disappointment and threw himself back into making movies. He appeared in big ones, such as *Monte Carlo or Bust!* (which packed as many stars into cars as *Those Magnificent Men* … had managed previously to push into planes); he appeared in small ones, such as the barely seen black comedy *Arthur? Arthur!* (which was financed by Ted Weiner, a Texan oil millionaire, on the understanding that, while he accepted that he would probably not make a profit, he did not expect to make a loss, either); and he appeared in one or two quirky ones, such as *2000 Years Later* (an over-cooked satirical sci-fi comedy, stuffed full of jump-cut vignettes and short breathless scenes, in which he played an advertising man seeking to exploit a time-travelling citizen from ancient Rome). While few, if any, of the movies that he made during this period struck him – let alone anyone else – as being even remotely aesthetically satisfying, they kept the cash coming in none the less, and made him feel a little less guilty about doing next to nothing back at the villa in Ibiza. The old T-T wanderlust, he admitted the next time he found himself stuck in a studio somewhere, had all but disappeared: 'I'd much rather be at home with my wife and family,' he confided to a friendly journalist, 'woodcarving, gardening or painting.'[117]

This quiet and eminently comfortable style of life still had its occasional crises and minor kerfuffles, however, and one of the oddest of them occurred on 13 May 1969, when Belinda's sister, Susan, married a man named Norman Scott at Kensington Register Office. The relationship had already been the cause of countless intra-family arguments and increasingly bitter internal divisions – because Scott, right from the start, had made no secret of the fact that he was a bisexual with a predominantly homosexual past – but the wedding itself witnessed the family feud grow even worse. Her parents boycotted the ceremony, appalled that one of their daughters had chosen to marry a 'well-known poofter', and Belinda was absent as well, but Terry-Thomas – attempting to play the peacemaker from a relatively safe distance – decided, by way of a wedding present, to give the couple the use of a cottage he owned at Milton Abbas in Dorset. They duly moved in, and Susan gave birth to their baby – a son – later that same year, but the marriage broke up shortly afterwards when Norman, claiming that he felt unable to cope with the added responsibility of being a father as well as a husband, promptly 'scarpered' from the scene.[118]

When, a decade later, Scott was suddenly thrust into the media spotlight because of his role at the centre of Britain's so-called 'Trial of the Century' at the Old Bailey – which saw Jeremy Thorpe, the former leader of the Liberal Party, accused of conspiring to kill his alleged former lover – Scott's connection with his famous former brother-in-law was largely overlooked. From his home in Ibiza, Terry-Thomas would none the less follow the coverage of the case with a kind of bemused fascination that, for obvious reasons, was peculiar to him and his family.

Back at the end of the 1960s, however, no such strange twists of fate were ever seriously envisaged. Problems were solved promptly, the odd emotional crease was soon smoothed out, and life returned swiftly to normal. Terry-Thomas did enough, well enough, out in the show-business world to ensure that he remained widely admired and in demand, and devoted the rest of his time to play and pleasure in the Mediterranean. 'Life was good,' he would reflect. 'I was successful and rich. I had a fine family and a magnificent house.' At the age of fifty-nine, he sat back, looked around at what a combination of labour and luck had won him, and observed: 'It all seemed too good to last.'[119]

He would soon, unfortunately, be proven right. It was.

CHAPTER SIX

An Absolute Shower

I say: what absolutely rotten luck!

IT LOOKED AS though it was going to be another delightful decade. The 1960s had seen Terry-Thomas work hard to acquire all of the fame and fortune that he desired. The 1970s seemed set to be the decade in which he relaxed and really enjoyed the many luxuries that his efforts had earned. The tragic thing that happened instead, however, was that Terry-Thomas became seriously, and increasingly, ill.

It did not happen immediately. He began the new decade in good health and even better spirits and with a very busy-looking diary. There was a movie to be made in France (a comedy set in wartime and entitled *Le Mur de l'Atlantique*, starring a very popular but now ailing French comic actor called Bourvil[1]), another one at Elstree (an unorthodox and relatively witty horror vehicle for Vincent Price entitled *The Abominable Dr Phibes*) and one based at various locations in Hertfordshire (a curious little low-budget vehicle for the pop singer Lulu called *The Cherry Picker*). There was also a stage play (the Michael Pertwee farce *Don't Just Lie There, Say Something!*) to perform for a two-month run in Australia,[2] while he was signed up to appear on both British and US television alongside Tony Curtis and Roger Moore in an episode of the popular crime-busting romp *The Persuaders!*[3]

Then there was an invitation from BBC Radio 4 to choose his *Desert Island Discs* (included among his eight selections would be Noël Coward's 'Alice is at It Again', Django Reinhardt and Stephane Grappelli's recording of 'Honeysuckle Rose' and a version of Chopin's Mazurka – accompanied, as his solitary luxury, by an unlimited supply of brandy);[4]

there was also an exceptionally well-remunerated commercial for, of all things, Birds Eye fish fingers (playing William Shakespeare opposite June Whitfield as Anne Hathaway); and there was a brand new BBC1 chat show, called *Parkinson*, for which he was booked as its very first guest.[5] These were just a few of the engagements he had scheduled for the first two years of the 1970s.

He was also well and truly settled with Belinda in Ibiza, and knew exactly how to make the most of each break from his busy routine. His two boys were growing up – both of them would soon be pupils, along with Jon Pertwee's son Sean, at the island's egregiously relaxed 'International School', which was run by three young teachers bedecked in colourful kaftans and beads – and he was enjoying watching their respective personalities evolve. He was keeping himself fit, in his own inimitable way, by water-skiing up and down the coast while listening to the BBC's *Test Match Special* on a mini-radio he had attached to one of his ears with a tight little coil of insulating tape. On one bold occasion, he even attempted to ski across the English Channel, and managed to stay 'at it' for almost three hours before he became bored (at which point he flagged down the speedboat and popped in for a drink at a friend's house he spotted on the coast near Dover).[6]

Things were going well – even the odd gamble at work came up trumps. *The Abominable Dr Phibes*, for example, proved to be not only an enjoyable movie to make (thanks in part to the presence of the playfully urbane Vincent Price, as well as to the input of the enthusiastic young designer-turned-director Robert Fuest), but also surprisingly successful at the box office (where its intriguing mixture of suspense, parody and camp black comedy elevated it more or less immediately to the status of a cult). Filmed towards the end of 1970, it was set in England (*circa* 1929 going on 1969), and starred Price as a musicologist and theologian called Dr Anton Phibes who, following a car crash, turns into a deformed madman intent on exacting revenge for the premature loss of his beloved wife. She died during a routine operation from which – due to his crash – he was absent, and so he proceeds to punish all of the physicians who failed to save her life.

One by one, he stages a series of ingeniously conceived deaths based upon the ten biblical plagues of ancient Egypt. A nurse has her head covered in liquefied Brussels sprouts and is then consumed by a swarm of hungry locusts; one doctor is eaten alive inside the cramped cockpit of his private plane by a bunch of rabid rats; another is attacked by a swarm of vampire bats; a third is impaled by the hard brass horn of a unicorn. Probably the most darkly comic demise of all is suffered by the discreetly louche Dr Longstreet – the character played (with immense and evident relish) by Terry-Thomas – who is interrupted at his home while watching a hand-cranked 'naughty' film featuring a belly dancer and a snake. He is rendered dazed and confused by Phibes's icy but alluring assistant Vulnavia (whose incessant violin playing would be enough to drive most people to suicide), and then Phibes appears, binds Longstreet to his chair and promptly drains him of every last drop of his blood – which is left on a nearby mantelshelf, next to a snifter of his sub-standard brandy, in eight pint-sized glass jars.

The unexpectedly broad appeal of the movie would pave the way not only for other, similarly artful, black horror-comedies (such as 1973's splendid Shakespearian-themed, tongue-through-cheek, *Theatre of Blood*), but also for a hurriedly made sequel of its own entitled *Dr Phibes Rises Again*. Released in 1972, the movie managed to include a logic-defying cameo from Terry-Thomas – whose return, blood-filled and unbowed as a shipping agent named Lombardo, at least guaranteed one or two smartly delivered comic lines (e.g. POLICEMAN: 'We're looking for a madman.' LOMBARDO: 'Well, you've bloody well *found* one! Do you know what *time* it is?') – but would prove in most other respects to be something of a damp squib.[7] The popularity of the original, however, gave a timely lift to the movie career of Terry-Thomas in the recently neglected British and American markets, and ensured that a rather better class of project from these regions would be sent in his direction in the near future.

He was also very much in demand on television's burgeoning talk show circuit – which pleased him greatly, because the talk show format suited his own tastes down to a 'T-T'. 'I am above all else a raconteur,' he had told the *New York Times* as long ago as 1961, but he felt that such a form of performance had fallen out of favour. 'The art of the raconteur hasn't really gone,' he explained, 'but the market has gone. A good story should not be hurried. It's worth waiting a half-hour to hear. I loathe the way stories are condensed and ruined these days.'[8] Now, at the start of the 1970s, he found that countless talk show hosts were queuing up to air his anecdotes (not to mention those comedy shows, such as BBC1's *The Two Ronnies*, that were pleased to sometimes recycle them[9]).

Apart from America's well-established *The Tonight Show* – hosted by that classic 'half-man, half-desk' talk show creature, Johnny Carson – a number of new outlets for televised chat had been opened up recently on both sides of the Atlantic. These included, in the US, a trio of high-profile shows hosted by Dick Cavett, Mike Douglas and Merv Griffin, and, in the UK, such exploratory efforts as Peter Cook's *Where Do I Sit?* and Derek Nimmo's *If It's Saturday It Must Be Nimmo*, as well as the more propitious-sounding *Parkinson*. All of a sudden, Terry-Thomas the storyteller felt spoilt for choice.[10] He went on *The Dick Cavett Show* in May 1970 and charmed his American audience,[11] and then did much the same in Britain the following year by turning his interview on the debut edition of *Parkinson* into a memorably artful comic turn. It was like one of his old cabaret performances, but compressed and refined for the even greater intimacy of television, and it was a treat from start to finish, setting an admirably high standard for the many other experienced actors who would go on to use the programme as a showcase for their skill as raconteurs.

It was one of the last times, however, that Terry-Thomas would feel genuinely relaxed and in command in front of a camera, because 1971 was also the year in which he first became aware of a potentially serious problem concerning his health. There had been the odd minor niggle, on and off, over the course of the previous few months – such as a strange, slightly throbbing sensation at the back of the head, sudden shifts in body temperature and energy levels, somewhat sluggish legs and the occasional bout of clumsiness – but nothing that had struck him as much more than a passing side-effect of a hectic schedule. Now, however, slowly but surely, things were beginning to get somewhat worse.

He was in the middle of his stint in Sydney, Australia, starring in

Don't Just Lie There, Say Something! at the city's Metro Theatre, when, during a routine check-up by a local doctor, he was asked if he was aware that his left hand, when stationary and relaxed, trembled slightly. He glanced down, saw the shake, and replied that it was the first time that he had noticed. The doctor smiled and told him that it was probably nothing too serious, but the observation continued to bother the actor throughout the rest of his time in Australia. He was therefore rather relieved when, once back in Britain, he had an opportunity to discuss it with his regular London GP.

The doctor, after conducting a basic examination, wasted little time in referring him to a neurological specialist for some further tests. When the results came back, he informed his patient, quite matter-of-factly, that he had Parkinson's Disease. T-T, knocked into a state of shock, joked that he had never even heard of the wretched Yorkshireman before agreeing to help launch his new talk show, but the doctor, ignoring the nervous stab at levity, launched straight into a standard account of what Parkinson's Disease actually was, and what kind of impact it was likely to have on the mind and body. Parkinson's Disease, the doctor explained, was named after Dr James Parkinson, the man who established it as a clinical entity – he called it 'the shaking palsy' – in 1817. It results from the progressive degeneration of the nerve cells in the brain (specifically in those two regions known as the *substantia nigra* and the *locus coeruleus*) that are responsible for producing dopamine. Dopamine is a kind of chemical messenger: a neuro-transmitter that stimulates those nerve cells – the motor neurons – that control the body's muscles. When dopamine production is depleted, therefore, some of the messages are either delayed or stay unsent, and the motor system nerves are unable to control movement and coordination. Anyone diagnosed as suffering from Parkinson's has probably already lost around 80 per cent or more of his or her dopamine-producing cells by the time that the symptoms first appear.

The tremor that Terry-Thomas now had in his left hand, he was told, was thus merely the first of a number of symptoms that he could expect to see develop, at various stages and to varying degrees, over the course of the next few years. As well as the possibility of tremors occurring in other parts of the body (such as the lower jaw and one or both of the arms and/or the legs), he might also start suffering from regular nightmares; depression; excess saliva; difficulty speaking, swallowing, turning over in bed, buttoning clothes or cutting food; and increasingly serious problems with walking. There was no cure, he was advised, but there was certainly a well-established system of treatment available, and he would be obliged to take certain drugs (such as levodopa) for the rest of his life.

Terry-Thomas left the surgery and wandered around central London in a daze. He understood what he had been told, but he could not quite believe that it was true. He still felt so fit and well. He did not feel as though he had a *disease*. It did not make sense. Nothing, at that horrible, nauseating, bewilderingly surreal moment, made any sense at all, except for one very obvious thing: if news of the diagnosis was made public, then his career, in the eyes of some of the most hardened and powerful of his show-business peers, would almost certainly be deemed to be over.

After breaking the news to his wife, he summoned those others who were closest to him, such as his cousin Richard Briers, to share the sad secret. As Briers would recall:

> We went to see him in his flat, Ye Cowshed in South Ken, and his wife, Belinda, was there, and her father and mother, and, as usual, Terry raised a glass of champagne and smiled, but then said, 'I have to tell you that I have a million pounds, after tax, in the bank – but I've got bloody Parkinson's!' And I thought: that's such an amazingly 'show business' story. At that moment, he had everything in the world that he might have wanted, he had a huge fortune, a world fame, and yet this terrible thing was going to do him.[12]

The next step was to get away and, for a while at least, withdraw from view while the full significance of the diagnosis sank in. He resolved, therefore, to fly back to Ibiza, spend some time with his family, try to come to terms with the nature of his condition and then, as soon as he felt able, return to work and do his best to behave in public as if nothing whatsoever was wrong.

The strategy worked quite well for a short while. He spent some time in Lazio, Paris and Madrid shooting a cameo role for an Italian movie comedy called *Colpo grosso, grossissimo … anzi probabile* (1972), and then flew back to Britain to film a spot for an international television special (marking the relocation of London Bridge to Lake Havasu City in Arizona[13]) as well as making his brief contribution to *Dr Phibes Rises Again*. Eager to keep the momentum going, he moved straight on to Egypt in order to start work on yet another international movie – an Italian-French-Spanish co-production entitled *The Heroes*[14] – in the company of the two Rods, Steiger and Taylor. Terry-Thomas, ironically, was the fittest-looking of the trio on the set, as Rod Taylor was suffering from severe constipation (and then, as a result of his attempt to 'cure' the condition by eating a plateful of green peppers, was struck down with an even worse bout of diarrhoea) and Rod Steiger, who was in the process of 'bulking up' his already burly body to help him portray Mussolini in his next movie project,[15] appeared to be baking slowly in the desert under the hot Egyptian sun.

T-T, in contrast, was on fine and mischievous form, happily celebrating his sixty-first birthday with all of the crew, breezing through each on-camera sequence and subtly baiting Rod Steiger on a regular basis until, when the time came to film his death scene, T-T's co-star seemed close to being ready to explode. After watching the somewhat hammy actor pretend to be struck by seven consecutive bullets and then, while mouthing a silent parting prayer, stagger hither and thither before finally biting the dust beneath the blood-red sky, Terry-Thomas wandered over to him, in the manner of someone who was about to bring a casual game of croquet to a close, and enquired brightly: 'I say, old boy, are you all right?' Long after departing from the set, Steiger was still to be found shaking his head and muttering to himself, 'I'm sure that Englishman was making fun of me, but I couldn't nail him down.'[16]

Barely pausing to draw breath, Terry-Thomas followed this exotic Egyptian excursion with a return visit to chilly Twickenham and the increasingly popular sub-genre of comedy-horror, playing (with a healthy amount of self-mockery) a deeply fastidious man who so upsets his well-meaning wife (Glynis Johns) with his obsessive insistence on keeping every single little thing in its 'proper' place ('My dear, inside the doors of this cupboard is a list of all the items in the cupboard. Against each item are three marks. Now, every time that you use one of the items ...') that she ends up cracking under the strain and hits him on the head with a hammer – and then divides his dismembered body very neatly between a number of smartly labelled jars. Forming part of a five-segment movie portmanteau (directed by Roy Ward Baker and featuring, among the rest of the stellar cast, the likes of Curt Jürgens, Denholm Elliott, Tom Baker, Michael Craig, and Daniel and Anna Massey) known collectively as *The Vault of Horror*, the Terry-Thomas episode worked rather well – but not well enough, alas, to redeem a movie that was described persuasively by *The Times* as 'a woefully diluted concoction'.[17] According to Daniel Massey, however, T-T still managed to have enough fun to make the filming seem tolerable:

> Like most great comedians, laughter clung to every syllable he breathed, and, I must say, he was as funny off as on, but a natural man with few airs and graces. In *Vault of Horror* he was, for once, required to be serious, and it was he who had to ask me to tell my particular story in that film. I blush to tell you that every time he turned to ask me, 'Well, come on, tell us about it,' I burst out laughing. Eventually, he started breaking up too, and Roy Baker sent us both home in disgrace. He was a darling man, but sometimes, I think, his great skills were hidden by the ease with which he seemed to work.[18]

T-T was just keen to keep working while he could, and so he continued with another (far more lucrative) ongoing project: providing the voice of Sir Hiss, a slimy and scheming animated snake, in the Walt Disney feature-length cartoon *Robin Hood* (1973). Although some critics (who were quick to find significance in the fact that this was the company's first animated feature not to have been overseen by Walt Disney himself) were left unimpressed by the mechanical style of direction and the absence of memorable songs, the movie – which, in addition to the unmistakable utterances of Terry-Thomas, also boasted the distinctive vocal talents of Roger Miller, Peter Ustinov, Brian Bedford and Phil

Harris – fared well with the general public. Grossing a reported $32,056,467 at the US box office alone, it attracted similarly large and appreciative audiences in numerous other parts of the globe.

A Walt Disney cartoon was one of the few viable movie projects during this period that did not seem to demean the 'old style' kind of star. The British film industry was now producing little other than cheaply made TV sitcom spin-offs (such as *Dad's Army, On the Buses* and *Steptoe and Son*), even cheaper and embarrassingly inept slapstick sex comedies (such as *Secrets of a Door-to-Door Salesman* and *Confessions of a Window Cleaner*) and increasingly coarse instalments from the *Carry Ons* (such as the woeful *Carry On Behind*). The traditional Hollywood studios, meanwhile, were in the grip of a serious financial depression, and were relying on shallow but crowd-pleasing spectacles like *The Poseidon Adventure* and *The Towering Inferno* to bail them out of trouble, whereas America's new breed of independent film-makers (led by Francis Ford Coppola, George Lucas and Martin Scorsese) were busy crafting the kind of gritty, edgy contemporary movies that had no place for Old World airs and graces or crafty comic charm. An ageing English actor like Terry-Thomas, therefore, was now placed so far down the pecking order that, in truth, no beak was really required.

He was by no means the only star who had slipped (or been pushed) into this unpropitious position. His old friend Peter Sellers, for example, spent the early 1970s making movies that either flopped at the box office (such as the Boulting Brothers' shamefully ill-conceived Second World War-era sex romp *Soft Beds, Hard Battles*) or failed to get released at all (such as Peter Medak's disastrous *Treasure Island* parody entitled *Ghost in the Noonday Sun*) before salvation arrived in 1975 in the form of the revived *Pink Panther* franchise. David Niven was another greatly respected and very popular figure who found himself reduced during the first half of the Seventies to appearing in such ill-suited vehicles as *The Statue* (which saw him search for the man whose private parts had posed as his own on the naked effigy his wife has just sculpted) and *Vampira* (a British-made horror spoof that never threatened to merit an American release) before carving out a splendid second career for himself as a best-selling writer and chat show raconteur.

Terry-Thomas was still an eminently popular choice for the talk shows, but, now that his health was in decline, the format held far less appeal: an evening spent in close-up under television's unforgiving studio lights represented a trickier proposition when one had potential speech and tremor problems to control. He did agree, however, to make a return visit (on 19 October 1974) to *Parkinson*, where his fine comic technique ensured that any momentary stumbles – such as the one that may or may not have occurred during a knowingly irrelevant aside about Noël Coward – were practically indistinguishable from the deliberate tics and slips in his delivery:

> He was in a restaurant, somewhere near Charing Cross Road – which is nothing to do with the story so you can dismiss it from your mind very quickly – and he was eating woodcock. And Margaret Rawling ... ah, no, no, Margaret *Leighton* was with him – not very good at names tonight ... – ah, but it was Margaret Leighton who was with him, and Trevor Howard wasn't there either. And she said, 'Is the woodcock all right?' and he said, 'Too much wood and not enough cock.'[19]

There were also tentative discussions with NBC executives in America, shortly after the death of Jack Benny at the end of 1974, with a view to him replacing the late comedian in a major one-hour television special that had been planned for the following year, but T-T decided to decline – partly out of respect for the memory of a performer he greatly admired, and partly out of a reluctance to subject himself to such a stressful-sounding 'second-hand' project (which he knew was likely, if it went well, to lead to the offer of a gruelling US network series all of his own). He turned down a similar proposal from London Weekend Television in Britain to play a recurring character in a forthcoming Elaine Stritch sitcom called *Two's Company*, because, once again, he could not face the potential strain of a series-long commitment.[20]

Commercials, on the other hand, were much easier for him to maintain, thanks to some discreetly sympathetic directors (who found a variety of ways to hide his left hand whenever it threatened to start to shake), but, in spite of their escalating budgets and exotic locations, they were no substitute for a revivified movie career. Even though it had been a long time since any movie project had really excited him (*Arabella*, back in 1967, had arguably been the last), he was not yet ready to stop appearing on the big screen.

There was precious little that Terry-Thomas could do, bearing in mind his private worries about his health (even now, with a mounting sense of desperation, he was still seeking out alternative medical diagnoses[21]), other than to keep on taking the least-worst option that was offered. Sometimes, when he went ahead and did so, the movie failed even to reach a cinema screen (as turned out to be the case with the 1973 Italian heist comedy, *Chi ha rubato il tesoro dello scia?*, and the Canadian-funded *Closed Up-Tight* – both of which ran out of funding before coming close to their completion[22]), and sometimes it was unfortunate enough to succeed in receiving a theatrical release.

An example of the latter was *The Bawdy Adventures of Tom Jones* – a movie that was to the classic Enlightenment novel by Henry Fielding what a packet of pork scratchings is to *haute cuisine*. Thrown together in 1975, it was written by Jeremy Lloyd (one half of the double-act responsible for the scripts of *Are You Being Served?*), starred Nicky Henson as the priapic protagonist and featured the likes of Trevor Howard, Arthur Lowe, Georgia Brown, Joan Collins, William Mervyn and Geraldine McEwan, as well as Terry-Thomas, in a wide variety of badly fitting supporting roles. *Monthly Film Bulletin* dismissed the movie as 'direly depressing', complaining that it had 'everybody pawing, ogling and jumping in, out of and under beds as though these very acts were wit enough'.[23] A criticism which, to be fair, could have been levelled at far too many of the movies that Britain was producing in the mid-1970s, but in this particular case it was certainly well-deserved.

Another dispiriting project completed in 1975 was Bruce Beresford's *Side by Side*: an utterly lamentable so-called 'comedy' in which T-T played an ageing night-club owner called Max Nugget, who, along with his sickly nephew Rodney (Barry Humphries), comes into conflict with his glam rock-loving rivals at the much trendier club next door. This movie was, if anything, even worse than its wretched predecessor, and was duly savaged by the critics both for its 'marshmallow plot' and the 'evident lack of enthusiasm' shown by most of its cast.[24] Terry-Thomas, straining to put on a brave face, had claimed before shooting began that he regarded the task of portraying a seedy showbiz traditionalist as 'a challenge' – 'it goes against the grain,' he tried to explain, 'to make oneself look old, tawdry, not to mention sleazy!'[25] – but he probably knew that he was fooling no one: it was just not his sort of role, and it was most definitely not his sort of movie.

Directed by the young Australian who would later make a name for himself in Hollywood with such disciplined productions as *Driving Miss Daisy* and *Tender Mercies*, but who was most recently responsible for bringing the crapulous cult favourite *Barry McKenzie Holds His Own* to the British screen, this low-budget piece of nonsense never seemed to know what it was really supposed to be doing – sometimes pausing to indulge the whims of its comedians, sometimes serving as a badly lit show reel for the wooden acting of Stephanie De Sykes (who was there to link the other characters to some of London's most fashionable – but cheap – young 'stars'), and sometimes providing a showcase for such here-today-gone-tomorrow British pop groups as the retro-Teds Mud and the doowop duplicates The Rubettes, alongside Dougie Squires' dog's dinner of a song-and-dance troupe Second Generation. Terry-Thomas wandered in and out of all of this looking dazed and disoriented, which was entirely understandable but thoroughly awkward to watch.[26]

A third movie made during this period, *Spanish Fly*, was only slightly better (or not quite as bad), but at least it brought together British cinema's best and next-best bounders: Terry-Thomas ('Hell-*oh*!') and his spiritual nephew, Leslie Phillips ('Hell-*oh*!'). Filmed in Minorca (conveniently close to both men's comforting Ibicencan retreats), the movie told the highly improbable story of Sir Percy 'Horsey' de Courcy (Terry-Thomas), a covertly penurious expat who buys 100,000 gallons of cheap local wine with the intention of re-labelling it as something fancy and French and selling it on at a suitably obscene profit ('With the right amount of snobbery attached, people will buy anything – especially the English'), only to discover that the so-called 'liquid gold' is practically undrinkable. His prospects improve dramatically after his manservant,

'Hell-o!' The earliest-known image of T-T in action on the stage, during the 1930s.

Courtesy Richard Hope-Hawkins

In cabaret: 'There isn't a more difficult medium,' he reflected. 'You must learn to project yourself against a background of chatter and take whatever comes to you in the way of barracking.'

Courtesy Richard Hope-Hawkins

Performing the epic sketch 'Technical Hitch'. Courtesy Richard Hope-Hawkins

Meet the T-Ts, take 1: Terry with his first wife, Pat Patlanski, and their dog, Archie.

Courtesy Richard Hope-Hawkins

Radio days: T-T with Leslie Mitchell and Joan Sims in the BBC variety series *Top of the Town*.

Courtesy Richard Hope-Hawkins

British TV's first major comedy show, *How Do You View?* A typically surreal scene here with T-T and his car-less chauffeur, Lockit (Peter Butterworth).

Express / Hulton Archive

'I say: grapes – how perfectly jolly!' A Tarzan sketch for TV in 1951, with a young Diana Dors as Jane.   **Popperfoto / Getty Images**

These film slides,
in sparkling colour, feature top-television star Terry-Thomas. Supplied FREE for use in your local cinema, each slide has a panel for your own name and address. Let Terry-Thomas help speed your sales—send for these slides today to Publicity Dept., Baird Television, 118 Baker Street, London, W.1.

The small screen's first big star: 'If television has made Terry-Thomas into a name,' one critic remarked, 'then equally Terry-Thomas has made television into an entertainment.'

Unusually for a Southerner, T-T was a great champion of the Northern comedy circuit: here he is 'larking about' at an open-air swimming pool in Southport during a break from summer season in 1953.

A 1957 cricketing fundraiser for Headley Parish Church. From left to right: Tony Britton, Peter Sellers, Kenneth Griffith, the Rev Lloyd-Jones, John Slater, Bonar Colleano, T-T and (*front*) Eric Sykes.
Arlow / Hulton Archive

This Englishman's home is 'Ye Cowshed': T-T's converted wooden barn in South Kensington just after the war.
Courtesy Richard Hope-Hawkins

A predictably defiant T-T in 1958 on his way to court after being charged with attempting to drive while under the influence of drink.
AP/PA Photos

'Now *this* is more like it!' Relaxing in style in his bathroom-cum-office at Queen's Gate Mews during 1959.   Mirrorpix

'Cheers!' A still from a photo shoot for his debut album, *Strictly T-T*, in 1958.

A rare role against type: T-T as the rough Cockney rascal Alfred Green in *Brothers in Law* (1956).

Miscast as the pretentious would-be novelist Bertrand Welch – disturbed here by Ian Carmichael's drunken hero – in *Lucky Jim* (1957). The fancy hairnet, however, was a typical T-T touch.

T-T with his new lover, Lorrae Desmond, in 1956. He would later describe her ('physically speaking') as 'the greatest love of my life'.

'I feel an absolute Charlie!' With Joyce Grenfell in *Blue Murder at St. Trinian's* (1957).

British Lion / The Kobal Collection

An awkward moment from *The Naked Truth* (1957). From left to right: Miles Malleson, Shirley Eaton, Peter Sellers and Terry-Thomas.

Everett Collection / Rex Features

Peter Sellers and T-T chat between takes for *Carlton-Browne of the F.O.* (1959).

Popperfoto / Getty Images

Temporary Special Ambassador Cadogan de Vere Carlton-Browne – a most reluctant Englishman abroad: 'It'll mean that I will miss Ascot!'

British Lion / The Kobal Collection

'You're a positive *shower*
– a *stinker* of the first order!'
T-T as Major Hitchcock is
left hopping mad by the
hapless Stanley Windrush
(Ian Carmichael) in *I'm All
Right, Jack* (1959).
Charter Films / British Lion Film
Corporation / The Kobal Collection

'Hard cheese!'
The arch one-upper
Raymond Delauney in
School for Scoundrels
(1960).
Associated British / The Kobal
Collection

T-T with Claire
Gordon and
Hattie Jacques
in *Make Mine
Mink* (1960).
Jacques has
just informed
him that
Gordon hopes to
come out as
a debutante.
He gasps: 'She's
halfway out
already!'
Rex Features

'Hell-*o* America!' T-T is twinkly charm personified in *The Judy Garland Show* (1963). **MPTV.net**

High-jinks at a health farm in the underrated comedy-thriller *Kill or Cure* (1962).

MGM / The Kobal Collection

Left: T-T and his body double preparing for *It's a Mad, Mad, Mad, Mad World* (1963). Above: Doing his own stunt in the same movie.

United Artists / The Kobal Collection

Those Magnificent Men in Their Flying Machines (1965) saw T-T (as Sir Percy Ware-Armitage) team up with Eric Sykes (as his manservant, Courtney, *right*) to memorable comic effect.

20th Century Fox / The Kobal Collection

Meet the T-Ts, take 2: Terry with his second wife, Belinda Cunningham, and their baby son Timothy (a.k.a. 'Tiger') in April 1964. A second son, Cushan, would follow four years later.

J. Wilds / Hulton Archive

Two images of T-T: above, a caricature from the 1950s; left, a portrait of the dandy as a very happy man.

Courtesy Richard Hope-Hawkins

Two of the self-designed Christmas cards he liked to send out to friends and fans.

Courtesy Richard Hope-Hawkins

A STRICTLY *TT* XMAS

Examples of T-T's personal stationery, including a slip bearing his special crest and motto: 'I shall not be cowed.'

Courtesy Richard Hope-Hawkins

With Compliments

TERRY-THOMAS

SHALL NOT BE COWED

Further confirmation that T-T had 'made it' as a British movie star arrived in the late 1950s: his very own cartoon strip in *Film Fun*.

Author's Collection

Various photo shoots from the 1950s: 'One has to play ball with the photographer chaps – it's part and parcel of how one does a professional job.' **Courtesy Richard Hope-Hawkins**

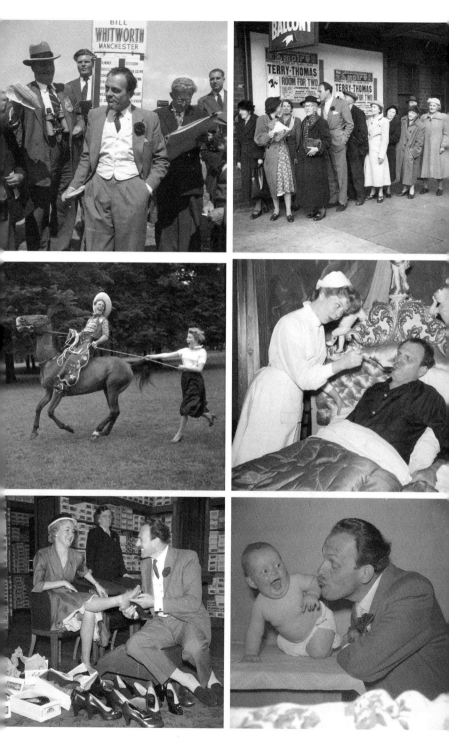

At home in Ibiza: T-T keeps an eye on his customised Mercedes (painted to match the pattern of his favourite Liberty shirt) with the aid of his trampoline.

Courtesy Richard Hope-Hawkins

Another big-budget international production, another British bounder: here T-T appears as Sir Cuthbert Ware-Armitage in *Monte Carlo or Bust!* (1969).

Paramount / The Kobal Collection

'Hard cheese, Mr Derek!' After missing out on a regular role opposite T-T in the BBC sitcom *The Old Campaigner*, Derek Fowlds makes do with T-T's puppet equivalent, Basil Brush. **BBC Photo Library**

Richard Hope-Hawkins visits T-T and his family in their cold and empty Barnes flat in 1989: 'It was heartbreaking to see him like that. I knew I had to do something to help.'

T-T with Belinda, Tiger and Cushan: now firmly in the grip of Parkinson's, he could barely even speak.

Raising funds to enable T-T to spend his final days in comfort: (*above right*) Phil Collins and (*right*) Richard Briers, Angela Douglas, Thorley Walters, Richard Hope-Hawkins, Hilary O'Neil and Jack Douglas.

A truly great British star: 'I say ... absolutely bang on!'   **Courtesy Richard Hope-Hawkins**

having added a number of random ingredients to the potion (including bits of the beetle responsible for 'Spanish Fly') in the hope of making the product vaguely palatable, turns it into an aphrodisiac.

When it is tested on Sir Percy's lecherous but currently impotent friend, a women's underwear salesman named Mike Scott (Leslie Phillips), the initial results are so impressive that Scott promptly purchases a thousand cases ('This is the best invention since the double-bed!'). Once it emerges, however, that the wine has an unfortunate side-effect, constricting the vocal cords temporarily to create canine-like sounds, Sir Percy feels obliged to execute an exceptionally sharp exit in a borrowed rowing boat ('Have you any idea where you're aiming for?' he enquires of his manservant. 'How about Ibiza?' comes the reply. 'Well, you can go anywhere,' Sir Percy declares, 'but do try and avoid Liverpool').

It was not an easy shoot – Leslie Phillips was greatly distressed to find his old friend (whom he still considered to be 'the raconteur of the island' that they shared[27]) now looking so frail and subdued ('Early morning conversation, before make-up, was non-existent; he was disorientated and shaky,' and 'in the evenings there was none of the usual banter and chat'[28]). On the screen, however, thanks to patient retakes and careful editing, Terry-Thomas still seemed more or less his old assured self playing the blinkered Englishman abroad ('Ah, what-ho, Domingo! How are you?' he asks a local café owner. 'Muy bien, señor! Magnifico! Fantástico!' cries the Spaniard. 'Sorry to hear that,' mutters Sir Percy sympathetically). Phillips did as well as could be expected in a role that often required him to behave in a manner that was simultaneously louche and limp, but – in spite of an advertising campaign that promised 'Terry-Thomas *versus* Leslie Phillips' – the screenplay failed to provide these two clever comedy actors with any decent scenes, or dialogue, to share. The nearest that they got to some relatively serviceable repartee was when Sir Percy first attempts to get Mike Scott to buy some of his doctored wine:

MIKE: Actually, Horsey, I think I'd prefer champagne.
SIR PERCY: *Champagne?* Champagne's a *poufy* drink. No offence,

    old chap. But look, Scotty, I would really like you to try this
    wine. I value your opinion.

MIKE: It's not that cat's piss again, is it?

SIR PERCY: No, no, no! This is really a very *fine* wine.

MIKE: [*Takes a sip*] Hmmm … it's quite pleasant.

SIR PERCY: 'Quite pleasant'? Don't *nibble* at it – give it a good
    bashing! It's a *lovely* wine. Chateau bottled, you know.

MIKE: I didn't know they had any châteaux in Morocco.

The rest of the movie preferred to keep Phillips, largely speechless and
trouserless, in the company of two or three winsome starlets, while T-T
was limited to the odd ogle at a naked model ('Absolutely *splehhhn-did*! There's a deckchair round there if you'd like to *pour* yourself into
it!').

The movie's director, Bob Kellett, would later recall how determined
T-T seemed to be, in spite of his obvious poor health, to strain his way
up to his old high standards – not only as an actor but also as an Englishman abroad:

> He was his usual immaculate self, and he was a very fussy dresser
> and wanted everything to be absolutely right, which was fine, but
> the problem was that he was wandering round in these immaculate
> suits and it was never, any day that we were shooting, less than 100
> degrees. Everybody was melting. All the crew were wearing shorts
> and T-shirts and drinking endless gallons of iced drink and Terry
> just managed to stay looking cool. God knows how he did it,
> wearing a jacket and tie – quite extraordinary.

Reflecting on the partnership between Leslie Phillips and T-T, he
noted how, although very similar in terms of their image, the two men
differed significantly as actors, with Phillips sticking firmly to the script
while the far more naturally funny and mischievous (and forgetful) T-T
liked to improvise more than the odd comic line. In one scene, for
example, Phillips had to stand on the shore while T-T stayed out on his
boat and a certain amount of dialogue had to be shouted out between
them – but every time that they tried it T-T kept coming up with another

idea. 'How can I say my line when he isn't giving me the feed?' Phillips complained to Kellett. 'He changes it every time. We rehearse all right and then when it comes to the shot he changes it!'

Kellett rowed out to the boat to convey the problem that Phillips was having, and T-T apologised profusely and suggested a fresh funny response that his fellow actor could use. Kellett rowed back to the shore, the revised lines were duly agreed on and delivered – only for T-T to then change the next block of dialogue. Phillips proceeded to groan all over again and Bob Kellett was left with no choice but to row back out to the boat and remind T-T of the ongoing problem. 'Oh dear,' the actor exclaimed, doing his best to look innocent and bewildered, 'have I been changing it?'[29]

Predictably, the only thing that most of the critics liked about the production was the fact that it was 'attractive to look at' whenever it paused to take in the beauty of the Balearic Islands.[30] After enduring several years of watching a succession of pallid-skinned and mullet-haired young men peep into bedroom and bathroom windows while various topless young women squeaked and squealed and squeezed, even the most indulgent of reviewers were showing signs of sleaze fatigue. 'Sadly,' *Films Illustrated* lamented, 'what passes for comedy in the British cinema these days – a few sniggers at the expense of the sexually deficient – does not contribute greatly to the entertainment quotient.'[31] *Monthly Film Bulletin* agreed, concluding that, 'apart from the moderate amusement to be had from Terry-Thomas being Terry-Thomas', *Spanish Fly* was 'a weak excuse for a comedy'.[32] There were no 'two thumbs up' – but plenty of flaccid digits drooping down.

Terry-Thomas, to his credit, did not pretend to be proud of the fact that he was now contributing to such an output. In an interview with a film magazine during 1976, he said of the current crop of British producers: 'They have the mistaken idea that what the public needs, or wants, is vulgarity, which I'm absolutely certain they don't.'[33] Warming to his theme, he went on to complain: 'Films don't have the quality they used to have. And one is depressed about that, but it can't go on forever. It's always ups and downs: I have known five downs and four-and-a-half ups. Everything seems to get worse and worse and then suddenly it gets better.' Explaining why he continued to appear in such movies, he claimed that he always felt capable of improving an indifferent script, but he acknowledged that, ideally, his career would be far better served elsewhere: 'Where I ought to be if I wanted to get in on the action is Los Angeles, where fantastically good films are being made. But it doesn't suit me to be there now. I don't want to up sticks.'[34]

Even his patience must have been strained close to snapping point, however, when he took part in his next couple of movies, *The Last Remake of Beau Geste* (1977) and *The Hound of the Baskervilles* (1978). The spoof of the 1939 Hollywood Foreign Legion epic *Beau Geste* (filmed in southern California during the summer of 1976) turned out to be an exasperating muddle of a movie: co-written by Marty Feldman, directed by Marty Feldman, narrated by Marty Feldman and starring Marty Feldman, it was a massive mistake by Marty Feldman, falling clumsily between a sharp *Monty Python*-style parody and a softer Mel Brooks-style pastiche. Few members of the large cast – which included Michael York, Ann-Margret, James Earl Jones, Peter Ustinov, Trevor Howard, Sinéad Cusack and Spike Milligan – looked comfortable in their roles, and too many of the attempts at humour – which ranged from whimsical routines redolent of the silent era to modish stabs at saucy slapstick – missed the mark. Terry-Thomas, playing a corrupt prison governor who allows himself to be seduced and used by the movie's *femme fatale*, Flavia Geste (Ann-Margret), was just one of a number of well-known actors who gave out the impression of having wandered on to the set by mistake. He dreaded having to film a bedroom scene alongside such an attractive young woman, because, ever since his days in amateur dramatics, he had been 'bothered by erections' whenever the action drew him close to any good-looking figure of the opposite sex: 'Ann-Margret was stunning, absolutely gorgeous,' he moaned, 'so acting with her at such close proximity was understandably hard-on me, so to speak.'[35] He did indeed look ill at ease throughout that brief scene, but then he looked ill at ease throughout all of his brief scenes; quite understandably, he looked as though he just wanted to get paid and then go away somewhere – anywhere – else.

He ended up getting away at the end of that autumn to South Africa, where he was due to attend a costume fitting in Johannesburg for his next scheduled movie, *King Solomon's Treasure*, before moving on to join the rest of the cast on location in Swaziland. It was while he was in Johannesburg, however, that he came perilously close to (in his words) 'snuffing it'.[36] He had caught a cold shortly after completing his modest contribution to *Beau Geste*, and, by the time he reached South Africa, he was beginning to show some of the symptoms associated with bronchial pneumonia and pleurisy, and was rushed on a stretcher straight from his hotel to a nearby hospital. Once a concerned citizen had tipped off the news agencies that an international movie star was either dying or dead in Johannesburg, the corridor outside T-T's room became clogged with photographers desperate to burst in and snatch some pictures of the great man on his death-bed. The news reached London on 30 November 1976, where *The Times* announced that 'Terry-Thomas (65)' was 'severely ill' in an unnamed Johannesburg clinic, and, soon after this, the producers of *King Solomon's Treasure* responded decisively by replacing him with Patrick Macnee.[37]

'I was given masses of medicaments as I struggled to hang on to life,' the actor would recall. 'I felt as if I were having a terrible attack of bilharziasis and the bubonic plague at the same time.'[38] His condition remained serious for some time, as Belinda and the boys – who had flown over as soon as they could once the first reports of his supposedly imminent demise had reached them – maintained a vigil by his bedside. Eventually, once the worst was deemed to be over, he was moved to a private nursing home on the outskirts of the city, where he remained until the doctors ruled that he was well enough to recuperate back home in Ibiza.

The following year should have seen him do precious little except rest, but, as the costs incurred during the period of his illness had proven to be prohibitive (he had not been insured at the time), he snapped straight back into action (to the point of attempting to water-ski across the English Channel, shortly after his sixty-sixth birthday, to raise funds for the newly formed Prince's Trust[39]) and then forced himself to resume his normal working routine. In the middle of July 1977, therefore, he duly arrived at Bray Studios in Berkshire to start work on a comedy version of *The Hound of the Baskervilles* – and was plunged into what soon came to seem like a season in hell.

The project had sounded promising enough when he first learned that it would feature Peter Cook as Sherlock Holmes and Dudley Moore as Dr Watson; having worked and socialised with the pair of them before on the set of *Monte Carlo or Bust!*, T-T (who had been invited to play the late Sir Charles Baskerville's executor, Dr Mortimer) felt sure that, after a run of movies in which he did little but grin while others were bearing it, some high-quality comedy was at long last on the cards. He reckoned, however, without the producers' perverse choice of director, the 'underground' American film-maker Paul Morrissey – a protégé of Andy Warhol's Factory,[40] a devotee of camp Hammer horrors and a very keen but breathtakingly ill-informed fan of British comedy films (especially the *Carry On* series).

The first thing that Morrissey did, once he had been handed control of the project, was to insist on rewriting the original script, inserting what he considered to be good bawdy British innuendo but which was, in fact, nothing better than crude and clumsy rubbish (e.g. 'All the Baskervilles have hearty dicks – dicky hearts, I mean!'). As if intent on making matters even worse, Morrissey then proceeded to force Cook and Moore to re-enact several of the most familiar 'Pete and Dud' sketches from their old *Not Only – But Also* television series, including the classic unidexter-auditions-for-Tarzan routine, 'One Leg Too Few' ('I've got nothing against your right leg. The trouble is – neither have you'), even though they obviously had no relevance whatsoever to Conan Doyle's famous tale of death, deception and demonic dogs on Dartmoor.

The all-British cast – which, in addition to Cook, Moore and Terry-Thomas, boasted such well-known names as Kenneth Williams, Joan Greenwood, Denholm Elliott, Hugh Griffith, Max Wall, Irene Handl, Roy Kinnear, Prunella Scales, Penelope Keith, Spike Milligan and Jessie Matthews – looked on with a mixture of bewilderment, exasperation and despondency as the American lectured visiting journalists on the nature of their own comic heritage, laughed out loud at the sound of a Jewish Sherlock Holmes and a Welsh Dr Watson, giggled at the sight of his own scene spoofing *The Exorcist* and appeared oblivious to the general mess that he was in the middle of making. It was painfully clear to everyone except Morrissey, for example, that his directing style, which relied on actors 'finding' their characters through extended improvisations, was at complete variance with the *Carry On* style of quick-fire gags, premature reactions and briskly methodical cutting that he now claimed to be championing, and the whole approach clashed with Cook and Moore's own very distinctive style, which was based on sharp observation, even sharper wit and an extremely well-structured script. Adding even more to the mounting misery, Morrissey was promptly struck down with hepatitis and shooting was delayed, thus robbing the movie of what little momentum it might have had, and then the very experienced cinematographer John Wilcox was diagnosed as being terminally ill and had to be replaced by a man whose name sounded unnervingly like one of Morrissey's clumsy tributes to the *Carry On* 'jokes': Dick Bush.

What all of this meant, as far as Terry-Thomas was concerned, was a protracted period of sheer torture. Still weak from the after-effects of his recent illness (which made the external signs of his Parkinson's Disease all the more difficult for him to hide), he looked awful and felt worse. The last thing that he needed at this moment in his life was to find himself part of a troubled production overseen by someone as spectacularly idiosyncratic as Paul Morrissey. 'According to him,' the ailing actor later complained, 'you could do anything that came into your head. As everybody's idea of comedy varied, this version of *The Hound of the Baskervilles*, consequently, made little sense.'[41] It did not take him long to come to the conclusion that the whole thing 'stank': 'In technical language, it was bad!'[42]

It was an opinion shared by most of those present on the set. John Preston, then a junior member of the crew (and who would go on to be a distinguished TV critic), recalled:

When the film was finished and everyone was fretting about how unfunny it was – one test screening in Oxford barely raised a titter – Dudley Moore decided that the music was too sombre. But by then there was no money left to pay for anyone to compose another score. Undaunted, Moore went off to a recording studio in Barnes where the film was projected up on screen while he sat at a piano playing along, improvising away like an accompanist at a silent movie. By the time the film was over, we had a new score. It didn't make it any funnier, but it was amazing to watch.[43]

Once the movie was released, in October 1978, the critics were quick to echo the insiders' collective verdict: a good cast had been 'thrown to the dogs', claimed *The Times*, and the production as a whole was 'awful'.[44] It would take all of three years before the movie was granted a US release – on the back of Dudley Moore's solo success with *10* (1979) and *Arthur* (1981) – but, as had been the case in Britain, both the public and the critical response was poor, and it played only to limited business at a handful of art-house locations.

Terry-Thomas never bothered to watch the completed movie – he had already seen the first batch of rushes, and had called there and then for *The Hound* to be put down. Dudley Moore raised some laughs with his additional cameo role as Holmes's pocket-sized Jewish mama (an amateur psychic who called Sherlock 'Sherl' as she rested her ample bosom on the back of his chair and warned him about taking poor 'Watty' for granted), but most of the other scenes were badly cut, the dialogue was often drowned out by an entirely unnecessary musical accompaniment and too many of the lines (at least, those that were audible) were plainly and simply unfunny. 'I should have got out of the business before ever agreeing to do it,' an embarrassed T-T later acknowledged.[45]

What made such appearances so distressing as well as depressing was the fact that he could no longer hide all of the physical effects of his Parkinson's Disease. By the late 1970s, the condition – though still far from seeming acute – had clearly begun to tighten its grip: 'I met Terry-Thomas,' Kenneth Williams recorded in his diary after their first encounter on set, 'and thought "Hallo! This one ain't going to know a line". He was shaking visibly & someone said it was Parkinson's Disease but it looks like a touch of your geriatrics as well. Rather frightening.'[46] What Williams was actually witnessing was not only the effects of

Parkinson's but also the extent to which pneumonia and pleurisy had taken their toll on a sixty-five-year-old who had come back to work far too soon, but, although T-T would soon regain some weight and strength and look considerably fitter than he had seemed most recently on the screen, the damage had certainly been done: too many people were now watching his health instead of his character.

Paul Morrissey had been under the impression that the actor was recovering from a stroke ('I said, "Great – I don't care if one-tenth of him is there; one-tenth of him is better than most other people"'[47]), whereas a number of others within the industry had been speculating for some time that he might have acquired a drink problem. It was time, he recognised reluctantly, for the truth to be made public: 'It was natural that people would think I was drunk,' he later reflected. 'I'd have thought the same seeing somebody behaving as I was. And as it was a condition that would get increasingly worse, I knew it would be hopeless to try to hide it.'[48]

After seeking out some advice from an old friend called Tony Kilmister – who had formerly been involved in show-business administration but by this time was executive director of the Parkinson's Disease Society – an announcement was duly made and, towards the end of 1977 inside his London home at Queen's Gate Mews, he recorded an appeal to be broadcast on BBC television on behalf of those involved in raising funds for further research into the disease.[49] It made him seem, if anything, somewhat worse than he actually was, as he had still not quite recovered fully from his recent bout of unrelated illness, but at least the spurious rumours were quashed once and for all. People now knew for certain not only that Terry-Thomas was suffering from a serious illness, but also that he was battling bravely against any further signs of decline.

One of the symptoms that was already becoming progressively more pronounced, however, was the frustrating and sometimes frightening combination of *akinesia* – an occasional inability to initiate an action – with *bradykinesia* – the slowing of the brain's ability to continue the body's movement, and the concomitant decline in its power to adjust any particular limb's position. T-T dreaded each occasion when, in the grip of this unpredictable and largely incomprehensible condition, the mind seemed imprisoned by a cage of lifeless flesh and bone:

It mostly comes on when I'm passing through a door but there is never any warning when it is about to happen. An invisible wall is built up, in my mind, and my foot refuses to budge. I never know how long I am going to remain stuck like that. When I do manage to free my foot, I shamble on quickly to catch up with my brain which seems as though it has already gone ahead. Some days it's worse than others. It's infuriating.[50]

On other distressing occasions, however, his body appeared, quite suddenly and unexpectedly, to be suffering from the opposite problem, refusing to allow him to relax and remain still: 'One minute I can be behaving in a perfectly normal manner; the next I have become a shaking mass of humanity.'[51]

Slowly but surely, it seemed, all of his favourite physical pastimes – which included horse riding, swimming, skiing, squash, tennis, table-tennis, 'standing on my head', painting, gardening, billiards, trampolining and 'sex-games' – were becoming harder and harder for him to do, let alone enjoy ('I lost my *joie de vivre* which is an English word meaning *gusto*'[52]). Even the most basic and prosaic of physical tasks, such as shaving, combing his hair, dressing, lifting a glass or using a knife and fork, were now a potential challenge – and the chronic anxiety that came from the fact that one could never be sure when such difficulties would occur served to blight even those days when everything worked more or less as it should. This very proud and still rather vain man adapted as best he could – replacing his now troublesome silk ties, for example, with a variety of smart scarves and cravats, and designing a range of looser, simpler clothes – but the self-confessed 'obsessive-perfectionist' was horrified by the thought that he was progressively losing control:

I often think, perhaps erroneously, that being an incurable perfectionist in everything from carving to cuddling makes having Parkinson's even more of a burden to bear than to people who do not set themselves such gruelling criteria. When your whole life has been a challenge to perform all that you do perfectly, it comes hard to have to accept that from now on there are going to be no impeccable performances.[53]

As if this was not bad enough, there were other, similarly demoralising signs that the condition was getting worse. His voice, which had once been so rich and flexible (enabling him, thanks to his unusually broad range of four-and-a-half octaves, to mimic everyone from operatic African-American tenors to reedy and squeaky silly-ass English toffs), had grown softer, and was not always particularly clear or distinct. His posture was also noticeably poorer, with his head sometimes bowed and his shoulders a little slumped, and there were moments when his famously bright and expressive face fell alarmingly dull and blank – as if a mask was hiding the man. The real T-T seemed to be slipping away, and he knew it, and it terrified him.

He put up a fight. There was no talk of retirement, but, understandably, the future of his movie career now mattered far less to him than that of his health, and he sought out plenty of medical specialists during this period in the hope of delaying – if not actually preventing – any further deterioration. There was always a second, third and fourth opinion on offer, and he wanted to hear them all – he was desperate. Relatively few people in those days knew much about either the nature or treatment of Parkinson's Disease (and the society that bore its name had only been in existence since 1969), so there was much that Terry-Thomas and his family still needed to discover and understand. He was advised, for example, that certain types of muscle-strengthening exercises would probably improve his balance, breathing and swallowing, while his voice could be strengthened through regular sessions with a speech therapist. He also consulted dieticians to deal with his digestive problems, started taking oil of evening primrose capsules and (surreptitiously) smoking marijuana to subdue some of the tremors, and dabbled in massage, chiropractic treatments, acupuncture, osteopathy, homeopathy, phytotherapy, aromatherapy, pressure therapy, reflexology and even (as a harmless supplement to certain drugs) some special fava bean salads – anything and everything that he read, heard or guessed might be of some help.

During the last two years of the 1970s, he spent far more time in consulting rooms than he did on studio sets. Medical men replaced movie men, and T-T found himself studying a series of clinical monographs instead of the usual succession of scripts. He even, quite coincidentally and rather bizarrely, had a 'pathological entity' named after him: in an article entitled 'The Terry-Thomas Sign' (published in the learned journal *Clinical Orthopaedics and Related Research*), Dr V.H. Frankel used the actor's name – with his full permission (he even provided pictures) – to signify, of all things, a type of dislocated wrist (a widened carpal joint space, reminiscent of the gap that separated T-T's two front teeth, between the scaphoid and lunate bones of the wrist, suggesting a rupture of the scapho-lunate ligament).[54] Anything that distracted him from his own problems, while keeping his name in circulation, was welcome at such an otherwise anxious time.

There had been few serious offers of work since news of his condition had first been made public, so, towards the end of 1979, Terry-Thomas was delighted to be told by a representative of the Ford motor company that, following extensive market research throughout the United States, he had beaten the likes of Sir Laurence Olivier, Sir Ralph Richardson, Wilfrid Hyde-White and Robert Morley to top the list of those actors whom Americans considered to be 'the most English, the most friendly and the most pleasant' – thus winning him a reasonably lucrative invitation (amounting to the equivalent of about £170,000 by today's rates for a six-day shoot) to advertise Ford's latest model of car.[55] He had been even more delighted and excited when told that the film director Derek Jarman wanted him (after being turned down by Sir John Gielgud) to play the part of the older Prospero in his own highly distinctive version of *The Tempest*; at the last minute, however, concerns about his health caused the deal to collapse,[56] and the role of a younger incarnation of the character went instead to Heathcote Williams. Another offer at this time – of a part in the Italian comedy *Le Braghe del Padrone* – fell through for the same reason. T-T did get to contribute his voice to the animated feature *Kingdom of Gifts* and the semi-animated ballet adaptation *The Mysterious House of Dr C* (both released in 1978), and he also managed to appear, albeit fleetingly, in a couple of minor European movies – the Franco-Spanish *La Isla de las Cabezas* (1979) and an Italian-German co-production called *Febbre a 40* (a.k.a. *Happy Birthday, Harry*, 1980) – but nothing came along to make up for the loss of the coveted role in *The Tempest*.

Such disappointments seemed to have a psychosomatic impact upon his health, as much of the old drive appeared to drain away from his body. He badly needed something to challenge him and excite him, but nothing looked likely to really do so. Hope had never felt so fragile. When, at the end of the decade, he returned briefly to British television as a surprise special guest on an edition of *This Is Your Life*[57] in honour of his old friend Eric Sykes, he was in a wheelchair, looking painfully strained and frail, and he seemed to be in danger of losing the will to fight.

He rallied a little again, however, and went on to make his most notable appearance in years during the summer of 1982, when he agreed to appear in a couple of episodes of a BBC2 documentary series entitled *The Human Brain*. The programmes – which examined the kinds of effects certain neurological disorders could have on both the mind and the body's mobility – allowed the seventy-two-year-old T-T to talk frankly and rather movingly about the impact of Parkinson's Disease on his life and career ('The best part of me now are my ear-lobes,' he joked in an attempt to make light of his plight; 'they're still firm and muscular'). In doing so, he helped educate a large viewing public – and many members of the media – about the true nature and implications of the condition. The programmes had an instant and positive impact, raising £32,000 for further research into Parkinson's Disease and heightening its public profile. Terry-Thomas was both surprised and touched to receive hundreds of letters from fans, fellow sufferers and well-wishers, and he was happy to continue doing whatever he could to support and promote the cause of the Parkinson's Disease Society.

Privately, however, he was becoming increasingly depressed as the new decade progressed. In spite of all of his and his family's efforts, he felt as though he was getting worse rather than remaining stable, and the prospect of any further decline filled him with a dark sense of despair. 'Deep down,' he would say, 'I like to think it's possible that I will be able to go back to work one day,' and, from his base in Ibiza (the Queen's Gate Mews flat in London had recently been sold to free up some finances), he did indeed continue to plan and discuss all kinds of possible projects, but, as the bad days began to outweigh the good, the battle against depression grew harder, and he more or less withdrew from view. 'Owing to the sense of confusion [the disease] causes,' he explained, 'I find it very difficult to behave naturally without shaking and I'm not keen to be seen like this in public, a shadow of my former self. I suppose it's my vanity that doesn't want people's image of a dashing T-T to be spoilt.'[58]

Now that both of their children were away completing their education, he and Belinda had fewer distractions, and the dark thoughts grew harder to dispel. He certainly felt the touch of a chill wind on his shoulder when Kenneth More, another warmly benign icon of old-fashioned Englishness as well as a fellow Parkinson's Disease sufferer, died in July 1982 after enduring many years of the same kind of pain, frustration, bewilderment and indignity. 'It was the most terrible thing to watch a friend endure [such a disease],' said T-T with real and very understandable feeling – for he feared that he had glimpsed his own fate.[59]

In June 1983, his sagging spirits were dragged down even lower by the news that his former wife Pat had died, aged eighty, at her home in Majorca. It was a hard blow for him to take, and, as he sat alone in his garden and reflected on what she had meant to him (and he to her: right up to her death, she had kept round her neck the silver locket, with both of their youthful portraits inside, that he had given her as a gift for one of their earliest wedding anniversaries), he was moved to tears. What made things even worse was the fact that each memory of the good times they had shared served to underline the terrible extent of his recent physical decline: there were days now when he could barely walk, and others when he could barely speak, and his somewhat mercurial but still devoted young wife had also become his nurse. She washed and dressed him every morning, gave him all of his pills at the right times, prepared him nutritional meals (presented in a style that satisfied his old perfectionist standards), assisted him in the bathroom and lavatory, opened and shut the buttons or zip of his flies (because he could not stand the idea of keeping them conveniently undone: 'A gentleman, even one with Parkinson's, doesn't do that'[60]) and helped move him from room to room and from chair to chair; there were some occasions, when he was suffering from prolonged attacks, when she stayed awake throughout the night, watching over him from a nearby armchair. He was, of course, profoundly humbled and grateful, but it broke his heart to see her worn down by so many of his needs, and found it hard to hide the fact that he now felt such a burden.

With time now seeming to fracture into frustrating little bits and pieces, and life riddled with palpable ellipses, he had never felt so helpless or scared. When, following his next scheduled check-up, a doctor told him that he probably had about four more years to live, he said that he hoped it would not turn out to be that long. 'Life is nothing for me now that I can't live as I like,' he complained. 'Nobody should have to suffer like this. It's a frightening thing to say but often I think I shall have to give in. Often, it seems the only way out is suicide. The trouble is, I have two excellent teenage sons and a wife who understands me. I don't want to leave them.'[61]

He still managed, every now and then, to travel back to his beloved England (which, he noted with a grimace, was now being run by a Prime Minister whose constituency happened to be none other than 'frightful' old Finchley[62]), visit a few favourite places and be reunited with some of his oldest and dearest friends, but such meetings were growing harder and harder to arrange and more distressing for both parties to experience. Richard Briers, for example, was one of those who was increasingly saddened and disturbed to see the arrival of each new phase in T-T's inexorable deterioration: 'The gaps between the meetings meant that you'd keep being struck by how much he'd changed. It was like he was just fading away.'[63]

It was not long after Pat's death, however, that T-T's own sense of loss prompted a constructive response: he resolved, with some encouragement from those around him, to write his memoirs. 'I've still got something useful to say before I die,' he announced, as much to himself as to anyone else. 'After all, I don't feel that T-T should just limp off the stage.'[64] He had written a volume of autobiography before, ostensibly, when he published a book called *Filling the Gap* in 1959, but that particular, wilfully eccentric effort had been far more notable for its omissions than for its commissions. Reading like an odd cross between *Tristram Shandy* and *The Code of the Woosters*, this was an autobiography that volunteered only the briefest and most basic details about the author's parents, only acknowledged his siblings to the extent of confirming how many of them there were and of what gender, and avoided saying anything at all about his marriage, his estranged wife or any other of his past and current girlfriends. Billing himself as a 'Perpetual Freeman of the Deckchairs, Margate', he told disconnected tales about 'T-T', the gent, bounder and jobbing comedy actor, included plenty of jokes, anecdotes and one or two whimsical illustrations, and alerted readers to several more examples – all of them imaginary – of his extant published output (including *How Many Times a Week is Bi-Annually?*, *A Bidet-Full of Fruit* and *The Freckled Ferret of Effingham*).[65] By 1983, however, he finally felt ready to record some rather more honest and serious thoughts, and so he enlisted an old friend of his, a journalist called Terry Daum, to act as his amanuensis.

Their collaboration started in October, soon after T-T and Belinda had reluctantly decided to put their beloved Ibicencan 'dream palace' on the market (the cost of all the medical bills – amounting to around £40,000 per year – was beginning to bite), and (after the still defiantly snobbish T-T had vetoed a suggestion to relocate to Malta: '*Malta?*' he exclaimed. '*MALTA?* You must be joking – it's one great big Sergeants' Mess!'[66]) move into the small Majorcan cottage, called 'S'Olivera', that Pat had bequeathed to her former husband in her will. Set in the hills behind Palma, it was a suitably pleasant and peaceful place in which the two men could meet and work, and, to begin with, the project progressed at a surprisingly brisk pace. Mornings were spent out in the garden beneath one of Pat's old palm trees, reminiscing about everything from the poky little offices at Smithfield Market to the cavernous sound stages in Hollywood, and then, once the inevitable fatigue had set in, T-T would sit back and speculate over a long and leisurely lunch as to whether he would be able to promote the book once it was completed ('I'd like to be in the public eye one more time,' he sighed[67]).

Although he was not always consistent in his aims for the book – sometimes he spoke of his desire for it to be 'a truthful, leave-nothing-out' sort of work, and sometimes he stressed the need to come up with something 'really funny' with plenty of entertaining 'goodies' ('people will expect that,' he explained)[68] – he was certainly fully committed to the project, straining every day to retrieve the right memories, jokes and words for each section even though there was now so much that eluded his grasp. 'Thank you for your tolerance,' he told Daum after yet another anecdote had faded away before reaching the intended end. 'This Parkinson's is a bugger, isn't it? How come you are so patient with me?'[69] By the middle of the following year, however, more and more of his responses to Daum's questions were becoming monosyllabic (DAUM: 'What about Shelly Winters, then?' T-T, after a painfully long pause: 'Fat!'[70]), and, even after the first draft of the book had been completed, he seemed disinclined to help speed the project towards publication.

He was obviously very tired and unwell, but there was more to his ambivalence than that: there was also the thought of what he would be doing once the daily sessions came to an end – nothing – and the fear that the book – which he took to referring to as his 'last fling', his 'final performance' and his 'epitaph' – would end up falling embarrassingly flat. So he took the manuscript away and struggled through the first few pages at a painfully pedestrian pace, re-editing each section as he went, suggesting innumerable deletions, revisions and additions, and chastising himself for what he judged to be the unevenness of his contribution. Month after month went by when he was too weak even to pick up a pencil, but still he refused to admit defeat and surrender the manuscript. 'I know I've not been as hilarious as I ought to have been,' he sometimes managed to whisper. 'Leave it with me. I'm going to go over it by myself and try to bung in a few more funny bits. People who buy books by comedians want value for their money.'[71]

The problem was that his own money was fast running out. By the start of 1987, Belinda was both physically and emotionally shattered, having spent so many weeks, months and years caring for T-T, and he, in turn, had become horribly thin, hollow-eyed and shrunken, and was seldom able to speak. The 250-page manuscript remained open on page 90, and the couple were close to being reduced to living on hand-outs. Although they would have much preferred to have stayed out in the sun, it was no longer possible, and so, with heavy hearts, they went home to London, where, following an urgent hernia operation for T-T and then a succession of short stays in a range of rented properties,[72] a church-linked housing association found them a small, three-roomed unfurnished flat in a property at 10 Laurel Road, Barnes. Bedding, a couple of carpets, a few items of basic furniture and a special adjustable bed were provided soon after they moved in thanks to generous donations from the Entertainment Artists' Benevolent Fund (EABF) and the Parkinson's Disease Society,[73] and life, lonely and miserable though it now was, went on.

Richard Briers and his wife were two of the first to visit the couple there, and were distressed at the sight they found:

> We'd always seen Terry at least once a year, when we used to go to a London hotel to see them all – him and the boys and Belinda – and, on this occasion, it seemed like such a sad and sorry end. This was a man who loved swimming and horse-riding, he was very physical, he liked the girls, you know, and he'd kept himself in wonderful condition, but now, sitting there, motionless, he was just a mere shadow. A crippled, crushed, shadow. It was really bloody awful.[74]

The multiple reversals were painfully apparent: sunshine had given way to clouds, warmth to cold, wealth to poverty, hope to despair and, it now seemed, fame to obscurity. It was hard, as one dismal day was replaced by another, not to feel forgotten and terribly alone. Belinda – who in truth had never been a particularly prudent home economist – now lost her way completely with the rapidly dwindling family finances, embraced the faith of a born-again Christian and seemed to become limply resigned to her fate, while a helpless T-T sat and suffered in silence.

Probably most of the British public – and, it seems, more than a few of his old colleagues, acquaintances and friends – had assumed that, by this time, Terry-Thomas was seeing out his remaining years in luxury at his grand Mediterranean villa. It came as quite a shock, therefore, when, on the morning of 9 December 1988, the *Daily Mirror* carried an article bearing the headline: 'Comic Terry's Life of Poverty'.[75] Written by the show-business journalist Tony Purnell, the piece told the story of how the actor was now a pathetic prisoner of Parkinson's Disease, practically bedridden and living hand-to-mouth with his wife in south-west London. 'It is very sad,' a representative of the EABF was quoted as saying; 'he is in a very bad way.'[76] The paper returned to the story the following morning, when Purnell reported on his visit to the couple's humble new home. Beneath a photograph of the seventy-seven-year-old actor looking grey, glazed and gaunt with an untidy beard and a shapeless woollen hat, Purnell revealed that 'the former funnyman' now 'simply stares into space' for much of each day, warmed by a one-bar electric fire, while being cared for round the clock by his wife. The long-suffering Belinda, it was said, no longer shaved her husband because she had grown too afraid of cutting him as he shook, and, now that her back was weak from lifting him in and out of bed, she dreaded him taking a fall. Underlining just how impoverished the couple had become, Purnell pointed out that any hot water had to be boiled in an old saucepan because they did not even own a kettle.[77]

Much was made of the fact that Terry-Thomas had apparently been either forgotten or abandoned by so many of his fellow stars. The newspaper noted that, apart from his ever-loyal cousin Richard Briers and his old friend and colleague George Cole (both of whom had visited several times and offered their enduring assistance), there had been no contact with other celebrities. 'I'm sure there are lots of friends who are unaware that we are even back in England,' Belinda was quoted as saying. 'A lot of them must have thought Terry was dead.'[78]

The response was immediate. The *Daily Mirror*, with traditional tabloid self-effacement, trumpeted the news that the show-business world had been 'stunned' by its 'exclusive' story that 'the film world's upper class gent is sadly on his uppers', and that various celebrities had started sending in cash and offering help. Bob Monkhouse was reported as saying, 'I thought he was still comfortably off and still living in the Spanish sunshine,' and contributed £1000. Michael Winner, one of T-T's old directors, was another who snapped into action, donating £250 and a few kind words, while, in America, Mickey Rooney spoke on behalf of the Hollywood community when he expressed his concern for 'one of the greatest purveyors of laughter there's ever been in the history of the motion picture business',[79] and promised some concerted support. The *Mirror*, meanwhile, managed to find enough spare cash in its budget to buy the ailing star six pairs of woollen socks, a two-slice toaster and a brand new electric kettle, and then launched an appeal for further financial assistance from among its predominantly working-class readership.[80]

The prospect of an additional source of support arose early the following year, when a lifelong admirer of T-T's, the writer and broadcaster Richard Hope-Hawkins, got in contact with Belinda and asked if it was at all possible to pay them a call ('We'd be delighted to see you,' she said; 'It would cheer Mac up'). He took his godfather, Thorley Walters, with him one winter's afternoon on a visit to the flat in Laurel Road. Walters, who had known the star ever since they appeared together in *Private's Progress* back in 1956, was shaken to the core by the sight of his plight. Hope-Hawkins would recall:

> Thorley couldn't really cope with it. He wasn't very good at han-
> dling people who were ill, and to find his old friend in that state,
> well, it was really harrowing. When we left, we walked outside and
> the cold winter sun hit us, and Thorley looked at me and I looked
> at him, and we both burst into tears. Thorley said, 'My goodness
> me, this is dreadful!' And I said, 'Yes, we've got to do something.'
> Thorley said, 'Yes, but what?' And I said, 'I don't know – I'll just
> have to think about it.'[81]

Later that same day, Hope-Hawkins went on a prearranged visit to see some friends who were appearing in a show at the Arts Centre in Horsham, and his distress was still evident to everyone there whom he met. 'All of them – Ed Stewart, Peggy Mount, Jack Douglas and the others – said, "What on earth is wrong with you, Richard?"' he would recall. 'I tried to avoid saying anything, but Jack insisted, so I told them where I'd been and what had happened.'[82] Alarmed by what he heard, Jack Douglas asked Hope-Hawkins to take him to see T-T as soon as was possible, so another trip to Laurel Road was duly arranged. Douglas came close to tears when he saw what had become of the individual whom he, like Hope-Hawkins, still considered a huge personal hero:

'He was wearing a balaclava and an army greatcoat, which completely swamped his now emaciated frame.' There was no hope of a conversation, so Douglas just knelt down, took hold of one of his fellow actor's frail and clammy hands and talked to him while searching for the occasional flicker of recognition in his dark and rheumy eyes. When the meeting was over, Douglas just managed to make it back out the door before breaking down in tears, asking Hope-Hawkins: 'How could a man like Terry, who'd brought such pleasure to millions of people, have ended up like that?'[83] Once back in their respective homes, the pair called each other and resolved to do what they could to help. 'You've got an idea, haven't you?' Douglas remarked. Hope-Hawkins said that he did: 'I've never done anything like it before, but why not have a gala and raise some money for Terry-Thomas?'[84] The pair agreed to proceed.

Hope-Hawkins was based in Bristol at the time, so he contacted a local PR company: 'I met this lovely couple, Sally and Derek Frise, who not only said they wanted to help but also threw open their offices for Jack and me, let us use all the staff facilities there, and even said, "Go out to lunch each day, do what you like and just put it on our account." They were so sweet.' He also sought advice from Michael Winner: 'He was a great help, all the way through, suggesting what could be done to get things moving.' The next step was to decide on the best and most plausible way to raise some money: 'I rang ITN – Jack was involved in this as well, of course – and said, "Will you come and film Terry-Thomas?" But I added: "There's one proviso: we only want one film crew in with Terry. So you *must* syndicate it." They agreed. So I drove from Bristol to Terry's flat in Barnes and we filmed it, and, of course, it really took off after that. The footage went all over the world.' Jack Douglas, in the meantime, had made contact with the hugely influential agent Dennis Selinger, and asked him if he could come up with a star big enough to act as a figurehead for the fund-raising project. 'Is Michael Caine big enough for you?' asked Selinger rhetorically. Douglas was delighted.[85]

Douglas and Hope-Hawkins then called on John Avery, who was the current head of the Moss Empires chain, and suggested staging a high-profile charity show. Avery agreed, promptly made the Theatre Royal,

Drury Lane, available at no charge ('If it's for Terry-Thomas, it's for free') and told the pair of them to go ahead and start assembling a cast. It did not take them long to enlist the services of a large and eclectic collection of British-based performers – ranging from a coterie of old friends and former colleagues (such as Richard Briers, Harry Secombe, Ronnie Corbett, Barbara Windsor, Lionel Jeffries, Joan Regan, Michael Winner, Jenny Seagrove, Eartha Kitt, Janet Brown, Ian Carmichael, Angela Douglas, Avril Angers and the re-formed Tiller Girls troupe) to a mixture of recent and longstanding fans (including Nigel Havers, Susan George, Kit and the Widow, Peter Goodright, Julia McKenzie, Russ Conway, Hannah Gordon, Roy Castle, Hilary O'Neil, various cast members from *'Allo, 'Allo, EastEnders, Emmerdale* and *Coronation Street* and one of the biggest international pop acts of the time, Phil Collins) – as well as attract the attention of the national media. Once Michael Caine had agreed to act as chairman of the organising committee, the interest extended far across the Atlantic.

On the evening of 22 March, several old friends and former colleagues gathered together at one of T-T's favourite American places, the very English-style King's Head pub in Santa Monica, and recorded their warmest wishes for him. Appeals were broadcast, messages of support were circulated and donations despatched. Fans in France, Italy, Spain, Germany, South America, Australia and elsewhere expressed their urgent concern. 'It was wonderful to find out just how much so many people genuinely cared about Terry,' Hope-Hawkins would recall. 'He was universally loved.'[86]

The next step was to enlist a broadcaster to film the event. 'I approached a friend of mine, Nick Dance of Serendipity Films,' Hope-Hawkins remembered, 'and Nick got together a free film crew – cameramen, lighting men, sound men, the whole lot – as well as Royston Mayoh as an online director. Then Badgerline, the Bristol bus company, gave us a free coach to take the crew and all the equipment to London.'[87] Back in Barnes, staring into space as though searching for an answer to an impossible question, T-T remained unaware of all that was happening, but he was now benefiting on a daily basis from the kindness of countless strangers.

Directed by Jack Douglas, the Terry-Thomas Benefit Concert took place on Sunday, 9 April 1989 in front of a full house of 2387 people. In addition to the more than 150 stars (both advertised and unbilled) who were present on the stage, the event also promised recorded contributions from the likes of Michael Caine, Jack Lemmon, Julie Andrews, Dudley Moore, Roy and Karen Dotrice, Mickey Rooney, Lynn Redgrave, Milton Berle, Ken Annakin, Glynis Johns and Shirley Ann Field.[88] 'On the night,' Hope-Hawkins would recall, 'it was like the premiere of a big Hollywood movie. You really couldn't move outside in the street. And I think I'm right in saying that it was the largest benefit show ever to have been held in a London theatre.'[89]

Some of those who appeared inside on the stage simply wanted to underline how much T-T still meant to them. The actor Melvyn Hayes, for example, recalled one particular private act of kindness:

Twenty-five years ago, I had a very bad accident. I was knocked down by a car and smashed up. And I was lying in hospital, my personal life was in a terrible mess and my body was in a terrible mess, and I was in traction and I'd got pneumonia – I was in a terrible state. And I'd been like this for two months when the phone rang by the side of my bed. And I picked up the telephone and a voice said: 'Hello, my name's Terry-Thomas, you don't know me, but I understand you need cheering up a bit. So what do you want to talk about?' And for about half an hour he gave me a one-to-one cabaret. He told me some of the funniest things and it was hysterical. Nobody knew about this except me and him. And at the end of half an hour he said: 'Well, I hope I've brought a little bit of happiness into your life.' And I'd just like to say: Terry, it's taken me twenty-five years – I've not had the opportunity – to say, 'Thank you.'

Another contributor, Ian Carmichael, sought to convey how much fun T-T used to be on a movie set, while Angela Douglas – the widow of Kenneth More – provided a poignant description of what it is like to watch a loved one slowly succumb to such a cruel disease as Parkinson's.

Most of those performers who participated enjoyed being part of the occasion so much that they overran by several minutes each, thus causing the event as a whole to continue far beyond the end of its official schedule: 'At about a quarter past midnight,' Hope-Hawkins would recall, 'Phil Collins got on stage and said, "I've shaved three times since I arrived in the theatre!" And then he was the last act on stage.'[90] The subject of the tribute, though sadly not well enough to attend, was shown a special video of the concert soon after, which he watched with tears rolling down his otherwise expressionless face.

The production raised over £75,000, and the subsequent television tribute added another £23,000, all of which was shared out between the newly created Terry-Thomas Trust and the Parkinson's Disease Society,[91] and enabled T-T to start living in comfort at the £200-per-week Busbridge Hall Nursing Home in Godalming, Surrey. 'I went to see how he was settling in,' Jack Douglas recalled, 'and found him sitting up in a comfortable bed wearing a smart red-check dressing gown. I took hold of his shaky hand and was relieved to discover that this time it felt warm, instead of icy cold.' Something, at last, had been done. 'This is to pay you back for all the laughter and entertainment you've given to us over the years, Terry,' said Douglas, who then added: 'But no chasing these nurses, mind.' T-T remained silent, staring ahead, but, after a while, Douglas felt that he understood: 'He gripped my hand and smiled with his eyes.'[92]

His health became more stable thanks to all of the expert care that he was now receiving, and, at times, he was even capable of uttering, very faintly, the odd expression of thanks, but the general physical and mental decline could not really be halted. Each time that Richard Briers went to visit, there seemed to be less and less of the real T-T remaining, and, on what would turn out to be the very last time that his cousin saw him, it was almost as though he was no longer really there:

> I saw him in the home near Guildford, and I didn't really know what to say – because, if you've ever tried to speak to someone with Parkinson's, you'll be aware that there's this horrible gap after you've said something. You'll say, 'How are you?' And a full minute

or more later, they'll answer. So I asked Terry, 'How are you?' and, after this gap, he said, '… Okay …' Then I said, 'Would you like a glass of champagne?' Then there was a long, long, long pause – I was holding his hand, and, as the pause went on and on, I was getting quite embarrassed, you know, because I really didn't know what the reaction would be – and then, after what seemed like an age, he said, 'Make it a *crate!*' So obviously, somewhere inside that poor unfortunate brain, was Terry, *our* Terry, which was very moving.[93]

The end came on the morning of Monday, 8 January 1990, when a member of the Busbridge Hall nursing staff found Terry-Thomas dead in his bed. He was seventy-eight years old, and had been suffering for some time from pneumonia. The rest of his family, sadly, had not been able to be by his side for the final hours: his devoted and uncomplaining wife Belinda had finally succumbed to the terrible strain of the past few years, and had recently been admitted to a nearby clinic after suffering a nervous breakdown; their two sons, Tiger and Cushan, were away in Ibiza, still trying to earn enough money to help with the cost of their father's nursing.

Once the news reached the media, the tributes began to pour in. George Cole described him as 'an impeccable man with impeccable timing and a delight to work with'; Eric Sykes said, 'I wish I was half the man that Terry was'; Sir Harry Secombe claimed that he was 'the finest raconteur ever'; Richard Briers just called him 'very special'; the *Guardian* remarked that 'as an upper-class twit or as a debonair rascal, Terry-Thomas had few equals'; the *New York Times* agreed, praising him for his ability as an actor to shift, 'seemingly without effort', between 'malevolent and naïve moods and characters'; the *Daily Telegraph* recalled him as 'British television's first "star comedian"' as well as an enduringly successful international movie actor; while the *Daily Mail* argued that behind 'the carefully scripted eccentricity and pomposity' of his screen persona 'lay something immensely attractive, and that was his Englishness'.[94]

The funeral, which took place on 17 January at St John the Baptist

Church in Busbridge, Godalming, was attended by Belinda and her two sons Tiger and Cushan (each of whom was wearing one of their father's famous custom-made waistcoats), along with such old friends and admirers as Eric Sykes, Denholm Elliott, Jon Pertwee, Phyllis Rounce, Thelma Wade, Jack Douglas, Thorley Walters and Richard Hope-Hawkins. The theme tune from *Those Magnificent Men in Their Flying Machines* played out in the background as, resting on a heart-shaped white lace cushion, a trio of famous T-T props – the monocle, the long silver cigarette holder and the fresh red clove carnation – were carried at the head of the procession by one of the late star's young nephews. The fine life was celebrated warmly, with many fond personal memories being shared, and the sad loss was mourned profoundly. A shorter and more private service was then held at the nearby Guildford Crematorium, where the final farewells occurred. When it was all over, as the tears were wiped dry and the first few faint smiles arrived, it was agreed, in the spirit of T-T, that things could have been even worse – it could have happened in Finchley.

Epilogue

I like me – I have to; I'm all I've got.

THE LAST WORDS that Terry-Thomas spoke about his memoirs before ill-health intervened to render them sadly incomplete were: 'I do want to be remembered as a *comedian*.'[1] The unfinished memoirs finally made it into print, shortly after his death, in a book entitled *Terry-Thomas Tells Tales*. In their own somewhat scattershot manner, they helped a little, but nowhere near enough.

Terry-Thomas merited something more and something better. This, after all, was the man who was the first to do on television the kind of things that would get lesser talents hailed as bold and imaginative innovators when they reprised them twenty, thirty, forty or even more years later. This was also the man who enhanced some of the best British movie comedies of the 1950s with his deftly timed and definitive parody of the nation's indigenous breed of bounder – which he then exported with such great success to the rest of the watching world.

This was also the man who was one of the best comic actors of his era. Terry-Thomas really did know how to be funny: for all of the flashy waistcoats and cheerfully fruity catchphrases, there was a subtlety there, and a keen intelligence, that made one relish every moment his character was visible and up to something on the screen. Go back and take another look at his performance as the bounderish baronet Sir Percy in *Those Magnificent Men in Their Flying Machines*: he took a role that could so easily have been flat and cartoon-like and turned it into something eminently watchable, making it funny by playing it straight when doing such things as using his manservant as a makeshift stepladder ('I trust your hands are *clean*, Courtney,' he remarks before treading on them with his boots). Take another look, while you are at it, at his portrayal of Major Hitchcock in *I'm All Right, Jack*: there, once again, is the kind of comic contribution that reveals a little more, and amuses a little more, each time that one sees it – especially when one notices how well his silent reactions serve to help us to read between the lines. Go back and take another look, in fact, at most of his performances during that memorable era, because, when taken together, they will form an invaluable masterclass in the art of light but precise comic character acting.

He impressed more or less everyone in the film world during the best years of his career. Few of his contemporaries – or, indeed, his successors – could point to such a large and loyal following not only in Britain and America but also in Italy, France, Germany, Spain, Australia and numerous other parts of the watching world. He did not just popularise a certain type of comic character; he also popularised a certain kind of comic sensibility. Indeed, he arguably did more for the image of his country abroad by mocking its bounders than countless 'straight' actors did by imitating its upright citizens, because, through doing so, Terry-Thomas exemplified one of his country's most enduringly attractive and admirable traits: the marked reluctance to take oneself too seriously. That was a rather fine moral lesson for him to have left behind.

Terry-Thomas left a few other things behind, too. His old villa in Ibiza, for example, is now the site of a holiday resort, the Hotel Can Talaias, run by his youngest son Cushan and his partner Laetitia, and visitors can stay there in some of the rooms – such as the set now known as 'The Terry-Thomas Suite' – where T-T used to socialise and relax; and his former London home at 11 Queen's Gate Mews now bears a Comic Heritage blue plaque to commemorate the many happy years that he spent there.[2] His two endearingly idiosyncratic albums, *Strictly T-T* and *Terry-Thomas Discovers America*, and his first collection of brazenly unreliable but entertaining anecdotes, *Filling the Gap*, have all become highly sought-after collectors' items, often changing hands for three-figure sums on internet auction sites.

Then there is the extraordinary range of abandoned or sadly neglected personal possessions that Richard Hope-Hawkins had the presence of mind to rescue from various odd and insalubrious places, including an over-stuffed skip in South Kensington and a dilapidated barn in North Devon: the items include numerous custom-made jackets, waistcoats and cigarette holders; several handwritten scripts for stand-up and radio routines; a bronze bust; and various letters, portraits, press cuttings, cartoons and calling cards. 'I still think,' he later said, 'that there's probably a Mercedes or a Rolls-Royce rotting away in a garage in LA somewhere, as well as many other of his belongings scattered worldwide.'[3]

Hope-Hawkins not only preserved what remained but also went on to use it in a succession of exhibitions to raise money for various charitable causes until, in the spring of 2006, a serious illness of his own intervened to force him, very reluctantly, to auction most of it off. The subsequent sale of the memorabilia – which took place over two days in March 2007 at the Dominic Winter auction house in South Cerney near Cirencester in Gloucestershire, raised about £6000 towards his own health care – which struck him as, in a sense, rather apt: 'I helped Terry in his hour of need,' he reflected, 'and now he's helping me.'[4]

T-T also left behind the story of his own brave struggle with Parkinson's Disease, which remains a standard reference point for those seeking new and better ways of living with and treating the condition. His cousin, Richard Briers, went on to honour his memory by campaigning, first as president and then as honorary vice-president, on behalf of the Parkinson's Disease Society in the UK, and the awareness of the very positive public response to the news of his illness has since encouraged many other well-known sufferers, including Muhammad Ali and Michael J. Fox, to use their own celebrity to promote further research into the affliction.

It is mainly for what Terry-Thomas left behind on the movie screen, however, that his memory will always deserve to be kept strong and sharp and cherished. He did what he said any serious artist – even those serious artists whose job it is to be funny – should do: he produced work that was 'really jolly good'.[5] Time and again, he took roles that required him to seem bright or dim, worldly or parochial, lascivious or aloof, and he made them all seem surprisingly real as well as wonderfully funny. With just a look, with just a line, he could make everyone who watched him break out into the broadest of smiles. That took real talent as well as great charm, and Terry-Thomas had both of those things in abundance.

One gap that has never been filled is where T-T used to be, sending himself, and us, up with such rare charm, skill and grace. Whenever, therefore, any bright-eyed character smiles and says, 'Hell-*o*,' 'Bang *on*' or 'Ding-*dong*,' the bell that it rings ought to remind us, for ever more, of a certain truly great comedian: Terry-Thomas.

Terry-Thomas: List of Performances

(HS = Home Service; LP = Light Programme; GOS = General Overseas Service; GFP = General Forces Programme; MHS = Midland Home Service; DVD = movie exists on DVD)

Theatre

Piccadilly Hayride
Prince of Wales Theatre, London
September 1946–January 1948

Royal Variety Performance
London Palladium
4 November 1946

Variety
London Palladium
13 September 1946

Variety
London Palladium
June 1948

Variety
London Palladium
27 September–4 October 1948

Cabaret
Paris
Spring 1949

The Gracie Fields Show
Empress Hall, London
15–23 May 1949

NSPCC Midsummer Ball
Dorchester Hotel, London
22 June 1949

Summer Season
New Royal Theatre, Bournemouth
1949

Cabaret
Palma House Night Club, Chicago
October–November 1949

Variety
The Chelsea Palace, London
10–17 April 1950

Summer Season
Opera House, Blackpool
1950

Out of this World
Opera House, Blackpool
5 October 1950

A Night of Variation
Bedford Theatre, London
12 November 1950

Jingle Bells
Wood Green Empire, London
December 1950

Cabaret
The Garter Club, Mayfair
31 December 1950

Cabaret
The Wedgwood Room, Waldorf
Astoria Hotel, New York
June 1951

Humpty Dumpty
London Palladium
22 December 1951–29 February 1952
(109 performances)

Top of the Town
Opera House, Blackpool
July 1952

Concert Party
Military Bases, Malaya
September 1952

Royal Variety Performance
London Palladium
3 November 1952

Dick Whittington
Johannesburg
December 1952/January 1953

Variety
Pier Pavilion, Llandudno
July 1953

Summer Season
Palace Theatre, Blackpool
1953

Fun and the Fair
London Palladium
7 October–19 December 1953
(138 performances)

Dick Whittington
Granada, Sutton; Granada,
Woolwich; Finsbury Park Empire
December 1953/January 1954

Summer Season
Winter Gardens Pavilion, Blackpool
1954

Room for Two
Prince of Wales's Theatre, London
7 March–2 April 1955
(48 performances)

Summer Season
Morecambe
1956

Charley's Aunt
Blackpool
August/September 1956

Variety
Prince of Wales Theatre, London
24–29 September 1956

King John
Adelphi, London
28 October 1956

Season of Variety
Prince of Wales Theatre, London
January 1957

Carroll Levis's Sensational TV Star Search
Shrewsbury
September 1957

Jingle Bells
Wood Green Empire, London
27 December 1957

Our Friends the Stars
Victoria Palace, London
13 March 1957

Large as Life
London Palladium
23 May–13 December 1958
(380 performances)

Cabaret
Savoy Hotel, London
1 January 1959

It's in the Bag
Provincial tour
March–May 1960
Duke of York's Theatre, London
25 May–4 June 1960

Revue
New South Wales
March–April 1963

Don't Just Lie There, Say Something!
Metro Theatre, Sydney
1971

Radio

6 June 1938	*Friends To Tea* (London Regional)
5 March 1943	*Anzac Hour* (GFP)
9 July 1943	*Anzac Hour* (GFP)
5 January 1944	*We're All Together Now* (HS)
29 November 1944	*Strike A Home Note* (GFP)
6 August 1945	*Band Party* (HS)
24 January 1946	*Out of the Hat* (HS)
1 April 1946	*Folly To Be Wise* (LP)

Bounder!

14 May 1946	*They're Out* (LP)
8 June 1946	*Victory Star Show* (GOS)
6 July 1946	*George Elrick's Band Party* (LP)
15 July 1946	*Caribbean Carnival* (GOS)
1 September 1946	*Variety Bandbox* (LP)
17 September 1946	*Cabaret* (MHS)
25 October 1946	*Workers' Playtime* (HS)
27 October 1946	*Variety Bandbox* (LP)
12 November 1946	*Happidrome* (LP)
8 December 1946	*The Carroll Levis Show* (LP)
23 December 1946	*Piccadilly Hayride* (HS)
25 December 1946	*Variety Bandbox* (LP)
10 January 1947	*Workers' Playtime* (HS)
26 January 1947	*The Carroll Levis Show* (LP)
23 February 1947	*Variety Bandbox* (LP)
28 February 1947	*Workers' Playtime* (HS)
4 March 1947	*Happidrome* (LP)
16 March 1947	*The Carroll Levis Show* (LP)
20 April 1947	*Variety Bandbox* (LP)
27 May 1947	*Workers' Playtime Anniversary Programme* (HS)
30 May 1947	*Accordion Club* (LP)
1 June 1947	*Variety Bandbox* (LP)
21 June 1947	*Up and Doing* (HS)
29 June 1947	*Variety Bandbox* (LP)
4 July 1947	*Workers' Playtime* (HS)
2 August 1947	*Up and Doing* (HS)
10 August 1947	*Variety Bandbox* (LP)

24 August 1947   *The Carroll Levis Show* (LP)

11 September 1947   *Accordion Club* (LP)

18 September 1947   *Navy Mixture* (HS)

19 October 1947   *Alhambra of the Air* (LP)

21 October 1947   *Workers' Playtime* (HS)

31 October 1947   *October Revue* (HS)

2 November 1947   *Variety Bandbox* (LP)

6 November 1947   *Accordion Club* (LP)

13 November 1947   *The Carroll Levis Show* (LP)

25 November 1947   *November Revue* (HS)

24 December 1947   *Christmas Crackers* (LP)

13 January 1948   *Night Shift* (LP)

23 January 1948   *Caribbean Carnival* (GOS)

3 February 1948   *Workers' Playtime* (HS)

4 February 1948   *Workers' Playtime* (HS)

25 May 1948   *Caribbean Carnival* (GOS)

30 May 1948   *Workers' Playtime* (HS)

15 June 1948   *Workers' Playtime* (HS)

16 June 1948   *Workers' Playtime* (HS)

1 August 1948   *Variety Bandbox* (LP)

7 September 1948   *Workers' Playtime* (HS)

8 September 1948   *Workers' Playtime* (HS)

23 September 1948   *Variety Hall of Fame* (LP)

5 October 1948   *Best Indian Rendezvous* (LP)

6 October 1948   *Alhambra of the Air* (LP)

12 October 1948   *To Town with Terry* (HS)

19 October 1948   *To Town with Terry* (HS)

Bounder!

26 October 1948	*To Town with Terry* (HS)
2 November 1948	*To Town with Terry* (HS)
9 November 1948	*To Town with Terry* (HS)
16 November 1948	*To Town with Terry* (HS)
23 November 1948	*To Town with Terry* (HS)
30 November 1948	*To Town with Terry* (HS)
7 December 1948	*To Town with Terry* (HS)
14 December 1948	*To Town with Terry* (HS)
20 December 1948	*To Town with Terry* (HS)
28 December 1948	*To Town with Terry* (HS)
4 January 1949	*To Town with Terry* (HS)
11 January 1949	*To Town with Terry* (HS)
18 January 1949	*To Town with Terry* (HS)
24 January 1949	*To Town with Terry* (HS)
31 January 1949	*To Town with Terry* (HS)
7 February 1949	*To Town with Terry* (HS)
21 February 1949	*To Town with Terry* (HS)
28 February 1949	*To Town with Terry* (HS)
7 March 1949	*To Town with Terry* (HS)
14 March 1949	*To Town with Terry* (HS)
21 March 1949	*To Town with Terry* (HS)
28 March 1949	*To Town with Terry* (HS)
16 April 1949	*Music Hall* (LP)
28 April 1949	*Workers' Playtime* (HS)
5 July 1949	*Caribbean Carnival* (HS)
7 July 1949	*The Vera Lynn Show* (LP)
23 October 1949	*Variety Bandbox* (LP)

1 January 1950	*Variety Bandbox* (LP)
11 January 1950	*Henry Hall's Guest Night* (HS)
21 January 1950	*Music Hall* (LP)
3 February 1950	*Variety Fanfare* (HS)
9 April 1950	*Variety Bandbox* (LP)
26 April 1950	*Henry Hall's Guest Night* (HS)
28 April 1950	*Workers' Playtime* (HS)
27 May 1950	*Something to Sing About* (LP)
13 July 1950	*Variety Fanfare* (HS)
13 August 1950	*Variety Bandbox* (LP)
27 August 1950	*Variety Fanfare* (HS)
31 August 1950	*Variety Fanfare* (HS)
16 September 1950	*Variety Fanfare* (HS)
16 October 1950	*Henry Hall's Guest Night* (HS)
25 October 1950	*Music Hall* (LP)
3 December 1950	*Variety Bandbox* (LP)
12 December 1950	*Can You Beat It* (HS)
17 December 1950	*Calling All Forces* (HS)
19 December 1950	*Can You Beat It* (HS)
22 December 1950	*Workers' Playtime* (HS)
25 December 1950	*Henry Hall's Guest Night* (HS)
26 December 1950	*Can You Beat It* (HS)
2 January 1951	*Can You Beat It* (HS)
9 January 1951	*Can You Beat It* (HS)
10 January 1951	*Henry Hall's Guest Night* (HS)
16 January 1951	*Can You Beat It* (HS)
19 January 1951	*Can You Beat It* (HS)

Bounder!

21 January 1951	*Calling All Forces* (HS)
6 February 1951	*Can You Beat It* (HS)
13 February 1951	*Can You Beat It* (HS)
20 February 1951	*Can You Beat It* (HS)
24 February 1951	*Music Hall* (LP)
27 February 1951	*Can You Beat It* (HS)
7 March 1951	*Henry Hall's Guest Night* (HS)
26 March 1951	*Can You Beat It* (HS)
27 June 1951	*Henry Hall's Guest Night* (HS)
4 July 1951	*Anglo-American Programme* (LP)
8 August 1951	*Top of the Bill* (LP)
18 August 1951	*Calling All Forces* (HS)
30 August 1951	*Happy-Go-Lucky* (LP)
23 February 1952	*Music Hall* (LP)
27 February 1952	*Dick Turpin* (LP)
9 April 1952	*Henry Hall's Guest Night* (HS)
5 May 1952	*Calling All Forces* (LP)
10 June 1952	*All Star Bill* (LP)
15 October 1952	*Henry Hall's Guest Night* (HS)
20 October 1952	*All Star Bill* (LP)
1 November 1952	*Star Show* (LP)
11 November 1952	*Forces Show* (LP)
23 May 1953	*Variety Playhouse* (HS)
25 May 1953	*Hip, Hip, Hooray* (LP)
1 June 1953	*BBC Ballroom* (LP)
5 June 1953	*Top of the Town* (HS) pilot
9 August 1953	*Star Bill* (LP)

27 August 1953	*Workers' Playtime* (HS)
30 September 1953	*Ignorance is Bliss* (LP)
25 October 1953	*Star Bill* (LP)
1 November 1953	*Top of the Town* (LP) series one
8 November 1953	*Top of the Town* (LP)
15 November 1953	*Top of the Town* (LP)
22 November 1953	*Top of the Town* (LP)
29 November 1953	*Top of the Town* (LP)
6 December 1953	*Top of the Town* (LP)
13 December 1953	*Top of the Town* (LP)
20 December 1953	*Top of the Town* (LP)
27 December 1953	*Top of the Town* (LP)
3 January 1954	*Top of the Town* (LP)
10 January 1954	*Top of the Town* (LP)
17 January 1954	*Top of the Town* (LP)
24 January 1954	*Top of the Town* (LP)
31 January 1954	*Variety at the Capitol* (LP)
7 February 1954	*Variety at the Capitol* (LP)
7 February 1954	*Top of the Town* (LP)
14 February 1954	*Top of the Town* (LP)
21 February 1954	*Top of the Town* (LP)
21 February 1954	*Variety at the Capitol* (LP)
4 April 1954	*Star Bill* (LP)
8 May 1954	*Variety Playhouse* (HS)
15 May 1954	*Royal Salute* (HS)
17 June 1954	*Thank Your Lucky Stars* (LP)
14 July 1954	*Blackpool Nights* (LP)

Bounder!

11 August 1954	*Blackpool Nights* (LP)
15 October 1954	*In Town Tonight* (HS)
31 October 1954	*Top of the Town* (LP) series two
7 November 1954	*Top of the Town* (LP)
14 November 1954	*Top of the Town* (LP)
21 November 1954	*Top of the Town* (LP)
28 November 1954	*Top of the Town* (LP)
6 November 1954	*Top of the Town* (LP)
20 December 1954	*Top of the Town* (LP)
27 December 1954	*Top of the Town* (LP)
3 January 1955	*Top of the Town* (LP)
10 January 1955	*Top of the Town* (LP)
17 January 1955	*Top of the Town* (LP)
24 January 1955	*Top of the Town* (LP)
6 February 1955	*Top of the Town* (LP)
13 February 1955	*Top of the Town* (LP)
20 February 1955	*Top of the Town* (LP)
27 February 1955	*Top of the Town* (LP)
13 February 1956	*Desert Island Discs* (HS)
26 February 1956	*Star Struck* (HS)
11 May 1957	*The Peers Parade* (LP)
28 December 1957	*Variety Playhouse* (HS)
26 March 1958	*The Laughtermakers* (HS)
24 March 1959	*Today Today* (LP)
21 November 1959	*In Town Tonight* (HS)
19 August 1961	*In Town Tonight* (HS)
17 February 1966	*Home This Afternoon* (LP)

21 March 1966	*Home This Afternoon* (LP)
24 November 1966	*Spoken Words* (US: WNYC-FM)
23 April 1970	*Open House* (BBC Radio 2)
6 June 1970	*Arthur Askey's Seventieth Birthday* (BBC Radio 4)
1 August 1970	*Desert Island Discs* (BBC Radio 4)

Television

Stars in Your Eyes (BBC TV)

30 January 1948	Terry-Thomas
27 October 1948	Terry-Thomas
8 January 1949	Anne Ziegler and Webster Booth, Bernard Miles, Terry-Thomas, Maurice Denham, Dinah Miller, The Wendy Toye Ballet-Hoo
6 May 1949	Terry-Thomas

How Do You View? series one (BBC TV)

26 October 1949	Terry-Thomas, Adèle Dixon, Ethel Revnell, Eric Robinson's Quartet
23 November 1949	Terry-Thomas, Adèle Dixon, Ethel Revnell, Eric Robinson's Quartet
5 December 1949	Terry-Thomas, Adèle Dixon, Ethel Revnell, Eric Robinson's Quartet
21 December 1949	Terry-Thomas, Adèle Dixon, Ethel Revnell, Eric Robinson's Quartet

How Do You View? series two (BBC TV)

5 April 1950	Terry-Thomas, Adèle Dixon, Herbert C. Walton, Leslie Mitchell, The Barrys, Eric Robinson and his Orchestra
19 April 1950	Terry-Thomas, Herbert C. Walton, Nigel Neilson, Lalage Lewis, Leslie Mitchell, The Barrys, Eric Robinson and his Orchestra
3 May 1950	Terry-Thomas, Herbert C. Walton, Nigel Neilson, Lalage Lewis, The Barrys, Eric Robinson and his Sextet
17 May 1950	Terry-Thomas, Herbert C. Walton, Nigel Neilson, Lalage Lewis, The Merry Macs, Brian Johnston, The Barrys, Eric Robinson's Sextet

Picture Page (BBC TV)

25 April 1950	Terry-Thomas and others

How Do You View? series three (BBC TV)

8 November 1950	Terry-Thomas, Avril Angers, Leslie Mitchell, Gordon Bell, Herbert C. Walton, Peter Butterworth, John and Daphne Barker
22 November 1950	Terry-Thomas, Avril Angers, Leslie Mitchell, Gordon Bell, Herbert C. Walton, Peter Butterworth, John and Daphne Barker
6 December 1950	Terry-Thomas, Avril Angers, Leslie Mitchell, Gordon Bell, Herbert C. Walton, Peter Butterworth, John and Daphne Barker
20 December 1950	Terry-Thomas, Avril Angers, Brian Johnston, Gordon Bell, Herbert C. Walton, Peter Butterworth, Victor Platt, John and Daphne Barker
3 January 1951	Terry-Thomas, Avril Angers, Brian Johnston, Gordon Bell, Herbert C. Walton, Peter Butterworth, Victor Platt, John and Daphne Barker, with Carole Carr

17 January 1951   Terry-Thomas, Avril Angers, Brian Johnston, Gordon Bell, Herbert C. Walton, Peter Butterworth, Victor Platt, John and Daphne Barker, with June Elvin

31 January 1951   Terry-Thomas, Avril Angers, Brian Johnston, Gordon Bell, Herbert C. Walton, Peter Butterworth, Victor Platt, John and Daphne Barker

14 February 1951   Terry-Thomas, Avril Angers, Brian Johnston, Gordon Bell, Herbert C. Walton, Peter Butterworth, Victor Platt, John and Daphne Barker

28 February 1951   Terry-Thomas, Avril Angers, Brian Johnston, Gordon Bell, Herbert C. Walton, Peter Butterworth, Victor Platt, John and Daphne Barker

Toast of the Town (US: CBS)

25 March 1951   Ed Sullivan, The Notre Dame Glee Club, Paul and Grace Hartman, Terry-Thomas

Vic Oliver Introduces … (BBC TV)

16 June 1951   Vic Oliver, Terry-Thomas and others

How Do You View? series four (BBC TV)

19 September 1951   Terry-Thomas, Diana Dors, Leslie Mitchell, Herbert C. Walton, Peter Butterworth, Michael Balfour, Sam Williams

3 October 1951   Terry-Thomas, Diana Dors, Leslie Mitchell, Herbert C. Walton, Peter Butterworth, Michael Balfour, Sam Williams

17 October 1951   Terry-Thomas, Diana Dors, Leslie Mitchell, Herbert C. Walton, Peter Butterworth, Michael Balfour, Sam Williams

31 October 1951   Terry-Thomas, Diana Dors, Leslie Mitchell, Herbert C. Walton, Peter Butterworth, Michael Balfour, Sam Williams

Bounder!

14 November 1951   Terry-Thomas, Diana Dors, Leslie Mitchell, Herbert C. Walton, Peter Butterworth, Michael Balfour, Sam Williams

28 November 1951   Terry-Thomas, Diana Dors, Leslie Mitchell, Herbert C. Walton, Peter Butterworth, Michael Balfour, Sam Williams

Hello Up There (BBC TV)

12 October 1951   Terry-Thomas and others

La Belle Hélène (BBC TV)

25 November 1951   Terry-Thomas (compère), Gerald Davies, Dennis Bowen, John Hargreaves, Edmund Donlevy, Ernest Frank, Harold Blackburn, Elster Kay, Ray Jackson, Barbara Rawson, Gertrude Holt, Eugénie Castle, Eunice Gayson, Eve Warren

Joan Gilbert at Home (BBC TV)

26 March 1952   Joan Gilbert, Terry-Thomas and others

How Do You View? series five (BBC TV)

2 April 1952   Terry-Thomas, Janet Brown, Herbert C. Walton, Leslie Mitchell, Benny Lee, Jimmy Young

16 April 1952   Terry-Thomas, Janet Brown, Herbert C. Walton, Leslie Mitchell, Benny Lee, Jimmy Young

30 April 1952   Terry-Thomas, Janet Brown, Herbert C. Walton, Leslie Mitchell, Benny Lee, Jimmy Young

4 May 1952   Terry-Thomas, Janet Brown, Herbert C. Walton, Leslie Mitchell, Benny Lee, Jimmy Young

28 May 1952   Terry-Thomas, Janet Brown, Herbert C. Walton, Leslie Mitchell, Benny Lee, Jimmy Young

11 June 1952   Terry-Thomas, Janet Brown, Herbert C. Walton, Leslie Mitchell, Benny Lee, Jimmy Young

How Do You View? special (BBC TV)

9 September 1953   Terry-Thomas, Avril Angers, Janet Brown, Herbert C.
                    Walton, Peter Butterworth, Benny Lee, Leslie Mitchell,
                    McDonald Hobley

For Your Pleasure (BBC TV)

28 October 1953   Leslie Mitchell, Jimmy Edwards, Terry-Thomas, Norman
                   Wisdom, Bill Fraser, Al Read, Pat Kirkwood, Helene
                   Cordet, Sally Barnes

Television's Christmas Party (BBC TV)

25 December 1953   Arthur Askey, Max Bygraves, Terry-Thomas, Julie Andrews,
                   Norman Wisdom, Shirley Abicair, Chan Canasta, John
                   Slater, The Beverley Sisters and others

The Name's the Same (BBC TV)

26 January 1954   Terry-Thomas and others

Variety Parade (BBC TV)

6 April 1954   Terry-Thomas and others

The Pat Kirkwood Show (BBC TV)

8 May 1954   Pat Kirkwood, Terry-Thomas and others

Celebration Music Hall (BBC TV)

15 May 1954   Gracie Fields, Terry-Thomas, Billy Cotton, McDonald
               Hobley, Sylvia Peters, Max Miller, Margaret Lockwood,
               Joan Hammond, Josef Locke

Stars at Blackpool (BBC TV)

15 July 1954   Terry-Thomas and others

Bounder!

In Town Tonight (TV: BBC TV/Radio: HS)

15 October 1954   Terry-Thomas and others

The Richard Hearne Show (BBC TV)

4 December 1954   Richard Hearne, Terry-Thomas

Variety Parade (BBC TV)

3 May 1955   Terry-Thomas and others

Around the Town (BBC TV)

1 October 1955   Terry-Thomas, Max Miller

Jack Hylton Presents 'Saturday Night at the London Palladium' (Associated-Rediffusion/ITV)

6 November 1955   Tommy Trinder, Ruby Murray, Terry-Thomas, Jimmy Jewell and Ben Warriss, Alma Cogan, Leslie Mitchell, Howard Jones, Reg Arnold and others

Dance Music (Associated-Rediffusion/ITV)

8 December 1955   David Jacobs, Anne Valery, Terry-Thomas, Jill Day and others

Bird in Hand (BBC TV)

25 December 1955   Jacqueline MacKenzie (Joan Greenleaf), Beatrice Varley (Alice Greenleaf), Herbert Lomas (Thomas Greenleaf), Eric Lander (Gerald Arnwood), Charles Victor (Mr Blanquent), Terry-Thomas (Cyril Beverley), William Mervyn (Ambrose Godolphin), Robert Speaight (Sir Robert Arnwood)

Strictly T-T (BBC TV)

12 January 1956   Terry-Thomas, Ken Griffith, Lorrae Desmond, Denis Kirkland, Gillian Lynne, Bob Sharples, Gerard Hoffnung

26 January 1956	Terry-Thomas, Ken Griffith, Lorrae Desmond, Denis Kirkland, Gillian Lynne, Bob Sharples, Harold Goodwin, Gerard Hoffnung
9 February 1956	Terry-Thomas, Ken Griffith, Lorrae Desmond, Denis Kirkland, Bob Sharples, Harold Goodwin, Gerard Hoffnung
23 February 1956	Terry-Thomas, Ken Griffith, Lorrae Desmond, Denis Kirkland, Bob Sharples, Harold Goodwin, Gerard Hoffnung
8 March 1956	Terry-Thomas, Ken Griffith, Lorrae Desmond, Denis Kirkland, Bob Sharples, Harold Goodwin, Gerard Hoffnung

My Wildest Dream series one (Granada/ITV)

15 May 1956	Terry-Thomas, Tommy Trinder, David Nixon, Alfred Marks. Host: Kenneth McLeod
22 May 1956	Terry-Thomas, Tommy Trinder, David Nixon, Alfred Marks. Host: Kenneth McLeod
29 May 1956	Terry-Thomas, Tommy Trinder, David Nixon, Alfred Marks. Host: Kenneth McLeod
5 June 1956	Terry-Thomas, Tommy Trinder, David Nixon, Alfred Marks. Host: Kenneth McLeod
12 June 1956	Terry-Thomas, Tommy Trinder, David Nixon, Alfred Marks. Host: Kenneth McLeod
19 June 1956	Terry-Thomas, Tommy Trinder, David Nixon, Alfred Marks. Host: Kenneth McLeod
26 June 1956	Terry-Thomas, Tommy Trinder, David Nixon, Alfred Marks. Host: Kenneth McLeod
3 July 1956	Terry-Thomas, Tommy Trinder, David Nixon, Alfred Marks. Host: Kenneth McLeod
10 July 1956	Terry-Thomas, Tommy Trinder, David Nixon, Alfred Marks. Host: Kenneth McLeod

17 July 1956   Terry-Thomas, Tommy Trinder, David Nixon, Alfred Marks. Host: Kenneth McLeod

24 July 1956   Terry-Thomas, Tommy Trinder, David Nixon, Alfred Marks. Host: Kenneth McLeod

31 July 1956   Terry-Thomas, Tommy Trinder, David Nixon, Alfred Marks. Host: Kenneth McLeod

7 August 1956   Terry-Thomas, Tommy Trinder, David Nixon, Alfred Marks. Host: Kenneth McLeod

14 August 1956   Terry-Thomas, Tommy Trinder, David Nixon, Alfred Marks. Host: Kenneth McLeod

21 August 1956   Terry-Thomas, Tommy Trinder, David Nixon, Alfred Marks. Host: Kenneth McLeod

28 August 1956   Terry-Thomas, Tommy Trinder, David Nixon, Alfred Marks. Host: Kenneth McLeod

4 September 1956   Terry-Thomas, Tommy Trinder, David Nixon, Alfred Marks. Host: Kenneth McLeod

11 September 1956   Terry-Thomas, Tommy Trinder, David Nixon, Alfred Marks. Host: Kenneth McLeod

19 September 1956   Terry-Thomas, Tommy Trinder, David Nixon, Alfred Marks. Host: Roy Rich

26 September 1956   Terry-Thomas, Tommy Trinder, David Nixon, Alfred Marks. Host: Roy Rich

3 October 1956   Terry-Thomas, Tommy Trinder, David Nixon, Alfred Marks. Host: Roy Rich

10 October 1956   Terry-Thomas, Tommy Trinder, David Nixon, Alfred Marks. Host: Roy Rich

17 October 1956   Terry-Thomas, Tommy Trinder, David Nixon, Alfred Marks. Host: Roy Rich

31 October 1956   Terry-Thomas, Tommy Trinder, David Nixon, Alfred Marks. Host: Roy Rich

7 November 1956   Terry-Thomas, Tommy Trinder, David Nixon, Alfred Marks. Host: Roy Rich

14 November 1956   Terry-Thomas, Tommy Trinder, David Nixon, Eddie Gray. Host: Roy Rich

21 November 1956   Terry-Thomas, Tommy Trinder, David Nixon, Alfred Marks. Host: Roy Rich

5 December 1956   Terry-Thomas, Tommy Trinder, David Nixon, Eddie Gray. Host: Roy Rich

Celebrity (ATV/ITV)

11 May 1956   Terry-Thomas

1-2-3 Click (ATV/ITV)

11 May 1956   Sheila Mathews, Maureen Pryor, Jack Allen, Terry-Thomas

The Holiday Show (BBC TV)

6 August 1956   Terry-Thomas, Joan Regan, David Berglas, Ormonde Douglas, Morris, Marty & Mitch, Billy Baxter, Jimmy Day, Gerry Singer, The George Mitchell Singers, Arthur Wilkinson, Peter Knight, Bob Sharples, Eric Robinson and his Orchestra

Jack Hylton Presents 'Friday Night' (Associated-Rediffusion/ITV)

10 August 1956   Terry-Thomas and others

24 August 1956   Terry-Thomas and others

7 September 1956   Terry-Thomas and others

We Are Your Servants (BBC TV)

27 October 1956   Terry-Thomas, Frank Muir, Denis Norden, Bob Monkhouse, Leslie Mitchell, Huw Wheldon, Harry Corbett, Petula Clark, Kenneth More, Eric Robinson, David Nixon, Gilbert Harding, Sylvia Peters, McDonald Hobley, Arthur Askey, J.B. Priestley, Alma Cogan, Henry Hall, Billy Cotton, Pat Kirkwood, Johnny Hutch, Richard

      Hearne, Jack Payne, Jerry Desmonde, Geraldo, Shirley
      Abicair and others

Off the Record (BBC TV)

12 November 1956 Terry-Thomas and others

Val Parnell's Sunday Night at the London Palladium (ATV/ITV)

9 December 1956 Brigitte Auber, Terry-Thomas, Lise Bourdin, Frankie
      Howerd, Martine Carol, Tommy Trinder, Nicolle
      Courcel, John Mills, Marion Neveu, Eric Sykes, Patachou,
      Violet Ford, Alta Riba, Genevieve Page, Nadine Tallier,
      Dora Doll, Eddie Constantine and guest artistes

The Harry Secombe Show (BBC TV)

31 December 1956 Harry Secombe, Terry-Thomas

My Wildest Dream series two (Granada/ITV)

30 January 1957 Terry-Thomas, Tommy Trinder, Eddie Gray, Alfred
      Marks. Host: Paul Carpenter

6 February 1957 Terry-Thomas, Tommy Trinder, Eddie Gray, Alfred
      Marks. Host: Paul Carpenter

11 February 1957 Terry-Thomas, Tommy Trinder, Eddie Gray, Alfred
      Marks. Host: Paul Carpenter

18 February 1957 Terry-Thomas, Tommy Trinder, Eddie Gray, Alfred
      Marks. Host: Paul Carpenter

25 February 1957 Terry-Thomas, Tommy Trinder, Eddie Gray, Alfred
      Marks. Host: Paul Carpenter

4 March 1957 Terry-Thomas, Tommy Trinder, Eddie Gray, Alfred
      Marks. Host: Paul Carpenter

11 March 1957 Terry-Thomas, Tommy Trinder, Eddie Gray, Alfred
      Marks. Host: Paul Carpenter

18 March 1957 Terry-Thomas, Tommy Trinder, Eddie Gray, Alfred
      Marks. Host: Paul Carpenter

25 March 1957	Terry-Thomas, Tommy Trinder, Eddie Gray, Alfred Marks. Host: Paul Carpenter
1 April 1957	Terry-Thomas, Tommy Trinder, Eddie Gray, Alfred Marks. Host: Paul Carpenter
8 April 1957	Terry-Thomas, Tommy Trinder, Eddie Gray, Alfred Marks. Host: Paul Carpenter
15 April 1957	Terry-Thomas, Tommy Trinder, Eddie Gray, Alfred Marks. Host: Paul Carpenter
22 April 1957	Terry-Thomas, Tommy Trinder, Eddie Gray, Alfred Marks. Host: Paul Carpenter.
30 April 1957	Terry-Thomas, Tommy Trinder, Eddie Gray, John Blythe. Host: David Nixon
11 June 1957	Terry-Thomas, Tommy Trinder, David Nixon, Alfred Marks. Host: Roy Rich

Jack Hylton's Music Box (Associated-Rediffusion/ITV)

| 8 February 1957 | Terry-Thomas, Leslie Mitchell, Rosalina Neri, Luigi Infantino, Ivy Benson and her Orchestra |

What's My Line? (BBC TV)

| 24 February 1957 | Terry Thomas and others. Host Eamonn Andrews |

Beat Up the Town (BBC TV)

| 22 April 1957 | Terry-Thomas, Bob Monkhouse, Cyril Fletcher, Vanessa Lee, Jill Day, The George Mitchell Singers |

Personal Appearance (ATV/ITV)

| 30 April 1957 | Terry-Thomas |

The Alma Cogan Show (BBC TV)

| 9 May 1957 | Alma Cogan, Terry-Thomas |

Bounder!

The Secombe Saga (BBC TV)

7 December 1957   Harry Secombe, Terry-Thomas, Bill Fraser

A Santa for Xmas (ATV/ITV)

26 December 1957   Hughie Green, Michael Miles, Leslie Mitchell, Dickie
Henderson, Terry-Thomas, Tommy Cooper, Geoffrey
Sumner, Arthur Askey, Anthea Askey, Robin Bailey, Joyce
Blair, Arthur Haynes, Joan Savage, Diana Decker, Jack
Parnell and his Orchestra, Paddie O'Neil, Avril Angers,
William Hartnell, Donald Gray, The Eleanor Fazan
Dancers and others

What's My Line? (BBC TV)

16 March 1958   Eamonn Andrews, Isobel Barnett, Pippa Stanley, Gilbert
Harding, Terry-Thomas

The Terry-Thomas Show (ATV/ITV)

29 March 1958   Terry-Thomas, Eric Sykes, Lorrae Desmond

The World Our Stage (BBC TV)

5 April 1958   Terry-Thomas, Jimmy Patton, Jeremy Hawk, Brian Patton,
Dickie Valentine, Patricia Cree, Wim Sonneveld

What's My Line? (BBC TV)

14 December 1958   Eamonn Andrews, Isobel Barnett, Pippa Stanley, Gilbert
Harding, Terry-Thomas

21 December 1958   Eamonn Andrews, Isobel Barnett, Pippa Stanley, Gilbert
Harding, Terry-Thomas

The Jack Paar Tonight Show (US: NBC)

16 November 1959   Jack Paar, Terry-Thomas and others

Armchair Theatre: Lord Arthur Savile's Crime (ABC/ITV)

3 January 1960   Terry-Thomas (Lord Arthur Savile), Robert Coote (Baines), Eric Pohlmann (Winkelkopf), Ernest Thesiger (Dean of Paddington), June Thorburn (Sybil), Ambrosine Phillpotts (Lady Julia), Arthur Lowe (Mr Podgers), Nora Nicholson (Clementina), Kynaston Reeves (Uncle Jasper), Michael Hitchman (Mr Pestle)

Close Up (Associated-Rediffusion/ITV)

23 June 1960   Neville Barker, Terry-Thomas

The Bing Crosby Show (US: ABC)

11 December 1961   Bing Crosby, Terry-Thomas, Sean Glenville, Miles Malleson, Ron Moody, Dave King, Marion Ryan, Julia Meade, Pat Coombs, Miriam Karlin, Shirley Bassey

Juke Box Jury (BBC TV)

2 June 1962   Terry-Thomas and others

The Perry Como Show (US: NBC)

31 October 1962   Perry Como, Terry-Thomas, Bobby Van

What's My Line? (BBC TV)

7 April 1963   Eamonn Andrews, Terry-Thomas and others

Terry-Thomas (BBC TV)

20 July 1963   Terry-Thomas, Sheree Winton, Donald Sutherland

The British at Play (Associated-Rediffusion/ITV)

21 August 1963   Stephen Potter, Terry-Thomas, Wendy Craig, Tony Tanner

The Judy Garland Show (US: CBS)

13 October 1963   Judy Garland, Terry-Thomas, Lena Horne

Burke's Law (US: ABC)

18 October 1963   Gene Barry (Capt. Amos Burke), Gary Conway (Det. Tim Tilson), Regis Toomey (Det. Les Hart), Leon Lontoc (Henry), Eileen O'Neill (Sgt Gloria Ames), Michael Fox (ME George McLeod), Carl Benton Reid (The Man), Terry-Thomas (Charlie Hill)

24 January 1964   Gene Barry (Capt. Amos Burke), Gary Conway (Det. Tim Tilson), Regis Toomey (Det. Les Hart), Leon Lontoc (Henry), Eileen O'Neill (Sgt Gloria Ames), Michael Fox (ME George McLeod), Carl Benton Reid (The Man), Terry-Thomas (Arthur Shelby)

24 February 1965   Gene Barry (Capt. Amos Burke), Gary Conway (Det. Tim Tilson), Regis Toomey (Det. Les Hart), Leon Lontoc (Henry), Eileen O'Neill (Sgt Gloria Ames), Michael Fox (ME George McLeod), Carl Benton Reid (The Man), Terry-Thomas (Gideon Auerbach)

Here's Edie (US: ABC)

16 January 1964   Edie Adams, Spike Jones, Terry-Thomas, Bettie Kovacs, Debbie Dawson, Don Chastain

What's My Line? (US: CBS)

17 May 1964   John Daly, Johnny Olson, Arlene Francis, Bennett Cerf, Dorothy Kilgallen, Jack Lemmon, Terry-Thomas

An Hour with Robert Goulet (US: CBS)

19 November 1964   Robert Goulet, Donald Voorhees, Terry-Thomas, Peter Genarro, Leslie Caron

The Andy Williams Show (US: NBC)

8 March 1965   Andy Williams, Shirley Jones, Terry-Thomas, Mongo Santamaría

Everybody's Got a System (US: ABC)

18 June 1965   Terry-Thomas (narrator)

The Man From U.N.C.L.E.: 'The Five Daughters Affair', parts 1 and 2
 (US: NBC)

31 March 1967   Robert Vaughn (Napoleon Solo), David McCallum (Illya
                      Kuryakin), Leo G. Carroll (Alexander Waverly), Curt
                      Jürgens (Carl Von Kesser), Herbert Lom (Randolph), Telly
                      Savalas (Count De Fanzini), Terry-Thomas (Constable),
                      Joan Crawford (Amanda True), Kim Darby (Sandy True),
                      Diane McBain (Margo), Jill Ireland (Imogen), Danielle
                      De Metz (Yvonne), Irene Tsu (Reikko), Jim Boles (Dr
                      True), Philip Ahn (Sazami Kyushu)

7 April 1967   Robert Vaughn (Napoleon Solo), David McCallum (Illya
                      Kuryakin), Leo G. Carroll (Alexander Waverly), Curt
                      Jürgens (Carl Von Kesser), Herbert Lom (Randolph), Telly
                      Savalas (Count De Fanzini), Terry-Thomas (Constable),
                      Joan Crawford (Amanda True), Kim Darby (Sandy True),
                      Diane McBain (Margo), Jill Ireland (Imogen), Danielle
                      De Metz (Yvonne), Irene Tsu (Reikko), Jim Boles (Dr
                      True), Philip Ahn (Sazami Kyushu)

The Red Skelton Hour (US: CBS)

22 May 1967   Red Skelton, Terry-Thomas, Joanie Sommers

Comedy Playhouse: **'The Old Campaigner'** (BBC1)

30 June 1967   Terry-Thomas (James Franklin-Jones), Derek Fowlds
                      (Peter Clancy), Lois Penson (Miss Pinto), Norman
                      Claridge (LB), John Devaut (hotel under-manager), Brian
                      Cullingford (porter), Erika Raffael (Yvette), Susan Jameson
                      (Isobel), Nadja Regin (Frederique Duval), Andrew
                      Andreas (waiter), Beatrice Mackay (Louise Tchernik),
                      Helena McCarthy (Karina Tabor), Julie Martin (Frances
                      Renaud), John Gerret (doctor), Andre Maranne
                      (businessman)

Bounder!

The Red Skelton Hour (US: CBS)

17 October 1967   Red Skelton, Terry-Thomas, Nancy Wilson

Rowan and Martin's Laugh-In (US: NBC)

4 March 1968   Terry-Thomas, Sally Field, John Wayne, Inge Nielsen, Joby Baker, Jerry Lewis, Godfrey Cambridge

Monte Carlo ... C'est la Rose (US: ABC)

6 March 1968   Princess Grace, Terry-Thomas, Françoise Hardy, Gilbert Bécaud

The Big Show (ATV/ITV)

7 April 1968   Terry-Thomas, The Dallas Boys, Neville King, Dorothy Loudon, Mireille Mathieu

That's Life (US: ABC)

29 October 1968   E.J. Peaker, Kay Medford, Robert Morse, Shelly Berman, Terry-Thomas, Ethel Merman, Lou Jacobi

The Old Campaigner (BBC1)

6 December 1968   Terry-Thomas (James Franklin-Jones), Jonathan Cecil (Peter Clancy), Lois Penson (Miss Pinto), Reginald Marsh (LB)

13 December 1968   Terry-Thomas (James Franklin-Jones), Jonathan Cecil (Peter Clancy), Lois Penson (Miss Pinto), Reginald Marsh (LB)

20 December 1968   Terry-Thomas (James Franklin-Jones), Jonathan Cecil (Peter Clancy), Lois Penson (Miss Pinto), Reginald Marsh (LB)

27 December 1968   Terry-Thomas (James Franklin-Jones), Jonathan Cecil (Peter Clancy), Lois Penson (Miss Pinto), Reginald Marsh (LB)

3 January 1969   Terry-Thomas (James Franklin-Jones), Jonathan Cecil
                  (Peter Clancy), Lois Penson (Miss Pinto), Reginald Marsh
                  (LB)

10 January 1969   Terry-Thomas (James Franklin-Jones), Jonathan Cecil
                  (Peter Clancy), Lois Penson (Miss Pinto), Reginald Marsh
                  (LB)

This Is Tom Jones (UK: ITV/US: ABC)

28 February 1969/ Tom Jones, Terry-Thomas, Dick Cavett, The Fifth
2 March 1969   Dimension, Sandy Shaw, Julie Driscoll with Brian
                   Auger and the Trinity

The Hollywood Palace (US: ABC)

22 March 1969   Phyllis Diller, Don Rickles, Terry-Thomas, The King
                  Family, Jack Walker, The Baja Marimba Band

The Liberace Show (LWT/ITV)

18 May 1969   Liberace, Terry-Thomas, Engelbert Humperdinck, Dana
                  Valery, Jack Wild, Richard Wattis, Georgina Moon

Howdy (US: NBC)

8 August 1969   Terry-Thomas and others

Music Hall (UK: LWT/Australia: 7 Network)

12 October 1969   Terry-Thomas, Tony Sadler, Ralph Young, Judy Carne,
                  Kaye Ballard, Jack Haig, Ann Sydney, Jack Parnell

Music Hall (UK: LWT/Australia: 7 Network)

19 October 1969   Terry-Thomas, Lena Horne and others

Bounder!

The Peapicker in Piccadilly (US: NBC/UK: ITV)

24 November 1969/ Tennessee Ernie Ford, Harry Secombe, Davy Jones,
31 December 1969   Terry-Thomas, Norman Wisdom

The Des O'Connor Show (ATV/ITV)

16 May 1970   Des O'Connor, Gene Barry, Dusty Springfield, Dyan
                       Cannon, Terry-Thomas with Jack Douglas, Jim Couton
                       and Rex, The Mike Sammes Singers, Jack Parnell and his
                       Orchestra

The Dick Cavett Show (US: ABC)

20 May 1970   Little Richard, Anthony Perkins, Terry-Thomas

The Kraft Music Hall TV Show (US: NBC)

1 July 1970   Des O'Connor, Terry-Thomas, Jo Ann Worley, Julie
                       London, Jack Douglas, The MacGregor Brothers

The Dickie Henderson Show (LWT/ITV)

23 April 1971   Dickie Henderson, Terry-Thomas, Teddy Peiro, Lionel
                       Blair, Shirley Bassey, Howard Keel

Parkinson (BBC1)

19 June 1971   Terry-Thomas, Arthur Ashe, Ray Bellisario

The Mike Douglas Show (US: KYW-TV)

2–6 August 1971   Terry-Thomas and others

The Kraft Music Hall TV Show (US: NBC)

1 September 1971   Des O'Connor, Terry-Thomas, Keith Michell, Connie
                       Stevens

The Hollywood Squares (US: NBC)

8–12 November 1971	Terry-Thomas, Michele Lee, Charley Weaver, Bob Clayton, Wally Cox, Rose Marie, Burt Reynolds, Totie Fields, Paul Lynde
15–19 November 1971	Terry-Thomas, Burt Reynolds, Teresa Graves, Charley Weaver, Wally Cox, Nanette Fabray, Vincent Price, Karen Valentine, Paul Lynde

The Persuaders! (ITC/ITV)

16 December 1971	Roger Moore (Lord Brett Sinclair), Tony Curtis (Danny Wilde), Laurence Naismith (Judge Fulton), Terry-Thomas (Archie), Suzy Kendall (Kay), Stephen Greif (Krilov), Frank Maher (Jones), John Orchard (Gregor), Michael Balfour (Donkey Cart Driver), Stanley Meadows (David Price), Geraldine Moffatt (Senka), Richard Burrell (Smith)

Rowan and Martin's Laugh-In (US: NBC)

21 February 1972	Sandy Duncan, Terry-Thomas, Johnny Cash, Paul Lynde, Jack Durant

Rowan and Martin's Laugh-In (US: NBC)

13 March 1972	John Wayne, Terry-Thomas, Jo Ann Pflug, Carol Channing, Steve Allen, Gene Hackman, Charles Nelson Reilly

Film Night (BBC1)

26 August 1972	Peter Curran, Terry-Thomas

The Dave Cash Radio Show (ATV/ITV)

16 November 1972	Dave Cash, Hilary Pritchard, Terry-Thomas, Gene Pitney, Chris Andrews, The Sweet

Bounder!

I Love a Mystery (US: NBC)

27 February 1973   Ida Lupino (Randolph Cheyne), Les Crane (Jack
(filmed in 1966)   Packard), David Hartman (Doc Long), Hagan Beggs
                     (Reggie York), Terry-Thomas (Gordon Elliott), Jack
                     Weston (Job Cheyne), Karen Jensen (Faith), Deanna
                     Lund (Hope), Melodie Johnson (Charity), Don Knotts
                     (Alexander Archer)

Russell Harty Plus (LWT/ITV)

20 January 1973   Russell Harty, Terry-Thomas, Patricia Neal, Georgie Fame
                     and Alan Price

The Special London Bridge Special (BBC2)

15 March 1973   Tom Jones, Jennifer O'Neill, Kirk Douglas, Terry-Thomas,
                     The Carpenters, Rudolf Nureyev, Merle Park, Hermione
                     Gingold, Jonathan Winters, Chief Dan George, Lorne
                     Greene, Charlton Heston, Michael Landon, George
                     Kirby, The Yankee Doodle Dandies, Elliott Gould,
                     Engelbert Humperdinck

Parkinson (BBC1)

19 October 1974   Terry-Thomas, Henry Cooper, Lawrence Durrell

The Circus World Championships (BBC1)

20 February 1981   Andrew Sachs, Joanna Lumley, Isla St Clair, Norman
                     Barrett, Terry-Thomas, Bobby Roberts and others

The Human Brain (BBC2)

31 May 1982   Terry-Thomas, Anthony Van Laast, Jackie Bevan, Colin
                     Blakely

21 June 1982   Richard Jameson, Terry-Thomas, Little Richard, Colin
                     Blakely

Inspector Gadget: 'All That Glitters' (UK: ITV/US: syndication)

26 November 1983   Don Adams (Gadget), Cree Summer (Penny), Melleny
Brown (Henrietta), Bernard Carez (Chef Gonthier), Terry-
Thomas (Archaeologist), Jeri Cradden (Detective), Patricia
Darnot (Sophie), Don Francks (MAD Agent #2), Victor
Désy (Docteur Gang), Hadley Kay (Chief Quimby),
Additional Voices: Dan Hennessey

A Tribute to Terry-Thomas (ITV)

23 September 1990   Richard Briers, Hilary O'Neil, Bonnie Langford, Kit and
the Widow, Melvyn Hayes, Barbara Windsor, Lionel Blair,
Susan George, Nigel Havers, Russ Conway, Roy Castle,
Sir Harry Secombe, Angela Douglas, Frazer Hines,
Frederick Pyne, Jean Rogers, Jimmy Cricket, The Roly
Polys, Ian Carmichael, Michael Winner, Jenny Seagrove,
Eartha Kitt, Richard Hope-Hawkins, The Palladium Girls,
Phil Collins

Movies

Early appearances

The Private Life of Henry VIII (1933)   Extra

The Ghost Goes West (1935)   Extra

Rhythm in the Air (1936)   Frankie, drunken cad

This'll Make You Whistle (1936)   Extra

When Knights Were Bold (1936)   Extra: Soldier speared by Saxon

Things To Come (1936)   Extra: Man of the future

Once in a Million (1936)   Extra: Auction room bidder

Cheer Up (1936)   Extra: Dancer

Bounder!

It's Love Again (1936)   Extra: Dancer in nightclub

Rhythm Racketeer (1937)   Extra

Climbing High (1938)   Voice of a cow

Sam Goes Shopping (1939)   Boyfriend

Flying Fifty-Five (1939)   Bit at racetrack

Under Your Hat (1940)   Cast member

For Freedom (1940)   News reader

Quiet Wedding (1941)   Extra

Major productions

The Brass Monkey (1947)
Carroll Levis (Himself); Carole Landis (Kay Sheldon); Herbert Lom (Peter Hobart); Avril Angers (Herself); Ernest Thesiger (Ryder-Harris); Edward Underdown (Max Taylor); Henry Edwards (Inspector Miller); Henry Worthington (Rodney); Terry Thomas (Himself); Campbell Cotts (A.J. Gilroy); Jack MacNaughton (Porter); Lyn Evans (Det. Sgt Richards); John Salew (Captain); Duncan Lewis (Steward); Michael Brennan (Wilks); Ida Patlanski (Accompanist); Gwyneth Vaughan (Miss Hamilton); The Ward Brothers (Themselves); John Lewis (Sailor); Peter Williams (Detective Fellows); Lionel Murton (Detective Mann); Vincent Holman (Chief Customs Inspector); Bruce Walker (1st Customs Man); Edward Hodge (2nd Customs Man); Alan Lawrence (PC Reynolds); Leslie A. Hutchinson (Himself).
Running time: 84 minutes. DVD.

Copy Book Please (1948)
Terry-Thomas (Himself).
Running time: 3 minutes.

Date with a Dream (1948)
Terry-Thomas (Terry); Jean Carson (Jean); Len Lowe (Len); Bill Lowe (Bill); Vic Lewis and his Orchestra; Wally Patch (Uncle Joey); Max Imshy (Porter); Alfie Dean (Joe); Ida Patlanski (Bedelia); Julie Lang (Madame Docherty); Harry Green (Syd Marlish).
Running time: 60 minutes. DVD.

If You Don't Save Paper (1948)
Terry-Thomas (Shop Assistant).
Running time: 3 minutes.

Melody Club (1949)
Bill Lowe; Len Lowe; Lilian Grey; Arthur Gomes; Sylvia Clark; Terry-Thomas (Freddy Forrester); Gwyneth Vaughan (Joan); Michael Balfour (Max).
Running time: 63 minutes.

Helter Skelter (1949)
Carol Marsh (Susan Graham); David Tomlinson (Nick Martin); Peter Hammond (Spencer Stone); Mervyn Johns (Ernest Bennett); Peter Haddon (Basil Beagle); Geoffrey Sumner (Humphrey Beagle); Judith Furse (Mrs Martin); Colin Gordon (Chadbeater Longwick); Wilfrid Hyde-White (Dr Jekyll); with Jimmy Edwards, Richard Hearne, Harry Secombe, Terry-Thomas, Jon Pertwee, Johnny Briggs.
Running time: 84 minutes.

Cookery Nook (1951)
Philip Harben, Terry-Thomas, Michael Bentine
Running time: 28 minutes.

The Queen Steps Out (1952)
Terry-Thomas
Running time: 19 minutes.

Private's Progress (1956)
Richard Attenborough (Pte Henry Percival Cox); Dennis Price (Brig. Bertram Tracepurcel); Terry-Thomas (Maj. Hitchcock); Ian Carmichael (Pte Stanley Windrush); Peter Jones (Arthur Egan); William Hartnell (Sgt Sutton); Thorley Walters (Capt. Bootle); Jill Adams (Prudence Greenslade); Ian Bannen (Pte Horrocks); Victor Maddern (Pte George Blake); Kenneth Griffith (Pte Dai Jones); John Warren (Sgt Maj. Gradwick); George Coulouris (Padre); Derrick De Marney (Pat); Ronald Adam (Doctor); Henry Longhurst (Mr Spottiswood); Miles Malleson (Mr Windrush Snr); Sally Miles (Catherine); David Kingwood (Gerald); Brian Oulton (MO at Gravestone Camp); Michael Trubshawe (Colonel Fanshawe); John Le Mesurier (Psychiatrist); Robert Raglan (General Tomlinson); Nicholas Bruce (German Officer); Theodore Zichy (German Agent); Henry Oscar (Art Expert); with Marianne Stone, Lloyd Lamble, Michael Ward, Ian Wilson, Christopher Lee.
Running time: 96 minutes. DVD.

The Green Man (1956)

Alistair Sim (Hawkins); George Cole (William Blake); Terry-Thomas (Charles Boughtflower); Jill Adams (Ann Vincent); Raymond Huntley (Sir Gregory Upshott); Colin Gordon (Reginald Willoughby-Cruft); Avril Angers (Marigold); John Chandos (McKechnie); Eileen Moore (Joan Wood); Peter Brough (Landlord); Dora Bryan (Lily); Richard Wattis (Doctor); Alexander Gauge (Chairman); Cyril Chamberlain (Sgt Bassett); Vivien Wood (Leader of Trio); Marie Burke (Felicity); Lucy Griffiths (Annabel); Arthur Lowe (Radio Salesman); Peter Bull (General Niva); Statesman (Willoughby Goddard); Waiter (Michael Ripper); Porter (Leslie Weston); Mrs Bostock (Doris Yorke); BBC Continuity Announcer (Terence Alexander).
Running time: 76 minutes. DVD.

Brothers In Law (1956)

Richard Attenborough (Henry Marshall); Ian Carmichael (Roger Thursby); Terry-Thomas (Alfred Green); Jill Adams (Sally Smith); Miles Malleson (Kendall Grimes QC); Raymond Huntley (Tatlock QC); Eric Barker (Alec Blair); Nicholas Parsons (Charles Poole); Kynaston Reeves (Mr Justice Lawson); John Le Mesurier (His Honour Judge Ryman); Irene Handl (Mrs Porter); Olive Sloane (Mrs Newton); Edith Sharpe (Mrs Thursby); Leslie Phillips (Shop Assistant); Brian Oulton (Client); John Welsh (Mr Justice Fanshawe); Peggyann Clifford (Mrs Bristow); Henry Longhurst (Rev. Arthur Thursby); Henry Hewitt (Treasurer); Gerald Fox (Clerk); Bob McNaughton (Robing Room Attendant); Llewellyn Rees (Farrant QC); Maurice Colbourne (Referee); Rolf Lefebvre (County Court Judge); Robert Raglan (Cleaver); Hugh Moxey (Golf Club Secretary); Everley Clegg (Mrs Barber); John Warren (Mr Venner); Stuart Saunders (Major Biddle); Penny Morrell (Rosalie Biddle); Margaret Lacey (Helper); Michael Ward (Photographer); Norma Shebbeare (Fashion Editor); John Boxer (Mr Johnson); Wyndham Goldie (Mr Smith); Basil Dignam (Mr Justice Emery); Ronald Cardew (Clerk); Susan Marryott (Barmaid); Kenneth Griffith (Hearse Driver); Ian Wilson (Hearse Attendant); John Schlesinger (Assize Court Solicitor); George Rose (Frost).
Running time: 76 minutes. DVD.

Lucky Jim (1957)

Ian Carmichael (Jim Dixon); Terry-Thomas (Bertrand Welch); Hugh Griffith (Professor Welch); Sharon Acker (Christine Callaghan); Jean Anderson (Mrs Welch); Reginald Beckwith (Porter); John Cairney (Roberts); Ronald Cardew (Registrar); Maureen Connell (Margaret Peel); Harry Fowler (Driver); Kenneth Griffith (Cyril Johns); Jeremy Hawk (Bill Atkinson); Charles Lamb (Contractor); Henry Longhurst (Professor Hutchinson); Jeremy Longhurst

(Waiter); Penny Morrell (Miss Wilson); Clive Morton (Sir Hector Gore-Urquhart); John Welsh (Principal); Ian Wilson (Singer).
Running time: 91 minutes. DVD.

Blue Murder at St Trinian's (1957)

Terry-Thomas ('Captain' Romney Carlton-Ricketts); George Cole (Flash Harry); Joyce Grenfell (Sgt Ruby Gates); Alistair Sim (Miss Amelia Fritton); Lionel Jeffries (Joe Mangan); Eric Barker (Culpepper Brown); Richard Wattis (Bassett); Thorley Walters (Major); Lloyd Lamble (Superintendent); Michael Ripper (Liftman); Judith Furse (Dame Maud Hackshaw); Lisa Gastoni (Myrna); Dilys Laye (Bridget); Jose Read (Cynthia); Rosalind Knight (Annabel); Patricia Lawrence (Mavis); Marigold Russell (Marjorie); Vikki Hammond (Jane); Sabrina (Virginia); Kenneth Griffith (Charlie Bull); Peter Jones (Prestwick); Lisa Lee (Miss Brenner); Guido Lorraine (Prince Bruno); Alma Taylor (Prince's Mother); Peter Elliott (Equerry); Charles Lloyd-Pack (Prison Governor); Cyril Chamberlain (Captain); Bill Shine (Policeman); Terry Scott (Police Sergeant); Raymond Rollett (Chief Constable); Ferdy Mayne (Italian Police Inspector); Ronald Ibbs (Lieutenant); Nicola Braithwaite (Daphne); Janet Bradbury (Mercia); Amanda Coxell (Tilly); Moya Francis (Bissy).
Running time: 86 minutes. DVD.

The Naked Truth (1957)

Terry-Thomas (Lord Henry Mayley); Peter Sellers ('Wee' Sonny McGregor); Peggy Mount (Flora Ransom); Shirley Eaton (Melissa Right); Dennis Price (Nigel Dennis); Georgina Cookson (Lady Mayley); Joan Sims (Ethel Ransom); Miles Malleson (Rev. Bastable); Kenneth Griffith (Porter); Moultrie Kelsall (Mactavish); Bill Edwards (Bill Murphy); Wally Patch (Paunchy Old Man); Henry Hewitt (Gunsmith); John Stuart (Police Inspector); David Lodge (PC); Joan Hurley (Author); Peter Noble (TV Announcer); Victor Rietti (Doctor).
Running time: 91 minutes. DVD.

Happy is the Bride (1957)

Ian Carmichael (David Chaytor); Janette Scott (Janet Royd); Cecil Parker (Arthur Royd); Terry-Thomas (Policeman); Eric Barker (Vicar); Edith Sharpe (Mildred Royd); Elvi Hale (Petula); Joyce Grenfell (Aunt Florence); Miles Malleson (1st Magistrate); Athene Seyler (Aunt Harriet); Irene Handl (Madame Edna); John Le Mesurier (William Chaytor); Thorley Walters (Jim); Nicholas Parsons (John Royd); Virginia Maskell (Marcia); Brian Oulton (2nd Magistrate); Joan Hickson (Mrs Bowles); Cardew Robinson (George the Verger); Sarah Drury (Miranda Royd); Victor Maddern (Shop Steward); Sam Kydd (Foreman); Richard Bennett (Denys Royd); Ian Wilson (Umpire); Rolf

Lefebvre (Clerk of Court); Pauline Winter (Ethel); Enid Hewitt (Lady Yeldham); Olive Milbourne (Miss Illingworth); Margaret Lacey (Miss Dacres). Running time: 84 minutes. DVD.

tom thumb (1958)
Russ Tamblyn (tom thumb); Alan Young (Woody); June Thorburn (Queenie); Terry-Thomas (Ivan); Peter Sellers (Anthony); Bernard Miles (Honest John); Jessie Matthews (Ann); Ian Wallace (Shoe Maker); Peter Butterworth (Band Master); Peter Bull (Major); with the voices of Stan Freberg (as the yawning man) and Dal McKennon (as the Chinese man and the Puppetoons). *Running time: 98 minutes. DVD.*

Carlton-Browne of the F.O. (1959)
Terry-Thomas (Cadogan de Vere Carlton-Browne); Peter Sellers (Señor Amphibulos, Prime Minister of Gaillardia); Her Serene Highness, Luciana Paoluzzi (Princess Ilyena); Ian Bannen (The Young King); Thorley Walters (Colonel Bellingham); Miles Malleson (Resident Advisor); Raymond Huntley (Foreign Secretary); John Le Mesurier (Grand Duke Alexis); Marie Lohr (Lady Carlton-Browne); Kynaston Reeves (Sir Arthur Carlton-Browne); Ronald Adam (Sir John Farthing); John Van Eyssen (Hewitt); Nicholas Parsons (Rodgers); Irene Handl (Mrs Carter); Harry Locke (Commentator); Basil Dignam (Security Officer); Sam Kydd (Signaller); Robert Bruce (Major in Commandos); John Glyn-Jones (Newsreel Interviewer); Marianne Stone (Woman in Cinema); Kathryn Keeton (Dancer); Margaret Lacey (Onlooker); Robert Young (Archivist).
Running time: 88 minutes. DVD.

Too Many Crooks (1959)
Terry-Thomas (William Delaney Gordon); George Cole (Fingers); Brenda De Banzie (Lucy Gordon); Bernard Bresslaw (Snowdrop); Sidney James (Sid); Vera Day (Charmaine); Delphi Lawrence (Secretary); John Le Mesurier (Magistrate); Sidney Tafler (Solicitor); Rosalie Ashley (Angelo); Nicholas Parsons (Tommy); Terry Scott (PC James Smith); Vilma Ann Leslie (Female Journalist); Edie Martin (Gordon's Mother); Tutte Lemkow (Swarthy Man); John Stuart (Inspector Jensen); Joe Melia (Whisper); with Gibb McLaughlin, Sam Kydd, Cyril Chamberlain, Wally Patch.
Running time: 86 minutes. DVD.

I'm All Right, Jack (1959)
Ian Carmichael (Stanley Windrush); Terry-Thomas (Maj. Hitchcock); Peter Sellers (Fred Kite/Sir John Kennaway); Richard Attenborough (Sidney De Vere Cox); Margaret Rutherford (Aunt Dolly); Dennis Price (Bertram Tracepurcel);

Irene Handl (Mrs Kite); Miles Malleson (Windrush Snr); Victor Maddern (Knowles); Liz Fraser (Cynthia Kite); John Le Mesurier (Waters); Marne Maitland (Mr Mohammed); Kenneth Griffith (Dai); Raymond Huntley (Magistrate); Malcolm Muggeridge (TV Presenter); Sam Kydd, Cardew Robinson, John Comer, Tony Comer, Bruce Wightman, Billy Rayment (Shop Stewards); Donal Donnelly (Perce Carter); Harry Locke (Union Official); John Glyn-Jones (Detto Executive); Fred Griffiths (Charlie); Basil Dignam (Minister of Labour); Ronnie Stevens (Hooper); Brian Oulton (Appts Board Examiner); Esma Cannon (Spencer); Martin Boddey (Num Yums Executive); Pauline Winter (Miss Forsdyke); Maurice Colbourn (Missiles Director); Jeremy White, Robin Ray (Young Chemists); Michael Bates (Henry Bootle); John Van Eyssen, Robert Bruce, Michael Ward, Stringer Davis, Tony Spear (Reporters); Arthur Skinner, William Peacock (Photographers); Eynon Evans (Truscott); Robert Young (Owens); Roy Purcell (Police Inspector); Marianne Stone (TV Receptionist); Terry Scott (Crawley); Marion Shaw (Tea Girl); Wally Patch (Workman); Alun Owen (TV Producer); Muriel Young (TV Announcer); Frank Phillips (BBC Announcer); Ian Wilson (Evangelist); Margaret Lacey (Empire Loyalist); George Selway, Alan Wilson (Union Flag Workmen); David Lodge, Keith Smith, Kenneth Warren (Card Players).
Running time: 105 minutes. DVD.

School for Scoundrels, or How to Win Without Actually Cheating (1960)
Ian Carmichael (Henry Palfrey); Terry-Thomas (Raymond Delauney); Alistair Sim (Mr S. Potter); Janette Scott (April Smith); Dennis Price (Dunstan Dorchester); Peter Jones (Dudley Dorchester); Edward Chapman (Gloatbridge); John Le Mesurier (Head Waiter Skinner); Irene Handl (Mrs Stringer); Kynaston Reeves (General); Hattie Jacques (1st Instructress, Miss Grimmet); Hugh Paddick (Instructor, Mr Pickthorn); Barbara Roscoe (2nd Instructress); Gerald Campion (Proudfoot); Monty Landis (Fleetsnod); Jeremy Lloyd (Dingle); Charles Lamb (Carpenter); Anita Sharp-Bolster (Maid).
Running time: 94 minutes. DVD.

Make Mine Mink (1960)
Terry-Thomas (Maj. Albert Rayne); Athene Seyler (Dame Beatrice); Hattie Jacques (Nanette Parry); Billie Whitelaw (Lily); Elspeth Duxbury (Pinkie); Jack Hedley (Jim Benham); Raymond Huntley (Inspector Pope); Kenneth Williams (Freddie Warrington); Noel Purcell (Burglar); Irene Handl (Madame Spolinski); Sydney Tafler (Spanager); Joan Heal (Mrs Spanager); Penny Morrell (Gertrude); Freddie Frinton (Drunk).
Running time: 100 minutes. DVD.

His and Hers (1961)

Terry-Thomas (Reggie Blake); Janette Scott (Fran Blake); Wilfrid Hyde-White (Charles Lunton); Nicole Maurey (Simone Rolfe); Joan Sims (Hortense); Kenneth Connor (Harold); Kenneth Williams (Policeman); Meier Tzelniker (Felix McGregor); Colin Gordon (TV Announcer); Joan Hickson (Phoebe); Oliver Reed (Poet); Francesca Annis (Wanda); Dorinda Stevens (Dora); Barbara Hicks (Woman); Billy Lambert (Baby).
Running time: 90 minutes. DVD.

A Matter of WHO (1961)

Terry-Thomas (Archibald Bannister); Sonja Ziemann (Michele); Alex Nicol (Kennedy); Richard Briers (Jimmy Jamieson); Honor Blackman (Sister Bryan); Carol White (Beryl); Guy Deghy (Ivanovitch); Clive Morton (Hatfield); Martin Benson (Rahman); Geoffrey Keen (Foster); Eduard Linkers (Linkers); Vincent Ball (Dr Blake); Michael Ripper (Skipper); Cyril Wheeler (Cooper); Andrew Faulds (Ralph); George Cormack (Henry); Bruce Beeby (Captain Brooke); Julie Alexander (Stewardess); Jacqueline Jones (Miss Forman); Ghulam Mohammed (Attaché); Roland Brand (US Sgt); Barbara Hicks (Margery).
Running time: 91 minutes. DVD.

Bachelor Flat (1961)

Terry-Thomas (Professor Bruce Patterson); Tuesday Weld (Libby Bushmill); Richard Beymer (Mike Pokski); Celeste Holm (Helen Bushmill); Francesca Bellini (Gladys Schmidlapp); Howard McNear (Dr Bowman); Ann Del Guercio (Liz); Roxanne Arlen (Mrs Roberts); Alice Reinheart (Mrs Bowman); Stephen Bekassy (Paul); Margo Moore (Moll); George Bruggeman (Paul Revere); Jessica the Dachshund (Jessica).
Running time: 91 minutes.

Operation Snatch (1962)

Terry-Thomas (Lieutenant 'Piggy' Wigg); George Sanders (Major Hobson); Lionel Jeffries (Evans); Jackie Lane (Bianca Tabori); Miklos Lee (Tabori); Dinsdale Landen (Captain Wellington); Jeremy Lloyd (Captain James); John Meillon (MO); Gerard Heinz (Colonel Waldock); John Gabriel (Major Frink); Warren Mitchell (Contact Man); Mario Fabrizi (Tall Man); Bernard Hunter (Captain Baker); Howard Lang (PT Sgt); Graham Stark (1st Soldier); John Scott (Lt General Hepworth); Ian Whittaker (Dyson); Mark Singleton (PM's Secretary); with Michael Trubshaw, James Villiers.
Running time: 83 minutes.

Kill or Cure (1962)

Terry-Thomas (Captain Jeroboam Barker-Rynde); Eric Sykes (Rumbelow); Dennis Price (Dr Crossley); Lionel Jeffries (Inspector Hook); Moira Redmond (Frances); Katya Douglas (Rita); David Lodge (Richards); Ronnie Barker (Burton); Hazel Terry (Mrs Crossley); Harry Locke (Higgins); Derren Nesbitt (Roger); Arthur Howard (Clerk); Tristram Jellinek (Assistant Clerk); Peter Butterworth (Barman); Patricia Hayes (Waitress); Anna Russell (Mrs Clifford); Julian Orchard (PC Lofthouse); with Sidney Vyvyan.
Running time: 88 minutes.

The Wonderful World of the Brothers Grimm (1962)

Laurence Harvey (Wilhelm Grimm); Karl Boehm (Jacob Grimm); Claire Bloom (Dorothea Grimm); Walter Slezak (Stossel); Barbara Eden (Greta Heinrich); Oscar Homolka (The Duke); Arnold Stang (Rumpelstiltskin); Martita Hunt (Story Teller); Ian Wolfe (Gruber); Betty Garde (Mrs Bettenhausen); Cheerio Meredith (Mrs Von Dittersdorf); Bryan Russell (Friedrich Grimm); Tammy Marihugh (Pauline Grimm); Walter Rilla (The Priest). *The Dancing Princess*: Yvette Mimieux (The Princess); Russ Tamblyn (The Woodsman); Jim Backus (The King); Beulah Bondi (The Gypsy); Clinton Sundberg (Prime Minister). *The Cobbler and the Elves*: Laurence Harvey (The Cobbler); Walter Brooke (The Mayor); Sandra Gale Bettin (The Ballerina); Robert Foulk (The Hunter); and The Puppetoons. *The Singing Bone*: Terry-Thomas (Ludwig); Buddy Hackett (Hans); Otto Kruger (The King); Robert Crawford Jnr (The Shepherd); Sydney Smith (The Spokesman).
Running time: 134 minutes.

The Mouse on the Moon (1963)

Margaret Rutherford (The Grand Duchess, Gloriana); Ron Moody (Mountjoy); Bernard Cribbins (Vincent); David Kossoff (Professor Kokintz); Terry-Thomas (Maurice Spender, MI5); June Ritchie (Cynthia); John Le Mesurier (British Delegate); John Phillips (American Delegate); Eric Barker (MI5 Man); Roddy McMillan (Benter); Tom Aldredge (Wendover); Peter Sallis (Russian Delegate); Clive Dunn (Bandleader); Hugh Lloyd (Plumber); Graham Stark (Standard Bearer); Mario Fabrizi (Valet); Jan Conrad (Russian Aide); John Bluthal (Von Neidel); Archie Duncan (American General); Guy Deghy (Russian Scientist); Richard Marner (Russian General); Allan Cuthbertson, Robin Bailey, Gerald Anderson (Members of Whitehall Conference); Gordon Phillott (Civil Servant); John Wood (Countryman); George Chisholm (Wine Waiter); Rosemary Scott (Launching Lady); Vincent Ball (Pilot); Frank Duncan (News Announcer); Ed Bishop, Bill Edwards (American Astronauts);

Laurence Herder, Harvey Hall (Russian Astronauts); Frankie Howerd (Himself).
Running time: 85 minutes. DVD.

It's a Mad, Mad, Mad, Mad World (1963)
Spencer Tracy (Captain C.G. Culpeper); Milton Berle (J. Russell Finch); Sid Caesar (Melville Crump); Buddy Hackett (Benjy Benjamin); Ethel Merman (Mrs Marcus); Mickey Rooney (Ding Bell); Dick Shawn (Sylvester Marcus); Phil Silvers (Otto Meyer); Terry-Thomas (Lt-Col. J. Algernon Hawthorne); Jonathan Winters (Lennie Pike); with Edie Adams, Dorothy Provine, Peter Falk, Eddie 'Rochester' Anderson, Jim Backus, Ben Blue, Joe E. Brown, Alan Carney, Barrie Chase, William Demarest, Andy Devine, Norman Fell, Paul Ford, Leo Gorcey, Sterling Holloway, Edward Everett Horton, Marvin Kaplan, Buster Keaton, Don Knotts, Charles Lane, Charles McGraw, ZaSu Pitts, Carl Reiner, Madlyn Ruhe, Arnold Stang, The Three Stooges, Jesse White, Jimmy Durante, Jack Benny, Tom Kennedy, Jerry Lewis.
Running time: 161 minutes. DVD.

Terry-Thomas in Tuscany (1963)
Terry-Thomas
Running time: 15 minutes.

Terry-Thomas in the South of France (1963)
Terry-Thomas
Running time: 19 minutes.

Terry-Thomas in Northern Ireland (1963)
Terry-Thomas
Running time: 16 minutes.

The Wild Affair (1963)
Nancy Kwan (Marjorie); Terry-Thomas (Godfrey Deane); Jimmy Logan (Craig); Bud Flanagan (Sgt Bletch); Gladys Morgan (Mrs Tovey); Betty Marsden (Mavis Cook); Paul Whitsun-Jones (Tiny Hearst); Donald Churchill (Andy); David Sumner (Ralph); Joyce Blair (Monica); Victor Spinetti (Quentin); Bessie Love (Mother); Joan Benham (Assistant); Bernard Adams (Bone); Diane Aubrey (Jill); Sheila Bernette (Tea Trolley Girl); Sidonie Bond (Sue Blair); Patience Collier (Woman in Travel Agency); Paul Curran (Father); Frank Finlay (Drunk); Penny Morrell (Tart); Claire Neilsen (Blonde Assistant); Fred Stone (Head Waiter); Frank Thornton (Manager).
Running time: 88 minutes.

How to Murder Your Wife (1965)
Jack Lemmon (Stanley Ford); Terry-Thomas (Charles Furbank); Virna Lisi
(Mrs Ford); Eddie Mayehoff (Harold Lampson); Claire Trevor (Edna
Lampson); Sidney Blackmer (Judge Blackstone); Jack Albertson (Dr Bentley);
Max Showalter (Tobey Rawlins); Alan Hewitt (District Attorney); Mary Wickes
(Harold's Secretary); with Barry Kelley, William Bryant, Charles Bateman,
Edward Faulkner, Laureen Gilbert, Howard Wendell, Khigh Dhiegh, K.C.
Townsend.
Running time: 118 minutes. DVD.

Strange Bedfellows (1965)
Rock Hudson (Carter); Gina Lollobrigida (Toni); Gig Young (Richard
Bramwell); Edward Judd (Harry Jones); Terry-Thomas (Assistant Mortician);
Arthur Haynes (Carter's Taxi Driver); Howard St John (J.L. Stevens); Nancy
Kulp (Aggressive Woman); with Dave King, Peggy Rea, Joseph Sirola, Lucy
Landall, Bernard Fox, Edith Atwater, James McCallion, Hedley Mattingly,
John Orchard.
Running time: 99 minutes. DVD.

*Those Magnificent Men in Their Flying Machines, or How I Flew from
London to Paris in 25 Hours and 11 Minutes* (1965)
Stuart Whitman (Orvil Newton); Sarah Miles (Hon. Patricia Rawnsley); James
Fox (Richard Mays); Alberto Sordi (Count Emilio Ponticelli); Robert Morley
(Lord Rawnsley); Gert Frobe (Count Manfred Von Holstein); Jean-Pierre
Cassel (Pierre Dubois); Irina Demick (Brigitte, Ingrid, Marlene, Francoise,
Yvette and Betty); Terry-Thomas (Sir Percy Ware-Armitage); Eric Sykes
(Courtney); Red Skelton (Neanderthal Man/Pioneer Flyers); Yujiro Ishihara
(Yama Moto); Benny Hill (Fire Chief Perkins); Flora Robson (Mother
Superior); Michael Vogler (Karl); Sam Wanamaker (George); Tony Hancock
(Harry Popplewell); Gordon Jackson (McDougal); Millicent Martin (Airline
Hostess); William Rushton (Gascoyne Tremayne); Fred Emney (Colonel
Willy); John Le Mesurier (French Painter); Eric Barker (French Postman);
Michael Trubshawe, Ronnie Stevens (Officials); Davy Kaye (Jean Pascac);
Jeremy Lloyd (Lt Parsons); Marjorie Rhodes (Chop 'n' Chips Waitress); Steve
Plytas (Reporter); Norman Rossington (Fireman); Jimmy Thompson
(Photographer); Cicely Courtneidge (Muriel the Memsahib); Maurice
Denham (Ship's Captain); James Robertson Justice (Narrator); with Zena
Marshall, Eric Pohlmann, Graham Stark.
Running time: 132 minutes. DVD.

You Must Be Joking! (1965)

Michael Callan (Lt Tim Morton); Lionel Jeffries (Sgt Major McGregor);
Denholm Elliott (Captain Tabasco); Wilfrid Hyde-White (General Lockwood);
Bernard Cribbins (Sgt Clegg); James Robertson Justice (Librarian); Leslie
Phillips (Young Husband); Gabriella Licudi (Annabelle Nash); Patricia Viterbo
(Sylvie Tarnet); Terry-Thomas (Maj. Foskitt); Lee Montague (Sgt Mansfield);
Irene Handl (Elderly Woman); Richard Wattis (Parkins); Miles Malleson
(Salesman); Gwendolyn Watts (Young Wife); Clive Dunn (Doorman); Tracy
Reed (Poppy Pennington); James Villiers (Bill Simpson); Graham Stark
(McGregor's Friend); Arthur Lowe (Member of Public); Peter Bull (Ferocious
Man in Library); David Jacobs (Himself); Norman Vaughan (Norman Stone);
Lance Percival (Young Man); Marianne Stone (Fan Club Worker); Jon
Pertwee (Storekeeper); Norman Mitchell (Fish Porter).
Running time: 100 minutes.

Our Man in Marrakesh (1966)

Tony Randall (Andrew Jessel); Senta Berger (Kura Stanovy); Herbert Lom (Mr
Casimir); Wilfrid Hyde-White (Arthur Fairbrother); Terry-Thomas (El Caid);
Gregoire Aslan (Achmed); John Le Mesurier (George C. Lilywhite); Klaus
Kinski (Jonquil); Margaret Lee (Samia Voss); Emil Stemmler (Hotel Clerk);
Helen Sanguineti (Madame Bouseny); Francisco Sanchez (Martinez); William
Sanguineti (Police Chief); Hassan Essakali (Motorcycle Policeman); Keith
Peacock (Philippe); Bert Kwouk (Export Analysis Manager).
Running time: 94 minutes. DVD.

The Sandwich Man (1966)

Michael Bentine (Horace Quilby); Dora Bryan (Mrs de Vere); Harry H.
Corbett (Mach); Bernard Cribbins (Harold); Diana Dors, Anna Quayle
(Billingsgate Ladies); Ian Hendry (Motorcycle Policeman); Stanley Holloway
(Park Gardener); Wilfrid Hyde-White (Lord Uffingham); Michael Medwin
(Sewer Man); Ron Moody (Rowing Coach); Terry-Thomas (Scoutmaster);
Norman Wisdom (Boxing Father); Donald Wolfit (Car Salesman); David Buck
(Steven Mansfield); Suzy Kendall (Sue); Tracey Crisp (Girl in Plastic Mac);
Alfie Bass (Model Yachtsman); Leon Thau (Rami); Earl Cameron (Bernard,
Bus Conductor); Hugh Futcher (Gogi); Peter Jones (Manfred the Magnificent,
Escapologist); John Le Mesurier (Abadiah, Religious Sandwich Man); Robert
Lang (Waiter); David Lodge (Charlie); Warren Mitchell (Gypsy Sid); Ewen
Solon (Blind Man); Aubrey Morris (Cedric); Sydney Tafler, Frank Finlay
(Billingsgate Porters); Ronnie Stevens (Drunk); Fred Emney (Sir Mervyn
Moleskin); John Junkin (Chauffeur); Jeremy Lloyd (Jeremy, Guards Officer);
Patrick Newell (Ferry Man); Michael Trubshawe (Guards Officer); Gerald

Campion (Fred); Roger Delgado (Abdul); Burt Kwouk (Ice Cream Salesman); Nosher Powell (Nosher); Michael Bentine (Indian Jazz Club Owner).
Running time: 95 minutes. DVD.

Munster, Go Home! (1966)

Fred Gwynne (Herman Munster); Yvonne de Carlo (Lily Munster); Al Lewis (Grandpa Al); Butch Patrick (Eddie Wolfgang Munster); Debbie Watson (Marilyn); Terry-Thomas (Freddie Munster); Hermione Gingold (Lady Effigie Munster); Robert Pine (Roger Moresby); John Carradine (Cruikshank); Bernard Fox (Squire Moresby); Richard Dawson (Joey); Jeanne Arnold (Grace Munster); Maria Lennard (Millie); Cliff Norton (Herbert); Diana Chesney (Mrs Moresby); Arthur Malet (Alfie); Ben Wright (Hennessey).
Running time: 86 minutes. DVD.

The Daydreamer (1966)

Paul O'Keefe (Chris); Jack Gilford (Papa Anderson); Jack Bolger (The Pieman); Mrs Margaret Hamilton (Klopplebobbler); and the voices of Cyril Ritchard, Hayley Mills, Burl Ives, Tallulah Bankhead, Victor Borge, Ed Wynne, Robert Harter, Patty Duke, Boris Karloff, Sessue Hayakawa, Robert Goulet, and Terry-Thomas (Brigadier Zachary Zilch).
Running time: 101 minutes. DVD.

Se tutte le donne del mondo ... (1966)

Dorothy Provine (Susan); Mike Connors (Kelly); Raf Vallone (Ardonian); Terry-Thomas (James/Lord Aldric); Margaret Lee (Grace); Oliver MacGreevy (Ringo); Nicoletta Rangoni (Sylvia); Sandro Dori (Omar); Beverly Adams (Karin); Marilu Tolo (Gioia); Seyna Seyn (Wilma Soong); Jack Gwillim (British Ambassador); Michael Audley (Major Davis); Nerio Bernardi (Papal Envoy); Andy Ho (Ling); Kruger H. Thoren (Kasai K. Wang); Edith Peter (Maria).
Running time: 106 minutes.

La Grand Vadrouille (a.k.a. *Don't Look Now*, 1966)

Terry-Thomas (Sir Reginald); Bourvil (Augustin Bouvet); Louis de Funès (Stanislas Lefort); Claudio Brook (Peter Cunningham); Marie Dubios (Juliette); Benno Sterzenbach (Major Achback); Colette Brosset (Madame Germaine); Andrea Parisy (Sister Marie-Odile); Mike Marshall (Alan MacIntosh); Mary Marquet (Mother Superior); Pierre Bertin (Punch and Judy Operator); with George Atlas, Gabriel Gobin, Paul Mercey, Nicolas Bang, Anne Berger, Sieghardt Rupp, Paul Preboisi, Alice Field, Henri Génès, Hans Meyer, Peter Jacob, Rudy Lenoir.
Running time: 116 minutes. DVD.

Bounder!

Jules Verne's Rocket to the Moon (1967)

Burl Ives (Phineas T. Barnum); Troy Donahue (Gaylord); Gert Frobe (Professor Von Bulow); Hermione Gingold (Angelica); Lionel Jeffries (Sir Charles Dillworthy); Dennis Price (Duke of Borset); Daliah Lavi (Madeleine); Stratford Johns (Warrant Officer); Graham Stark (Grundle); Jimmy Clitheroe (General Tom Thumb); Judy Cornwell (Electra); Joachim Teege (Bulgeroff); Edward De Souza (Henri); Joan Sterndale Bennett (Queen Victoria); Allan Cuthbertson (Scuttling); Derek Francis (Puddleby); Anthony Woodruff (Announcer); Hugh Walters (Carruthers); Donald Bissett (Flood); Cecil Nash (Chambers); Vernon Hayden (Mr Brown); John Franklyn Robbins (Railway Guard); Harry Brogan (Professor Dingle); Derek Young (French Officer of Guard); Renata Holt (Anna); Terry-Thomas (Captain Sir Harry Washington-Smythe).
Running time: 101 minutes. DVD.

Ragazza del Charleston (a.k.a. *Arabella*, 1967)

Virna Lisi (Arabella Danesi); James Fox (Giorgio); Margaret Rutherford (Princess Ilaria); Terry-Thomas (Felloni the Hotel Manager/General Sir Horace Gordon/Duke Pietro Moretti Trivulzano/Insurance Manager); Giancarlo Giannini (Saverio); Antonio Casagrande (Filberto); Paola Borbon (Duchess Moretti); Milena Vukotic (Graziella); with Esmeralda Ruspoli, Valentio Macchi, Renato Romano, Renato Chiantoni, Giuseppe Addobbatti.
Running time: 105 minutes.

The Perils of Pauline (1967)

Pat Boone (George); Terry-Thomas (Sten Martin); Pam Austin (Pauline); Edward Everett Horton (Caspar Colman); Hamilton Camp (Thorpe); Doris Packer (Mrs Carruthers); Kurt Kasznar (Consul General); Vito Scott (Frandisi); Leon Askin (Commissar); Aram Katcher (Vizier); Ric Natolill (Prince Benji).
Running time: 98 minutes.

A Guide for the Married Man (1967)

Walter Matthau (Paul Manning); Robert Morse (Ed Stander); Inger Stevens (Ruth Manning); Sue Anne Langdon (Mrs Johnson); Claire Kelly (Harriet Stander); Linda Harrison (Miss Stardust); Terry-Thomas (Technical Advisor/ 'Tiger'); Jackie Russell (Miss Harris); Aline Towne (Mousey Man's Wife); Eve Brent (Blowsy Blonde); Marvin Brody (Cab Driver); Majel Barrett (Mrs Fred V); Marian Mason (Mrs Rance G); Jason Wingreen (Harry Johnson); with Elaine Devry, Michael Romanoff, Jason Wingreen, Fred Holliday, Pat Becker, Lucille Ball, Jack Benny, Polly Bergen, Joey Bishop, Sid Caesar, Art Carney,

Wally Cox, Jayne Mansfield, Hal March, Louis Nye, Carl Reiner, Phil Silvers,
Ben Blue, Ann Morgan Guilbert, Jeffrey Hunter, Marty Ingels, Sam Jaffe.
Running time: 91 minutes. DVD.

Arriva Dorellik (a.k.a. *How to Kill 400 Duponts*, 1967)
Johnny Dorelli (Dorellik); Agata Flori (Charlotte); Riccardo Garrone (Vladimir
Dupont); Terry-Thomas (Commissioner Green); with Margaret Lee, Alfred
Adam, Jean-Pierre Zola, Rossella Como.
Running time: 96 minutes.

Top Crack (1967)
Terry-Thomas (Charles); Gaston Moschin (Karl); Didier Haudepin (Uno);
Stella Interlenghi (Due); Lorna Palombini (Tre); Consuelo Aranyi (Quattro);
Oreste Lionello (Peter); Mirella Maravidi (Agatha); with Anna Degli Uberti,
Antonio Altoviti, Cesare Gelli, Christiane Maybach, Ferdinando Brofferio, Gia
Sandri, Gianluigi Polidoro, Liana Ferrakian, Luigi Zerbinati, Mario Frera,
Marisa Busetto, Rossella Labella, Valentino Macchi, Victor Francen.
Running time: 90 minutes.

Don't Raise the Bridge, Lower the River (1967)
Jerry Lewis (George Lester); Terry-Thomas (H. William Homer); Jacqueline
Pearce (Pamela Lester); Bernard Cribbins (Fred Davies); Patricia Routledge
(Lucille Beatty); Nicholas Parsons (Dudley Heath); Michael Bates (Dr Spink);
John Bluthal (Dr Pinto); Sandra Caron (Pinto's Nurse); Pippa Benedict (Fern
Averback); Harold Goodwin (Six-Eyes Wiener); Richard Montez (Arab); Henry
Soskin (Bearded Arab); Al Mancini (Portuguese Chauffeur); John Moore
(Digby); John Barrad (Zebra Man); Robert Lee (Bruce); Francisca Tu (Chinese
Telephonist); Colin Douglas (Barman); Alexandra Dane (Masseuse); Nike
Arrighi (Portuguese Waitress); Jerry Paris (Baseball Umpire).
Running time: 99 minutes. DVD.

Danger: Diabolik (1967)
John Phillip Law (Diabolik); Marisa Mell (Eva Kant); Michel Piccoli
(Inspector Ginco); Adolfo Celi (Valmont); Claudio Gora (Police Chief); Mario
Donen (Danek); Renzo Palmer (Minister's Assistant); Annie Gorassini
(Valmont's Girlfriend); Carlo Croccolo (Lorry Driver); Lidia Biondi
(Policewoman); Andrea Bosic (Bank Manager); Federico Boido, Tiberio Mitri,
Isarco Ravaioli, Wolfgang Hillinger, Francesco Mule (Valmont's Henchmen);
Giorgio Sciolotte (Doctor at Morgue); Terry-Thomas (Minister of Finance);
Edward Fobo Kelleng (Sir Harold Clark); Giulio Donnini (Doctor Vernier);

Giorgio Gennar (Rudy); Giuseppe Fazio (Tony); with Caterina Boratto, Lucia Modugno.
Running time: 101 minutes. DVD.

How Sweet It Is! (1968)
James Garner (Griff Henderson); Debbie Reynolds (Jenny); Maurice Ronet (Philippe); Paul Lynde (Purser); Marcel Dalio (Louis); Terry-Thomas (Mr Tilly); Gino Conforti (Agatzi); Donald Losby (Davey); Hilarie Thompson (Bootsie); Alexandra Hay (Gloria); Mary Michael (Nancy Leigh); Walter Brooke (Haskell Wax); Elena Verdugo (Vera Wax); Ann Morgan Guilbert (Bibi); Patty Regan (Midge); Vito Scotti (Cook); with Chris Ross, Larry Hankin, Jerry Riggio, Jack Colvin, Leigh French, Erin Moran, Belia Bruch.
Running time: 99 minutes.

Uno scacco tutto matto (a.k.a. *Checkmate for McDowell*, 1968)
Edward G. Robinson (Sir George McDowell); Terry-Thomas (Il Direttore Dorgeant); Maria Grazia Buccello (Monique); with Adolfo Celi, Jorge Rigaud, Manuel Zarzo, Loris Bazzocchi, José Bódalo, Rossella Como, Gaetano Imbró, Franca Dominici, Ana Maria Custodio.
Running time: 87 minutes.

Where Were You When the Lights Went Out? (1968)
Doris Day (Margaret Garrison); Robert Morse (Waldo Zane); Terry-Thomas (Ladislaus Walichek); Patrick O'Neal (Peter Garrison); Lola Albright (Roberto Lane); Steve Allen (Morgan Cline); Jim Backus (Tru-Blue Lou); Ben Blue (Man with Razor); Pat Paulsen (Conductor); Dale Malone (Otis J. Hendershot Jnr); Robert Emhardt (Otis J. Hendershot Snr); Harry Hickox (Det. Capt. Peroy Watson); Parley Baer (Dr Dudley Caldwell); Randy Whipple (Marvin Reinholtz); Earl Wilson (Himself).
Running time: 94 minutes.

Sette volte sette (1968)
Lionel Stander (Sam); Gastone Maschin (Lord Benjamin Barton Brain); Raimondo Vianello (Bodoni, '229'); Gordon Mitchell (Big Ben); Paul Stevens (Bingo); Neno Zamperla (Bananas); Theodor Corra (Briggs); Erika Blanc (Mildred); Terry-Thomas (Police Inspector); Turri Ferro (Bernard); Adolfo Celi (Governor); Neil McCarthy (Mr Docherty); Christopher Benjamin (Mr Clerk); David Lodge (Police Sergeant); Gladys Dawson (Miss Higgins); Lionel Murton (Walker); Geoffrey Copleston (Police Commissioner); Charles Borromel (Officer Issuing Prison Uniform); Janos Bartha (1st Coal Shoveller); Ray Lovelock (Mildred's Boyfriend); with Paolo Bonacelli, Adalberto Rossetti, Claudio Trionfi.
Running time: 100 minutes.

2000 Years Later (1969)
Terry-Thomas (Charles Goodwyn); Edward Everett Horton (Evermore); Pat Harrington Jnr (Franchot); Lisa Seagram (Cindy); John Abbott (Gregorius); John Myhers (Air Force General); Tom Melody (Senator); Myrna Ross (Miss Forever); Mati Rock III (Tomorrow's Leader); Michael Christian (The Piston Kid); Casey Kasem (DJ); with Tony Gardner, Buddy Lewis, Milton Parsons. *Running time: 80 minutes.*

Una su 13 (a.k.a. 12+1, 1969)
Vittorio Gassman (Mario Bereti); Orson Welles (Markan); Vittorio Di Sica (Di Seta); Sharon Tate (Pat); Mylene Demongeot (Judy); Terry-Thomas (Albert); Tim Brooke-Taylor (Jackie); Lionel Jeffries (Randomhouse); Gregoire Aslan (Psychiatrist); with Isa Miranda, William Rushton. *Running time: 96 minutes.*

Monte Carlo or Bust! (1969)
Bourvil (Monsieur Dupont); Lando Buzzanca (Marcello); Walter Chiari (Angelo); Tony Curtis (Chester Schofield); Terry-Thomas (Sir Cuthbert Ware-Armitage); Eric Sykes (Percy Perkins); Peter Cook (Major Dawlish); Dudley Moore (Lt Barrington); Mireille Darc (Marie-Claude); Marie Dubois (Pascale); Gert Frobe (Willi Schickel/Horst Muller); Susan Hampshire (Betty); Jack Hawkins (Count Levinovitch); Nicoletta Machiavelli (Dominique); Peter Schmidt (Otto); Jacques Duby (Motorcycle Gendarme); Hattie Jacques (Female Journalist); Derren Nesbitt (Waleska); Nicholas Phipps (Golfer); William Rushton (John O'Groats Official); Michael Trubshaw (German Rally Official); Richard Wattis (Golf Club Secretary); Walter Williams (German Customs Official). *Running time: 125 minutes.*

Arthur? Arthur! (1969)
Shelley Winters (Hester Green); Donald Pleasance (Arthur Brownjohn/Sir Easonby); Terry-Thomas (Clennery Tubbs); Tammy Grimes (Lady Joan Mellon); Margaret Courtenay (Clare Brownjohn); Michael Bates (Mr Harrington); Raymond Huntley (George Payne); Judith Arthy (Patricia 'Pat' Parker); Mark Eden (Jack Parker); Peter Bayliss (Doctor Hubble); Joan Benham (Mrs Payne); Basil Henson (Coverdale); Patsy Smart (Miss Bonnamie); Oliver Tobias (Peter Jackson 'Bobo'); Angie Grant (Cynthia); Robin Ellis (Ames); Margery Withers (Susan); Keith Marsh (Lillywhite); Erik Chitty (Uncle Ratty); Stanley Lebor (Analyst); Mike Carrell (Postman); Frank Crawshaw (Dustman); Jeffrey Sirr (Waterboy); Harry Shacklock (Attendant); Rafiq Anwar (Major Domo); Garry Marsh (Golfer); with Victor Brooks, Maurice Good. *Running time: 94 minutes.*

Bounder!

Le Mur de l'Atlantique (1969)
Bourvil (Leon Duchemin); Peter McEnery (Jeff); Jean Poiret (Armand); Sophie Desmarets (Maria Duchemin); Reinhard Kalldehoff (Heinrich); Sara Francheti (Juliette Duchemin); Pino Caruso (Friedrick); Roland Lesaffre (Le Faux Resistant); Jean-Pierre Zola (Colonel Muller); George Staquet (Le Chef des Resistants); Jacques Balutin (Gendarme); Robert Le Beal (English Officer); Jacques Preboist (Ernest); Billi Koarnes (Camp Commandant); Norman Mitchell, Stephen Yardley (Policemen); Gerald Campion, Frank Williams (Clergymen); William Mervyn (English Bishop); Bill Horsley (RAF Orderly); Peter Myers (RAF Colonel); Terry-Thomas (Perry).
Running time: 135 minutes.

The Abominable Dr Phibes (1971)
Vincent Price (Dr Aston Phibes); Joseph Cotten (Dr Vesalius); Terry-Thomas (Dr Longstreet); Sean Bury (Lem Vesalius); Susan Travers (Nurse Allen); David Hutcheson (Dr Hedgepath); Edward Burnham (Dr Dunwoody); Alex Scott (Dr Hargreaves); Peter Gilmore (Dr Kitaj); Maurice Kaufmann (Dr Whitcombe); Peter Jeffrey (Detective Inspector Trout); Derek Godfrey (Crow); Norman Jones (Sergeant Schenley); John Cater (Waverley); Alan Zipson, Dallas Adams (Police Officials); James Grout (Sergeant); Alister Williamson, Thomas Heathcote, Ian Marter, Julian Grant (Policemen); Hugh Griffith (Rabbi); Aubrey Woods (Goldsmith); John Laurie (Darrow); Barbara Keogh (Mrs Frawley); Charles Farrell (Chauffeur); John Franklyn (Graveyard Attendant); Walter Horsbrugh (Ross the Butler); Virginia North (Vulnavia); Caroline Munro (Victoria Regina Phibes).
Running time: 93 minutes. DVD.

The Cherry Picker (1971)
Lulu (Nancy); Bob Sherman (James Burn III); Wilfrid Hyde-White (Dobson); Spike Milligan (Mr Lal); Robert Hutton (James Burn II); Priscilla Morgan (Mrs Trulove); Arthur Blake (Dan Haydock); Barry Wilsher (Vicar); Bruce Boa (Dr Softman); Henry McGee (Pilkington); Jack Hulbert (Sir Hugh Fawcett); Fiona Curzon (Maureen); Marianne Stone (Mrs Lal); Terry-Thomas (Appleby).
Running time: 92 minutes.

Tunisia – Yesterday and Today (1972)
Terry-Thomas (Commentator)
Running time: 16 minutes.

Colpo grosso, grossissimo … anzi probabile (1972)
Terry-Thomas (Pierre Le Compte); Nino Castelnuovo (Sandro); Luciana
Paluzzi (Jacqueline); Edda di Benedetto (Valentina); Linda Sini (Sandro's
Mother); Anita Durante (Monsignor's Mother); Stefano Oppedisano (Antonio
Lavacca); Rosalbo Neri (Pierre's Wife); Umberto D'Orsi (Monsignor); Luigi
Antonio Guerra (Policeman); Fulvio Mingozzi (Police Commissioner); with
Lopez Vasquez, Juanjo Menendez, Giancarlo Badessi, Jose Luis, Eduardo
Calvo.
Running time: 97 minutes.

Dr Phibes Rises Again (1972)
Vincent Price (Dr Anton Phibes); Robert Quarry (Darius Biederbeck); Valli
Kemp (Vulnavia); Peter Jeffrey (Inspector Trout); John Cater (Waverly); Fiona
Lewis (Diana Biederbeck); Peter Cushing (Captain); Beryl Reid (Mrs
Ambrose); Terry-Thomas (Lombardo); Hugh Griffith (Ambrose); Gerald Sim
(Hackett); John Thaw (Shavers); Keith Buckley (Stuart); Lewis Flander (Baker);
Milton Reid (Manservant).
Running time: 89 minutes. DVD.

Gli Eroi/The Heroes (1973)
Rod Steiger (Gunther Von Lutz); Rosanna Schiaffino (Kathrin); Rod Taylor
(Bob Robeson); Claude Brasseur (Raphael Tibaudet); Terry-Thomas (John
Cooper); with Schreiber Gianni, Garko Spartaco, Aldo Giuffri, Miguel Bose,
Antonio Pica, Nino Sequirin, Angel Aranda.
Running time: 105 minutes.

The Vault of Horror (1973)
Terry-Thomas (Arthur Gritchit); Glynis Johns (Eleanor); John Forbes-
Robertson (Wilson); Marianne Stone (Jane); Dawn Addams (Inez); Tom Baker
(Moore); Michael Craig (Maitland); Denholm Elliott (Diltant); Edward Judd
(Alex); Curt Jürgens (Sebastian); Anna Massey (Donna); Daniel Massey
(Rogers); Robin Nedwell (Tom); Geoffrey Davies (Jerry); with Terence
Alexander, Maurice Kaufmann, Ishaq Bux, Sylvia Marriott, Arthur Mullard,
Tony Hazel, Michael Pratt, Jasmina Hilton, John Witty, Eric Chitty, Roy
Evans, Frank Forsyth, Tommy Godfrey, Genine Graham, Geraldine Hart,
Daniel Jones, Elsa Smith, Tony Wall, Jerold Wells.
Running time: 83 minutes. DVD.

Robin Hood (1973)
Voices of: Roger Miller (Allan-a-Dale); Peter Ustinov (Prince John/Prince
Richard); Terry-Thomas (Sir Hiss); Brian Bedford (Robin Hood); Monica
Evans (Maid Marion); Phil Harris (Little John); Andy Devine (Friar Tuck);

Bounder!

Carole Shelley (Lady Kluck); Pat Buttram (Sheriff of Nottingham); George
Lindsay (Trigger); Ken Curtis (Nutsy); Billy Whitaker (Skippy); Dana Laurita
(Sis); Dora Whitaker (Tagalong); Richie Sanders (Toby Turtle); J. Pat O'Malley
(Otto); Candy Candido (Tournament Crocodile); Barbara Luddy (Mother
Rabbit); Beulah Bondi (Mother Church Mouse); John Fielder (Church
Mouse).
Running time: 83 minutes. DVD.

The Bawdy Adventures of Tom Jones (1975)
Nicky Henson (Tom Jones); Trevor Howard (Squire Western); Terry-Thomas
(Mr Square); Arthur Lowe (Dr Thwackum); Georgia Brown (Jenny Jones/Mrs
Waters); Joan Collins (Black Bess); William Mervyn (Squire Alworthy); Murray
Melvin (Blifil); Madeline Smith (Sophia); Geraldine McEwan (Lady
Bellaston); Jeremy Lloyd (Lord Fellemar); Jane Greenspun (Daisy); Michael
Bates (Madman); Hilda Fenemore (Mrs Belcher); Patricia MacPherson (Molly
Seagram); Isabel Dean (Bridget); James Hayter (Briggs); Frank Thornton
(Whitlow); Gladys Henson (Mrs Wilkins); Joan Cooper (Nellie); Maxine
Casson (Prudence); Judy Buxton (Lizzie); Arthur Howard (Old Vicar); John
Forrest (Captain Blifil); Arnold Diamond (Noisy Reveller); Claire Davenport
(Mrs Bakewell); Griffith Davies (Tilehurst); Christine Ozanne (Miss Skillett);
Tricia Newby (Betty); Eric Chitty (Sam); Roy Evans (Major Domo); Michael
Forbes Robertson, Susan Shaper (Coach Passengers); Angela Crow (Woman
Prisoner); Jeanne Collings, Penny Irving, Zena Clifton (Serving Wenches);
Patrick Westwood, Donald Bisset, Max Faulkner (Gentlemen of the Hunt);
Jean Gilpin (Lady at Ball); Colin Cunningham, Eric Longworth (Men at Ball);
Terence Seward (Bellaston's Footman); Maggy Maxwell, Patsy Smart,
Rosamund Greenwood (Village Gossips).
Running time: 94 minutes.

Side by Side (1975)
Barry Humphries (Rodney); Terry-Thomas (Max Nugget); Stephanie De Sykes
(Julia); Billy Boyle (Gary); Dave Mount (Flip); Frank Thornton (Inspector
Crumb); Jennifer Guy (Violet); Sheila Collings (Bessie); Geoffrey Sumner
(Magistrate); with Gerry Yates, Neil McCarthy, Maggie Wright, The Second
Generation, Mud, Kenny, The Rubettes, 'Fox' MOP, Joe Baker, Alan Rebbeck,
Michael Travers, Wilfrid Grove, Andre Cameron, Debbie Greenhill, Lauri
Lupino Lane.
Running time: 84 minutes.

Spanish Fly (1975)
Leslie Phillips (Mike Scott); Terry-Thomas (Sir Percy de Courcy); Graham

Armitage (Perkins); Nadiuska (Julie); Frank Thornton (Dr Johnson); Ramiro Oliveros (Juan); Sue Lloyd (Janet Scott); Andrea Allan (Bruce); Sally Farmiloe (Francesca); Jaleh Haddeh (Annette); Nina Francis (Isabel); Sergio Mendizabal (Pons Prades); Emiliano Redondo (Clean Domingo); Fernando Villena (Dirty Domingo); Marisa Porcel (Maria); Jose Luis Lifante (Pedro).
Running time: 86 minutes. DVD.

The Last Remake of Beau Geste (1977)
Marty Feldman (Digby Geste); Ann-Margret (Flavia Geste); Michael York (Beau Geste); Peter Ustinov (Markov); James Earl Jones (Sheik Abdul the Disgusting); Trevor Howard (Sir Hector Geste); Henry Gibson (General Pecheur); Terry-Thomas (Prison Governor); Roy Kinnear (Boldini); Spike Milligan (Grumble); Avery Schreiber (Camel Salesman); Hugh Griffith (Judge); Irene Handl (Miss Wormwood); Sinead Cusack (Isabel Geste); Ted Cassidy (Blind Man); Burt Kwouk (Father Shapiro); Henry Polic II (Captain Merdmanger); Val Pringle (Dostoevsky); Gwen Nelson (Woman in Courtroom); Philip Bolland (Young Beau, aged 6); Nicholas Bridge (Young Beau, aged 12); Michael McConkey (Young Digby, aged 12); Bekki Bridge (Young Isabel); Roland MacLeod (Dr Crippen); Martin Snaric (Valentine); Stephen Lewis (Henshaw); Ed McMahon (Arab Horseman); special guest star: Gary Cooper.
Running time: 85 minutes.

The Hound of the Baskervilles (1978)
Peter Cook (Sherlock Holmes); Dudley Moore (Dr Watson/Mrs Ada Holmes/ Mr Spiggott); Denholm Elliott (John Stapleton); Joan Greenwood (Beryl Stapleton); Hugh Griffith (Franklyn); Irene Handl (Mrs Barrymore); Terry-Thomas (Dr Mortimer); Max Wall (Arthur Barrymore); Kenneth Williams (Sir Henry Baskerville); Roy Kinnear (Seldon the Axe Murderer); Dana Gillespie (Mary); Lucy Griffiths (Medium's Assistant); Penelope Keith (Massage Parlour Receptionist); Jessie Matthews (Mrs Tinsdale); Prunella Scales (Glynis); Josephine Tewson (Nun); Mohammad Shamsi, Patsy Smart (Young Masseuses); Rita Webb (Elderly Masseuse); Henry Woolf (Post Office Clerk); Helena McCarthy (Enid); Geoffrey Moon (Perkins); Spike Milligan (Country Policeman); Anna Wing (Sausage and Mash Woman); Ava Cadell (Marsha the Maid); Mollie Maureen (Mrs Oviatt); Vivien Neves, Jacqui Stevens (Nuns); Sidney Johnson, Pearl Hackney (Rail Passengers).
Running time: 85 minutes. DVD.

The Mysterious House of Dr C (1978)
Walter Slezak (Dr Coppelius); Claudia Corday (Swanilda); Eileen Elliott (Brigitta); Caj Selling (Franz); Terry-Thomas (The Bull).
Running time: 88 minutes.

La Isla de las cabezas (1979)
Norman Briski, Lola Gaos, Jean-François Garreaud, Claudia Gravy, Piéral, Terry-Thomas.
Running time: 85 minutes.

Kingdom of Gifts (1978)
Voices of: Gemma Craven (The Unhappy Princess); Douglas Fairbanks Jnr (The Proud King); Peter Sellers (The Slightly Larcenous Mayor); Terry-Thomas (The Bumbling Chancellor).
Running time: 79 minutes.

Febbre a 40 (a.k.a. Happy Birthday, Harry, 1980)
John Richardson (Harry Petersen); Carole André (Patty); Marisa Mell (Linda Martin); Terry-Thomas (Dr Christopher); Leonora Fani (Sandy Temple); Gordon Mitchell (Sandy's Husband); Isarco Ravaioli (Robert); Marina Hedman (Rosalind); Margaret Rose Keil (Sylvia); Marina Daunia, Zaira Zuccheddu (Photo Shoot Models).
Running time: 79 minutes.

Albums

Solo

Strictly T-T (London LL 3292, 1958/Decca LK4398, 1961/London LP 5764, 1963)

> *Side one*
> 1. Bring Back the Cat
> 2. A 'Reasonable' Rhyme
> 3. Ram in a Jam
> 4. Mixed Bathing
> 5. Jo the Carrier Lad

6. Mishap in Mayfair/Baby, It's Cold Outside
7. The Vegetarian Beefeater

Side two

1. The Poy Friend
2. Amazing
3. Nouvelle Vague (or How Vague Can Some People Be?)
4. Send For Me
5. Mary Bella Crawfish Esq.

Terry-Thomas Discovers America (Warner Bros W1558, 1964)

Side one

1. It Could Have Been So Pleasant
2. Booking The Beatles
3. You Haven't Lived
4. Home Sweet Home
5. One of the Gang

Side two

1. The Ring Fell Under the Sofa
2. PTA Meeting
3. Hello Mater, Hello Pater
4. Joan of Arc and the Mouth Piece

As cast member

Jeeves (CAEDMON TC1137, 1958/Harper Audio 1559940042, 1989)

The Wonderful World of the Brothers Grimm (MGM 1E/SIE/E-3, 1962)

Three Billion Millionaires! (United Artists UXTL-4, 1963)

The Daydreamer (Columbia LP OL-6540/OS-2940, 1966)

Robin Hood (Buena Vista 3810, 1973)

Singles

(As 'Terry-Thomas, Esq., & His Rock 'n' Roll Rotters'/'R.S.M. Terry-Thomas and the Band of the W.R.E.C.S.'):
'A Sweet Old-Fashioned Boy'/'Lay Down Your Arms' (78rpm, Decca F10804, 1956)

(As Terry-Thomas):
'The Phantom Grenadier Strikes Again' (Produced and circulated privately by Terry-Thomas, 1959)

Notes

Prologue

1   Reginald Bosanquet, *Let's Get Through Wednesday* (London: New English Library, 1980), p. 148.
2   *Ibid.*, p. 146.
3   Reginald Bosanquet, 'Dance With Me' Pye Records (7P-167), 1980. The single came top of DJ Kenny Everett's 1980 Capital Radio poll to find 'The World's Worst Record'.
4   See Chris Welch and Lucian Randall, *Ginger Geezer: The Life of Vivian Stanshall* (London: Fourth Estate, 2001).
5   Terry-Thomas, *Terry-Thomas Tells Tales* (London: Robson, 1990), p. 62.
6   See F. Scott Fitzgerald, *The Great Gatsby* (Harmondsworth: Penguin, 1950), p. 95.
7   Terry-Thomas, *Filling the Gap* (London: Max Parrish, 1959), p. 22.
8   The motto, which was accompanied by an illustration of a rampant cow with a cigarette holder in its mouth, was used to decorate the cover and title page of his memoirs, as well as his calling cards and letterheads.
9   Jules Barbey D'Aurevilly, *Dandyism* (New York: P.A.J., 1988), p. 55.
10 *Filling the Gap*, p. 27.
11 *Terry-Thomas Tells Tales*, p. 2.
12 Dustin Hoffman made explicit the connection between his character and Terry-Thomas in most of the promotional interviews he gave at the time of *Hook*'s release (see also Roger Lewis, *The Life and Death of Peter Sellers* (London: Century, 1994), p. 449). In 2004, Rupert Everett explained the inspiration for his vocal approach to the animated *Shrek 2* villain: '[The character of Prince Charming] reminds me of, I don't know if you know of an actor called Terry-Thomas, an old English character actor. He was kind of vocally my role model while I was doing it. You know, that guy who's very brash up until the moment that someone frightens him and then he turns into a whiney, bratty, spoiled child. So Terry-Thomas was my role model, although the character doesn't look like Terry Thomas' (Fred Topel,

'Rupert Everett interview', About.com, 2004, p. 1, web page address: http://actionadventure.about.com/cs/weeklystories/a/aa051204_p.htm).

13 Vic Reeves, 'One-2-One' campaign, Chelsea Pictures, 1997.
14 London *Evening Standard*, 12 March 1999.
15 Propellerheads, 'Bang On!' released in 1998 (Wall of Sound, WALL D039).
16 John Dillon, 'Eubank: I'm Naz Advisor', *The Daily Mirror*, 11 December 1998, p. 55.

1 Hell-*o*!

1 Finchley – part of the London Borough of Barnet since 1965 – was a borough in its own right during the period when Terry-Thomas was living there.
2 *Filling the Gap*, p. 11.
3 *Terry-Thomas Tells Tales*, p. 2.
4 *Filling the Gap*, pp. 14–15; *Terry-Thomas Tells Tales*, p. 4.
5 *Terry-Thomas Tells Tales*, pp. 2, 4.
6 *Ibid.*, p. 4.
7 *Ibid.*, pp. 2–3.
8 *Ibid.*, p. 3.
9 *Filling the Gap*, p. 13.
10 *Terry-Thomas Tells Tales*, p. 3.
11 *Ibid.*
12 *Filling the Gap*, p. 13.
13 *Ibid.*
14 *Ibid.*, p. 11.
15 *Ibid.*, p. 14.
16 *Terry-Thomas Tells Tales*, p. 4.
17 *Ibid.*, p. 12.
18 *Ibid.*, p. 5.
19 *Ibid.*, p. 3.
20 *Ibid.*
21 Richard Briers, interview with the author, 8 November 2007.
22 *Filling the Gap*, p. 15.
23 *Terry-Thomas Tells Tales*, p. 8.
24 W.M. Thackeray's 'Little Billee' (see Carolyn Wells, ed., *A Nonsense*

Anthology, public domain text: available via Project Gutenberg) goes as follows:

> *There were three sailors of Bristol City*
> *Who took a boat and went to sea,*
> *But first with beef and captain's biscuits,*
> *And pickled pork they loaded she.*
>
> *There was a gorging Jack, and guzzling Jimmy,*
> *And the youngest he was little Billee.*
> *Now when they'd got as far as the Equator,*
> *They'd nothing left but one split pea.*
>
> *Says gorging Jack to guzzling Jimmy,*
> *'I am extremely hungaree.'*
> *To gorging Jack says guzzling Jimmy,*
> *'We've nothing left, us must eat we.'*
>
> *Says gorging Jack to guzzling Jimmy,*
> *'With one another we shouldn't agree!*
> *There's little Bill, he's young and tender,*
> *We're old and tough, so let's eat he.'*
>
> *'O Billy! We're going to kill and eat you,*
> *So undo the button of your chemie.'*
> *When Bill received this information,*
> *He used his pocket-handkerchief.*
>
> *'First let me say my catechism,*
> *Which my poor mother taught me.'*
> *'Make haste! make haste!' says guzzling Jimmy,*
> *While Jack pulled on his snicker-snee.*
>
> *Then Bill went up to the main-top-gallant-mast,*
> *And down he fell on his bended knee,*
> *He scarce had come to the Twelfth Commandment*
> *When up he jumps – 'There's land I see!*
>
> *'Jerusalem and Madagascar,*
> *And North and South Amerikee,*
> *There's the British flag a-riding at anchor,*
> *With Admiral Napier, K.C.B.'*

> *So when they got aboard of the Admiral's,*
> *He hanged fat Jack and flogged Jimmee,*
> *But as for little Bill, he made him*
> *The captain of a Seventy-three.*

Terry-Thomas would recall his distinctive performance of the ballad: 'When I got to the bit: "And down he fell on his bended knee," I introduced a frightfully clever bit of business. I fell down on mine' (*Filling the Gap*, p. 12).

25 *Filling the Gap*, p. 15.

26 *Ibid.*, p. 16.

27 *Ibid.*

28 *Ibid.*, pp. 16–17.

29 *Ibid.*, p. 14.

30 *Ibid.*

31 *Terry-Thomas Tells Tales*, p. 6.

32 *Ibid.*

33 *Ibid.*

34 *Ibid.*

35 See *Filling the Gap*, pp. 6–7.

36 *Terry-Thomas Tells Tales*, p. 6.

37 *Ibid.*, p.7.

38 *Filling the Gap*, p. 19.

39 *Ibid.*, p. 22.

40 *Terry-Thomas Tells Tales*, p. 8.

41 *Ibid.*

42 *Ibid.*

43 *Filling the Gap*, pp. 24–6.

44 *Ibid.*, p. 24.

45 *Terry-Thomas Tells Tales*, p. 9.

46 Richard Briers, interview with the author, 8 November 2007.

47 *Terry-Thomas Tells Tales.*, p. 10.

48 *Ibid.*

49 Richard Briers, interview with the author, 8 November 2007

50 *Terry-Thomas Tells Tales*, p. 10.

51 *Ibid.*, p. 11.

52 *Filling the Gap*, p. 29.

53 *Ibid.*, pp. 29–30.

54 The voice of the cow was for the 1938 Jessie Matthews movie *Climbing High*.

55 *Terry-Thomas Tells Tales*, p. 12.

56 *Sam Goes Shopping* was released in 1939, and *For Freedom* followed in 1940.

57 *Terry-Thomas Tells Tales*, p. 57.

58 *Ibid.*

59 *Filling the Gap*, p. 35.

60 *Ibid.*, p. 34.

61 *Terry-Thomas Tells Tales*, p. 13.

62 Official documents in the UK, including a marriage certificate, spell the maiden name of Terry-Thomas's first wife 'Patlansky', but both she and he always spelled it 'Patlanski'.

63 *Terry-Thomas Tells Tales*, p. 14.

64 *Ibid.*, p. 14.

65 *Ibid.*

66 Her most recent husband had been Ernest Stern.

67 *Terry-Thomas Tells Tales*, p. 16. The marriage of Thomas Terry Hoar Stevens to Ida Florence Stern (née Patlansky) took place in the first quarter of 1938, on 3 February, at Marylebone, as recorded in volume 1a, page 1003 of the official register.

68 *Ibid.*, p. 18.

69 *Ibid.*, p. 19.

70 He recalled one such pre-war 'striptease auction' in an interview with *Answers* magazine (3 July 1954, p. 7): 'It was a tricky job. I was compering the show and at one stage I had to auction a girl's clothes. Of course, she was warned that she must not take off the ... er ... ultimate garment until the lights were doused. But she was Spanish ... impetuous ... warm-blooded and all that, and on one terrible night she took off the lot before the stage manager could do his stuff with the lights. I had visions of us all appearing in court, but we were lucky.'

71 *Terry-Thomas Tells Tales*, p. 18.

72 *Ibid.*, p. 19.

73 *Ibid.*

74 *Ibid.*, p. 20.

75 *Ibid.*, p. 21.

76 *Ibid.*, p. 22.

77 *Ibid.*, pp. 22–3.

78 *Ibid.*, p. 23.

2 I Say!

1 I am grateful to Richard Hope-Hawkins for allowing me to consult Terry-Thomas's Soldier's Service and Pay Book, in which this date is recorded.

2 *Filling the Gap*, p. 43; *Terry-Thomas Tells Tales*, p. 22.

3 *Terry-Thomas Tells Tales*, p. 22.

4 *Filling the Gap*, p. 43.

5 *Terry-Thomas Tells Tales*, p. 23.

6 *Ibid.*

7 *Filling the Gap*, pp. 48–9.

8 *Ibid.*, p. 45.

9 See John Graven Hughes, *The Greasepaint War* (London: New English Library, 1976), p. 124.

10 The decision was made on 19 October 1942.

11 Hughes, *The Greasepaint War*, p. 124.

12 The inspiration for the 'Technical Hitch' sketch dated back to 15 October 1940. The London Blitz had started on 7 September, and five weeks later the BBC's Broadcasting House took its first hit. A delayed action bomb crashed through a window on the seventh floor, and came to rest two levels down in the music library. Moments later, as teams of firemen rushed to the scene, it exploded, killing seven people. Bruce Belfrage was reading the news on air at the time, and his microphone picked up the sound of the blast. Belfrage, although shaken and covered in dust and soot, read on regardless.

13 Terry-Thomas, quoted by Richard Fawkes, *Fighting for a Laugh* (London: Macdonald and Jane's, 1978), p. 45.

14 See *Terry-Thomas Tells Tales*, pp. 24–5.

15 The routine was not, strictly speaking, original, as (although Thomas himself seemed unaware of the fact) similarly themed sketches had been performed before by the comedians Leslie Strong and Eric Barker.

16 *Terry-Thomas Tells Tales*, p. 25.

17 T-T was promoted to the rank of sergeant on 4 September 1944.

18 Basil Brown, quoted by Fawkes, *Fighting for a Laugh*, p. 45. According to the actor Lionel Jeffries, who later became a good friend, there was one particular occasion when, even by T-T's usual standards, his sheer audacity was truly astounding: 'He told me that, in order to make a few bob, he dressed up as a captain, and he got a friend of his to be his batman, and they purloined an Army lorry, and they purloined a large consignment of very good quality carpets from the American PX [Postal Exchange] in France

after the occupation, and resold them to the Officers' Mess back with the British!' (speaking on an edition of the Channel 4 series *Heroes of Comedy*, first broadcast on 17 November 1995).

19 *Filling the Gap*, p. 28.

20 Terry-Thomas, quoted by Susan d'Arcy, 'Terribly, Terribly Terry-Thomas', *Films Illustrated*, vol. 6, no. 61, September 1976, pp. 32–3.

21 An unnamed Army sergeant, quoted in *Filling the Gap*, p. 50.

22 See Richard Stone's memoir, *You Should Have Been In Last Night* (Lewes: The Book Guild, 2000), p. 56.

23 The actual puppet Basil Brush was co-designed by Ivan Owen and the very influential illustrator and animator Peter Firmin.

24 Terry-Thomas, quoted by Hughes, *The Greasepaint War*, p. 166.

25 *Terry-Thomas Tells Tales*, pp. 25–6.

26 *Ibid.*, p. 26.

27 Philip Hindin, *The Call Boy*, vol. 38, no. 1, Spring 2000, p. 18.

28 The earliest communication sent by Jack Adams about Terry Thomas and preserved in the BBC Written Archives is a brief letter dated 26 February 1946 to a 'Miss Cotter' (presumably a booker), informing her of Thomas's imminent availability and recommending him for new and current shows (BBC WAC: Terry-Thomas Artist's File I: 1938–50).

29 At least two memos (dated 7 and 12 March 1946) were circulated within the BBC about Spear's interest in Thomas's proposal; although others were not persuaded by the appeal of the idea, Spear was allowed to proceed. The project, however, did not progress much further. (Source: BBC WAC: Terry-Thomas Artist's File I: 1938–50.)

30 Terry-Thomas, quoted by Frank Muir in *A Kentish Lad* (London: Transworld, 1997), p. 114.

31 Letter from Jack Adams to a Miss Piggott, 26 April 1946, and letter from L.M. Barry to Arthur Brown on 30 April 1946 (BBC WAC: Terry-Thomas Artist's File I: 1938–50).

32 J.B. Priestley, 'Sid Field', *Particular Pleasures* (New York: Stein and Day, 1975), p. 162.

33 Arthur Askey, *Before Your Very Eyes* (London: Woburn Press, 1975), p. 143.

34 See, for example, *The Times*, 19 March 1943, p. 6 and 12 October 1946, p. 6. An excellent critical essay on Sid Field, written in the 1950s, is included in Kenneth Tynan's *Profiles* (London: Nick Hern Books, 1989), pp. 12–15.

35 'King John', written by Frederick Burtwell and reproduced in John Fisher's now out-of-print *Sid Field* (London: Seely, Service, 1975), p. 156.

36 *Terry-Thomas Tells Tales*, p. 74.

37 *Ibid.*, p. 26.

38 *Filling the Gap*, p. 55.
39 He bought the property for what was then the bargain price of £1800 –
    equivalent to about £45,000 by today's rates.
40 *Filling the Gap*, pp. 55, 59.
41 T-T's measurements (according to the records kept by Maxwell Vine in
    Mayfair) were as follows:

Chest	42½″
Waist	37½″
Seat	45″
Neck to waist	18½″
Jacket length	31″
Half back	9¼″
Sleeve length	32½″
Inside leg	32½″
Outside leg	45″
Width of shoulder	6⅝″
Hat size	7¼″
Shoes	11 (English)
	12 (American)
Collar (outside)	16½″.

42 Years later, the actor Peter Jones, who worked with T-T on the movie
    Private's Progress (playing a character called Arthur Egan), actually saw the
    bespoke underpants when the two men were changing costumes between
    scenes:

> I never really knew Terry-Thomas and we had very little to do together in
> *Private's Progress*. But we did once share a dressing room in the wardrobe
> department, and while we were having our uniforms adjusted I noticed
> his striking vests and pants. They were pale blue with white piping round
> the edges – 'binding' is probably the correct word. Anyway, they were
> unusual enough for me to comment on them and Terry told me he had
> them made to measure. He is the only man I have known to wear custom-
> made underwear. But it established him as a man of some style.

(I am very grateful to the comedy historian Glyn Roberts for allowing me to
reproduce this quotation from an interview he conducted with Peter Jones
in the early 1990s.)
43 *Filling the Gap*, p. 23.
44 Other founder members included the actors Jon Pertwee and Peter
    Cushing, and T-T's fellow Old Ardinian, the racing driver Mike Hawthorn.

45 *Terry-Thomas Tells Tales*, p. 31.

46 *Filling the Gap*, p. 27.

47 *Terry-Thomas Tells Tales*, p. 31.

48 *Ibid.*, p. 58.

49 Interviewed by Jack Lewis, 'Terry-Thomas Takes It Lying Down', *Reynolds News*, 15 November 1959, p. 11.

50 *Terry-Thomas Tells Tales*, p. 33.

51 Reported in *The Times*, 11 May 1960, p. 8.

52 Reported in *The Times*, 21 April 1960, p. 8.

53 Reported in the *Daily Telegraph*, 21 April 1960, p. 12.

54 *Filling the Gap*, p. 57.

55 *Ibid.*, p. 110.

56 *Ibid.*

57 *Terry-Thomas Tells Tales*, p. 28.

58 See 'The Broadcaster', *Radio Times*, 8 October 1948, p. 5.

59 *Filling the Gap*, p. 136.

60 *Ibid.*, p. 53.

61 *Ibid.*, p. 35. (No documentation appears to exist that clarifies the matter, but it should be noted here that Terry-Thomas's agent at the time, Phyllis Rounce, later claimed that *she* had been the one who came up with the idea of using the hyphen in his name: see Cliff Goodwin, *When the Wind Changed: The Life and Death of Tony Hancock* (London: Century, 1999), p. 77.)

62 Letter from Phyllis Rounce, on behalf of International Artistes, to the BBC, dated 28 April 1948 (BBC WAC: Terry-Thomas Artist's File I: 1938–50).

3 T-T on TV

1 Source: Post Office/National Television Licence Records Office.

2 There was also a significant change in the kind of personnel who were running BBC TV. As the actor Richard Bebb – who appeared on both radio and television during this period – recalled, with only slight exaggeration, for Kate Dunn in her *Do Not Adjust Your Set: The Early Days of Live Television* (London: John Murray, 2003; pp. 57–8): 'In 1950, the whole of [British] television was run from Broadcasting House by people who hated television. Every administrative job – [such as] head of drama, head of

variety – was filled by people from Broadcasting House. They wanted to keep their hands on television and to starve it.' A year or so later, however, things had changed: 'there was a complete palace revolution and everyone from Broadcasting House was thrown out and the major jobs were offered to television people'.

3 'The Broadcaster', *Radio Times*, 8 October 1948, p. 5.

4 *Filling the Gap*, p. 129.

5 His debut appearance was broadcast live on 11 October 1947. He had turned down the chance to contribute a similar spot the year earlier due to other, more pressing commitments.

6 Cecil Madden to Michael Mills, 15 February 1949 (BBC WAC: Terry-Thomas TV Art 1: 1946–55, File 1).

7 See my *Dad's Army: The Story of a Classic Television Show* (London: Fourth Estate, 2001), pp. 41–3.

8 Michael Mills to Cecil Madden, 16 February 1949 (BBC WAC: Terry-Thomas TV Art 1: 1946–55, File 1).

9 Terry-Thomas, quoted by Wilfred Greatorex, 'Terry-Thomas – Specialist in Fine-Grain Comedy', *Radio Times*, 14 September 1951, p. 47.

10 BBC WAC: Terry-Thomas Artist's File II: 1951–4.

11 Peter Black, *The Biggest Aspidistra in the World* (London: BBC, 1972), p. 155.

12 Hal Burton, an early BBC TV drama producer, quoted in Denis Norden et al., *Coming To You Live!* (London: Methuen, 1985), p. 3.

13 *Filling the Gap*, p. 139.

14 *Ibid.*, p. 140. Bill Ward would tell Glyn Roberts in an unpublished interview recorded on 11 February 1994,: 'Terry and Walton didn't hit it off at all. In fact, to put it mildly, Terry hated his guts. He had no faith in his ability.' (Reproduced here with Glyn Roberts' kind permission.)

15 Terry-Thomas, 'Meet T-T, TV's First Star', *Answers*, 6 October 1951, p. 13.

16 Terry-Thomas to Walton Anderson, sent from the Prince's Hotel in Folkestone, on 28 September 1949 (BBC WAC: Terry-Thomas TV Art 1: 1946–55, File 1).

17 *Filling the Gap*, p. 140.

18 Bill Ward, interviewed by Glyn Roberts, 11 February 1994.

19 *Ibid.*

20 Terry-Thomas and Pat Patlanski set off from Avonmouth on the SS *Bayano* and arrived in Kingston, Jamaica, on 5 March 1950; they returned to England on 15 March (source: list of passengers, ref. PRO/BT26/1257/1438, Public Records Office).

21 Bill Ward, interviewed by Glyn Roberts, 11 February 1994.

22 Avril Angers, one of T-T's fellow cast members, would recall: 'He was the
    first television personality to use a stand-in. At rehearsal, he used to go up
    into the control room, and he had a stand-in who used to do his part in the
    show so he could see how it looked. Which I thought was brilliant and very
    sensible' (unpublished interview by Glyn Roberts, 10 February 1994,
    reproduced here with his permission).

23 *Filling the Gap*, p. 145. Terry-Thomas wrote to Pat Hillyard, the BBC's
    Assistant Head of Variety, on 12 April 1950 complaining about the 'nuisance'
    of performing in front of a live studio audience, explaining that it sometimes
    'ruined my timing' and arguing that it was best to do without any audience
    in future (BBC WAC: Terry-Thomas TV Art 1: 1946–55, File 1). In *Terry-
    Thomas Tells Tales* (p. 29), he added: 'I did not want the home viewers'
    enjoyment spoilt by controlled laughter in the studio. I knew I was able to
    time my delivery to allow for the people sitting at home to have their chortle
    without missing the next joke. While most comedians found it impossible to
    be funny without an audience to play to, I was adamant that we had no
    need of one.'

24 Norman Collins, letter to Terry-Thomas, 19 May 1950 (BBC WAC: Terry-
    Thomas TV Art 1: 1946–55, File 1).

25 *Terry-Thomas Tells Tales*, p. 30.

26 'Meet T-T, TV's First Star', *Answers*, 6 October 1951, p. 13.

27 Sarah Miles, correspondence with the author, 17 February 2008.

28 *Terry-Thomas Tells Tales*, p. 30.

29 Ronald Waldman, 'Creating Light Entertainment in Television', *Radio
    Times*, 23 February 1951, p. 46.

30 Greatorex, 'Terry-Thomas – Specialist in Fine-Grain Comedy'.

31 The first recorded reference to *The Hammetts* is a programme suggestion
    from Neil Munro, dated 22 February 1950. Munro then wrote to Michael
    Standing, the Head of Radio Variety, on 2 May 1950 notifying him that both
    Terry-Thomas and Ethel Revnell were interested in the project, which
    could be put into production by October of that year with an estimated
    budget of £250. Neither Standing nor his assistant, however, was prepared to
    pursue the idea, as they had doubts as to whether the two co-stars would 'hit
    it off' and were also unconvinced about Munro's suitability (BBC WAC:
    Terry-Thomas Artist's File I: 1938–50).

32 BBC WAC: Terry-Thomas Artist's File II: 1951–4.

33 See, for example, 'Meet T-T, TV's First Star', *Answers*, 6 October 1951, p. 13.

34 *Terry-Thomas Tells Tales*, p. 56.

35 Terry-Thomas, 'The Camera Doesn't Do Me Justice', *Radio Times*,
    6 January 1956, p. 9.

36 *Filling the Gap*, p. 99.

37 Janet Brown, quoted by Robert Ross, *The Complete Terry-Thomas* (London: Reynolds & Hearn, 2002), p. 60. In her autobiography – *Prime Mimicker* (London: New English Library, 1987), p. 79 – she added: 'I never knew him take a laugh line from anybody. If it was funny, it was good for the show.'

38 Georgina Cookson, speaking to Glyn Roberts in the early 1990s (and reproduced here with his kind permission).

39 Ronald Waldman, letter to BBC TV's Controller of Programmes, dated 2 October 1952. His colleague replied, later the same day, assuring Waldman that he agreed and was 'here to help you' (BBC WAC: Terry-Thomas Artist's File II: 1951–4).

40 See June Whitfield, *… and June Whitfield* (London: Corgi, 2001), p. 168.

41 Pat Patlanski was now living in an apartment T-T was renting for her at 7a Clareville Grove in Chelsea.

42 *Terry-Thomas Tells Tales*, pp. 36–7.

43 *Top of the Town* – a *Variety Bandbox*-style showcase – ran for two series (the first from 1 November 1953 to 21 February 1954, the second from 31 October 1954 to 27 February 1955) on the BBC's Light Programme. It only reached the airwaves, however, after a protracted period of haggling by T-T's agent for a satisfactory fee from the BBC. On 21 July 1953, for example, an obviously exasperated Bookings Manager, Pat Newman, wrote an admonishing letter to Terry-Thomas ('What a fellow you are …!'), complaining about the delays and reminding him of the 'good' old days 'when the unfortunate guinea-a-day bloke was not in a position to go on strike as it seems he can in the year 1953!' Newman added that the BBC was a 'jolly decent firm all round' and urged him to reach an agreement to make the series. Eventually a deal was indeed struck, with T-T receiving a fee of 75 guineas per programme (BBC WAC: Terry-Thomas Artist's File II: 1951–4).

44 Among these theatres was Leeds Empire, where one of T-T's future scriptwriters, Barry Cryer, went to see him while still a student at Leeds University: 'I had evolved a routine of dropping in a note to stars at the stage door on the Monday and hoping for a reply. Terry was unable to see me, but made a reference to the university when he was on stage. He received an appreciative noise from our gang in the gallery. "*I* was at Leeds University," he said, "and it was a lovely day out"' (letter to the author, 29 January 2008).

45 The 78rpm single (see List of Performances for more details) featured the military-style spoof 'Lay Down Your Arms' on the other side, credited to 'R.S.M. Terry-Thomas and the Band of the W.R.E.C.S.' It was released in 1956.

46 Terry-Thomas, quoted by Gerald Scheff, 'The Private Dreams of Terry-Thomas', *TV Times*, 27 May–2 June 1956, p. 6.

47 *Terry-Thomas Tells Tales*, pp. 88–9.

48 *The Times* (26 May 1960, p. 6), for example, judged *It's in the Bag* 'an unfunny and rather tasteless contrivance' that placed too much of a burden on the shoulders of its star: 'The actor finds himself in the position of giving a music hall turn which goes on too long. Again and again he registers shock in exactly the same way. He is not resourceful enough to give his predicaments a genuine momentum of their own. He is at his best when life becomes altogether too much for him and he enters into a comic nervous breakdown.'

49 Richard Briers, interview with the author, 8 November 2007.

50 According to Terry-Thomas's own account of the show (*Filling the Gap*, p. 76):

> I should explain that one of those good-looking fillies with legs right up to the top paraded before the audience with a card on which was written the challenger's wildest dream. We, on the panel, had to guess what it was … We used to telefilm three of these programmes in an afternoon, during which we smoked ourselves silly, and drank endless glasses of water supplied free by Granada … Tommy Trinder, I remember, always insisted upon having the last word and, with the help of his oxy-acetylene voice, usually got it.

51 *Terry-Thomas Tells Tales*, p. 77.

52 *Ibid.*

53 See, for example, *The Times*, 20 February 1956, p. 7. Bill Ward would confirm to Glyn Roberts (11 February 1994): 'There was no doubt as to where Terry was heading. Films were clearly his big ambition.'

4 Hollywood

1 Dick Richards, *Answers*, 10 July 1954, p. 7.

2 *Filling the Gap*, p. 6.

3 *Terry-Thomas Tells Tales*, p. 58.

4 *Ibid.*, p. 119.

5 *Ibid.*, pp. 37–8. Terry-Thomas would appear on *The Toast of the Town* (the forerunner of *The Ed Sullivan Show)* on 25 March 1951.

6 See my *Morecambe & Wise* (London: Fourth Estate, 1998), p. 157.

7 See *Filling the Gap*, p. 146.

8 John Redway was a casting director at the Associated British Picture Corporation before becoming an independent theatrical agent in 1953. He went on to form a partnership with his fellow agent Dennis Selinger, and both Terry-Thomas and Peter Sellers were among the first artists on their books.

9 See *Terry-Thomas Tells Tales*, p. 90.

10 Ian Carmichael, quoted by Ross, *The Complete Terry-Thomas*, p. 93.

11 *Terry-Thomas Tells Tales*, p. 91.

12 Another characterisation inspired by Sid Field's spiv 'Slasher Green' would be James Beck's portrayal of Private Joe Walker in *Dad's Army.*

13 *Films and Filming*, November 1957, p. 26.

14 *Terry-Thomas Tells Tales*, p. 92.

15 Jean Anderson, interviewed by Glyn Roberts in the early 1990s (reproduced here with his kind permission).

16 Kingsley Amis, *Memoirs* (London: Hutchinson, 1991), p. 177.

17 *Ibid.*

18 *Ibid.*, p. 178.

19 *Ibid.*

20 *Ibid.*

21 *Terry-Thomas Tells Tales*, p. 38.

22 *Ibid.*, p. 52.

23 *Ibid.*, pp. 52–3.

24 *Ibid.*, p. 48.

25 *Ibid.*

26 *Ibid.*, p. 55. Terry-Thomas said of his long-term relationship with Lorrae Desmond: 'I don't know if I was Lorrae's only fellow; I have a feeling I was. But I had other girl-friends. It is quite extraordinary when I think how many there were.'

27 *Ibid.*, p. 53. T-T's friend and former co-star, Avril Angers, would tell Glyn Roberts in their unpublished interview on 10 February 1994 that Pat Patlanski had once confided in her about Lorrae Desmond: 'I wouldn't let him marry *her* – she wasn't right for him.'

28 *Ibid.*, p. 54.

29 *Ibid.*

30 Peter Sellers, quoted by Lewis, *The Life and Death of Peter Sellers*, p. 568.

31 *Films and Filming*, January 1958, p. 24.

32 *Terry-Thomas Tells Tales*, p. 93.
33 *Ibid.*, p. 92.
34 *Ibid.*, p. 94.
35 Terry-Thomas claimed in *Filling the Gap* (p. 150) that he was arrested on
Friday, 2 December 1957; apart from the fact that 2 December fell on a
Monday in 1957, the newspaper reports of the time clearly state that the
arrest came on Monday 23 December 1957.
36 Ian Carmichael recalled one such incident for John Fisher's Channel 4
Heroes of Comedy tribute to T-T (first broadcast on 17 November 1995):

> I don't think he took authority very gladly. There was an occasion in
> *School for Scoundrels* when we were on location in Hendon. It was a
> beautiful summer's day. And Terry had a blue drophead Jaguar at the
> time, and the hood was down, and he'd parked it on a kerb in the residen-
> tial part of Hendon where obviously he shouldn't have parked it. We were
> standing by talking, and I suddenly saw two policemen coming along the
> other side of the street, and they were just going to cross over and talk to
> us. And I realised that what they were going to say was, 'What are you
> doing parked here – you're not allowed to park here.' And Terry had on
> the back seat of the car a toy Thompson sub-machine gun which you
> loaded with ping-pong balls. And he let these officers get within spitting
> distance of him – 'Oh, good *morning*, officers!' he said – and then, when
> they were within range, he suddenly bent down, picked this toy Thomp-
> son machine gun up from the back of the car and fired a whole volley, a
> burst, of these ping-pong balls at the policemen. And I've never seen two
> rozzers hit the deck so fast in all my life!

37 See *The Times*, 27 December, 1957, p. 4.
38 *Filling the Gap*, p. 152.
39 See *The Times*, 17 January 1958, p. 5.
40 *Filling the Gap*, p. 152.
41 *Ibid.*, p. 154.
42 See *The Times*, 15 March 1958, p. 4.
43 See *The Times*, 17 January 1958, p. 5.
44 *Terry-Thomas Tells Tales*, p. 49. (See also *The Times*, 27 December 1957,
p. 4 and 15 March 1958, p. 4. He celebrated winning the case with a lavish
dinner at a Berkeley Square night club, where, for the benefit of the press,
he bit the heads off three marzipan policemen before toasting everyone with
champagne and brandy: see the *Daily Sketch*, 15 March 1958, p. 7.)
45 *Ibid.*, p. 93.
46 *Filling the Gap*, p. 61.

47 Born in Trani, southern Italy, in 1892 and brought up in Rome, Filippo del
    Giudice worked as a lawyer for, among others, the Vatican before fleeing
    from the Fascists in 1933 and moving to England, where, in partnership with
    the film-maker Mario Zampi, he founded the production company Two
    Cities. After surrendering control to the Rank Organisation, he resigned in
    1947 and established a new company, Pilgrim Pictures. Three movies were
    made – the Boulting Brothers' *The Guinea Pig* (1948), Peter Ustinov's
    Private Angelo (1949) and Bernard Miles' *Chance of a Lifetime* (1950) – but
    none were box-office successes and it proved too much of a struggle to raise
    further finance. Del Giudice returned to Italy in 1950, and, although he
    made a number of dubious attempts to resume his involvement in the
    movie industry, he never produced another project, dying in Florence on
    New Year's Eve, 1962. When Peter Sellers was struggling to 'get' the
    character of the Levantine prime minister in *Carlton-Browne of the F.O.*,
    Roy Boulting stepped in: 'As well as I could, I gave Peter my impression of
    Del [Giudice] and, within two minutes, on the sidewalk, he proceeded to
    improvise dialogue and put on an act as a man he'd never seen which was
    more "Del" than himself' (quoted by Alexander Walker, *Peter Sellers*
    (London: Macmillan, 1981), p. 99).

48 Ian Bannen, who played the character of the young King Loris, later told
    Glyn Roberts what it was like to work with T-T:

> Clearly from the start this was a very amusing man – much larger than life
> – an anecdote took over quarter of an hour – studded with laughter –
> totally exhausting to spend a quiet afternoon with – one was sick with
> laughter. Acting with him was even more exhausting – one was con-
> fronted by this face whose eyes would disappear above and under the
> eyelids leaving only the whites to contemplate and the ridiculous mouth,
> teeth, moustache and outsize vowels. Giggling was an ever-present danger
> both for you and him.

49 *The Times* (9 March 1959, p. 5), for example, remarked that Terry-Thomas
    'shows something like genius in converting a vacant stare into the
    semblance of a stiff upper lip'.

50 A.H. Weiler, *New York Times*, 15 June 1960, p. 50.

51 See Arthur Marwick, *British Society Since 1945* (Harmondsworth: Penguin,
    1982), p. 165.

52 Roy Boulting, interviewed in Brian McFarlane's *An Autobiography of
    British Cinema* (London: Methuen, 1997), p. 79.

53 *Daily Telegraph*, 15 August 1960, p. 7. (£4000 in 1960 was equivalent to
    about £160,000 by today's rates.)

54 Bosley Crowther, *New York Times*, 1 May 1960, p. X1; 25 December 1960, p. X3.

55 Stanley Kauffman, *A World On Film* (New York: Delta, 1966), p. 52.

56 Ian Carmichael, interviewed by Clyde Jeavons at the National Film Theatre, 8 December 2002 (transcript published on the web site: http://www.bfi.org.uk/features/interviews/carmichael.html).

57 Ian Carmichael recalled: 'When I came to do the tennis match … it wasn't scripted at all. [The director Robert Hamer] said just carry on playing and I'll photograph it and I'll cut it up later. That was a bit too loose in style for me.' Quoted by Geoffrey McNab, 'Ealing Tragedy', *Independent*, 12 March 2004.

58 *Films and Filming*, May 1960, p. 23.

59 *Make Mine Mink* was a movie about a group of misfits who, almost by accident, begin a spree of stealing fur coats, 'redistributing' the profits to deserving causes. In one memorable scene Terry-Thomas, as the gang's supposed organiser, Major Rayne, enters what he takes to be a seedy-looking pub and attempts to find a 'fence' for his gang's stash of stolen goodies:

> RAYNE: Interested?
> MAN: What in?
> RAYNE: … Fencing.
> MAN: What – swords and suchlike?
> [*A waiter arrives with a coffee. Rayne thinks the man has reacted to the threat of eavesdropping*]
> RAYNE: That was quick thinking – I didn't see him coming – congratters! [*Glances nervously from one side to the other*] I'm interested in a … fence.
> MAN: Buying or selling?
> RAYNE: Selling, naturally. Well …?
> MAN: You're wasting your time, mate. Nobody round here's got a garden!

60 John P. Shanley, 'On Television Tomorrow – Terry-Thomas', *New York Times*, 10 December 1961, p. X21.

61 Although I cannot cite an official source for this, I have had it confirmed by several reliable sources involved in various aspects of the 1961 production, as well as by the British producer Sydney Rose, who recalled (22 May 2006) being told of the offer by Terry-Thomas himself shortly before he decided to turn it down.

62 *Terry-Thomas Tells Tales*, p. 56.

63 *Ibid.*, p. 122.

64 Ian Carmichael had turned down the role that Terry-Thomas ended up being offered. Carmichael had received part of the script shortly before setting off on a long-awaited family holiday in the South of France, and was not in a receptive mood. A second section was sent to him during his first week away, with an invitation to fly to Los Angeles forty-eight hours later if he wished to participate. Unimpressed with the writing and disinclined to cut short his vacation, Carmichael declined. T-T was the next choice on the list.

65 *Terry-Thomas Tells Tales*, pp. 119–20. (Although Terry-Thomas spelt the surname as 'Gerts', it was in fact spelt 'Gertz'.)

66 *Ibid.*

67 Previously, Terry-Thomas had used either Phyllis Rounce or Thelma Wade as his agent for most of his major stage, radio, TV or movie projects, but he was coming to the end of such long-term relationships. So stung was he by the Gertz episode that he would never bother having another regular agent for the rest of his career, preferring instead to negotiate contracts either on his own or with the help of his occasional business associate and solicitor, Clive Nicholas.

68 *Terry-Thomas Tells Tales*, pp. 121, 123, 125–6.

69 *Ibid.*, p. 121.

70 *Ibid.*, p. 126.

71 See Sheridan Morley, *Tales from the Hollywood Raj: The British Film Colony On Screen and Off* (London: Weidenfeld & Nicolson, 1983).

72 *Terry-Thomas Tells Tales*, pp. 134–5.

73 *Kill or Cure* is worth watching for the delightful double-act that Terry-Thomas formed with Eric Sykes. T-T starred as the slightly seedy Captain J. Barker-Rynde (the 'J' being an abbreviation of 'Jeroboam' – 'I was weaned on champagne'), 'a fully paid-up member of the Private Detectives' Association'; Sykes appeared as the stuffy health clinic consultant, Mr Rumbelow. First suspecting each other of being a poisoner, the pair eventually join forces to track down the real murderer who is lurking somewhere in the grounds of the health farm. The movie also featured Moira Redmond (playing Frances Roitman, the attractive young secretary of an elderly guest called Mrs Clifford), who later told Glyn Roberts of her memories of working with T-T on the project:

> First impressions were unfortunate. I met him originally in a drinking/gambling private club in Sloane Street called, I believe, 'The Village'. We got into a conversation and he gave his opinion of the film *The Hustler* as being 'rubbish', and I said I thought it was a very fine film indeed. He

flew into an extraordinary rage with swearing, abuse and obscenity which left a deeply dismayed impression. I was naïve enough not to realise that he was very drunk. Later, when I found I was going to make a film with him, I was somewhat worried!

But don't you worry. It gets better as we continue – but there are still some obstacles to overcome!

I sat on the tube reading the script I was about to do with Terry and Eric Sykes. Eric I had worked with before – and I was very fond of him, so he would protect me from that horrid man! It was a marvellous script, very funny, and I cast them in the parts they should have been playing, as I thought. Unfortunately they were, I discovered later, cast the wrong way round. Which is why the film flopped, I believe.

The first day of filming, I came down on to the set to show the director various outfits that had been designed for me. The two comics looked at me and Terry said, 'Why have they made you look like a lesbian?' (Lesbians were not as yet in fashion, nor indeed, the androgynous look.) I was, of course, mortified. But, when we started to rehearse, often Eric had said how nice I looked. Although the two actors were of equal excellence, in my eyes Eric deferred a great deal to Terry, who deferred to no one. But gradually, as the day progressed, I was aware of the fact that he greatly admired Eric. We had a mutual appreciation situation. And gradually Terry became human and enchanting and funny and loving and lovable. I will never know if he ever remembered our 'row' at 'The Village'. I have to admit I rather fell for him! And the two of them were a great team, and worked together wonderfully.

74 The cameo role – although far from being one of the best of his career – won Terry-Thomas his sole nomination for a Golden Globe.

75 These short travelogues were filmed during 1961–2, and produced by Thomkins Productions Ltd (the short-lived production company that Terry-Thomas had set up with his friend Douglas Rankin – he had previously established, on 9 March 1954, the more durable Terry-Thomas Films Limited with his co-director Clive Nicholas). The best of the three was, without doubt, the first – *Terry-Thomas in Tuscany* – even though, by his own admission (*Terry-Thomas Tells Tales*, pp. 65–6), not all of the footage was actually shot in Italy:

I couldn't get away from London [for one particular scene], so we decided to do it on Hampstead Heath.... I found the first assistant and he set up a scene outside a restaurant where people were eating. We hung a few bottles of Chianti around for the authentic Italian touch and photographed it in the beautiful pink rays of the setting sun. It turned out as good as anything in the film. I bet more than one person felt nostalgic for Pisa when they saw our dastardly clever bits done on Hampstead Heath.

He did manage, however, to travel to Italy to film the rest of the twenty-minute short, meeting, among others, the artist Pietro Annigoni and the designer Emilio Pucci. Neither the second nor the third film was up to the same standard: the South of France travelogue was mainly shot on the Ile de Levant – a nudist island whose nudists T-T found 'a pretty unhealthy, shapeless and uninspiring lot'; the Northern Ireland short mainly featured little more than 'a lot of drunks'. The series, which Terry-Thomas had hoped would run for two or three more episodes, thus came to an abrupt halt, and the production company folded.

76 The tracks on *Strictly T-T* included the weird and wonderful self-penned monologue 'Bring Back the Cat' – about a Cockney he encounters in a pub, The Old Cow and Crumpet ('Plenty of old cows, but not much …'), and his prodigiously gifted piano-playing pussy ('He did knock out a very amusing little tune. And I said to the fellow, "What a wonderful cat!" I said, "And this lovely tune that it's playing – what is it?" He said, "I don't know. He writes all his own music." I said, "No, no, no, you're pulling my paw!" He said, "No, honest – he writes every note." I said, "But that's the most *beautiful* tune. It's a *lovely* tune. Why don't you get it orchestrated?" Do you know, that cat was out of the room before you could say …'); some of T-T's and Sid Colin's old TV routines (including the 'Vegetarian Beefeater' sketch they had written specially for the Queen's visit to the BBC studios); another delightful tall story called 'The Poy Friend'; and a predictably T-T version of 'Baby, It's Cold Outside'. His sleeve notes urged listeners to 'give the servants the day off, and make yourself as comfortable as your furniture will allow and have a nice bottle of wine within easy reach' – and 'give the ruddy thing a chance'. (It is interesting to compare this record, and his 78rpm single 'A Sweet Old-Fashioned Boy'/'Lay Down Your Arms', with similar recordings of the time by Peter Sellers; T-T's range of characterisations, and voices, suggest a versatility that – in contrast to Sellers' own splendid efforts – would often go largely unnoticed.)

77 *Strictly T-T* was first released in the UK in 1958 (London LL3292), then by Decca in 1961 (Decca LK4398) and then in the US in 1963 (London LP5764); *Terry-Thomas Discovers America* was first released in the US in 1964 (Warner Bros W1558). Another recording, *Jeeves* (Caedmon TC1137) – which consisted of two P.G. Wodehouse stories ('Indian Summer of an Uncle' and 'Jeeves Takes Charge') performed by a cast headed by Terry-

Thomas and Roger Livesey – had originally been released in the US in 1958, was also 're-promoted' during 1963.

78 His performances also serve as a moral lesson to those British actors today who, in spite of their avowed dislike of many aspects of contemporary US political and cultural imperialism, have still agreed to mock their compatriots in the most contemptuous manner in exchange for a large fee and extensive stateside exposure. See, for example, the execrable antics of various British actors in the 'London' episodes of *Friends* ('The One With Ross's Wedding', parts 1 and 2, 7 May 1998, and 'The One After Ross Says Rachel', 24 September 1998) and in the painfully clichéd British-based US movie 3 *Men and a Little Lady* (1990).

79 *Terry-Thomas Tells Tales*, p. 77.

80 Stanley Kramer, interviewed in the early 1990s by Glyn Roberts (and reproduced here with his kind permission).

81 *Terry-Thomas Tells Tales*, p. 103.

82 Edie Adams, quoted by Ross (no primary source identified), *The Complete Terry-Thomas*, p. 140.

83 *Terry-Thomas Tells Tales*, p. 76.

84 Nicholas Parsons, *The Straight Man* (London: Weidenfeld & Nicolson, 1994), pp. 176–7.

85 *Terry-Thomas Tells Tales*, p. 188.

86 The movie had been released in the US on 7 November, and in the UK on 2 December 1963; then, after reaching several other countries in the early part of the following year, it opened in Finland on 4 September, Sweden on 11 September and Australia on 3 December 1964.

87 *Terry-Thomas Tells Tales*, p. 105.

88 *Ibid.*

89 Jack Lemmon, correspondence with Glyn Roberts in the mid-1990s (and reproduced here with his kind permission).

90 Raymond Durgnat, *Films and Filming*, October 1965, pp. 24–5.

91 Bosley Crowther, *New York Times*, 27 January 1965, p. 29.

92 *Time*, 29 January 1965, p. 28.

93 *Filling the Gap*, p. 136.

5 A Bit of Fun

1   Terry-Thomas, *TV Times*, 1957: quoted in *Terry-Thomas Tells Tales*, p. 156.
2   *Terry-Thomas Tells Tales*, p. 156.
3   *Ibid.*, p. 110.
4   *Ibid.*, p. 157.
5   *Ibid.*, p. 159.
6   *Ibid.*, p. 64.
7   *Ibid.*, pp. 64–5.
8   *Ibid.*, p. 139.
9   *Filling the Gap*, pp. 59–60. He also took part in celebrity flat races; he came a close second, for example, to George Formby in a show-business 'Petit Prix' at Squires Gate, near Blackpool in Lancashire, on 3 August 1950.
10 *Ibid.*
11 The incident was confirmed to me by T-T's friend, Richard Hope-Hawkins.
12 *Terry-Thomas Tells Tales*, pp. 79–80.
13 The story was told me by Eric Sykes (15 December 2004); the incident took place during the 1958 run of *Large as Life* at the London Palladium. England were playing a series against New Zealand at the time: Sykes could not remember the specific match, but, judging from the details he mentioned (including a catch by Fred Trueman on the following day), the drinks session probably occurred on Friday night/Saturday morning during the Second Test at Lord's in June 1958.
14 See John Antrobus, *Surviving Spike Milligan* (London: Robson, 2003), p. 56.
15 Ian Carmichael, interviewed in the mid-1990s by Glyn Roberts (reproduced here with his kind permission).
16 Thomas Wiseman, 'The Dandy On Horseback Says "I Shall Act"', *Evening Standard*, 27 April 1955, p. 6.
17 *Filling the Gap*, p. 12.
18 *Terry-Thomas Tells Tales*, p. 1.
19 Sidney Gilliat, interviewed in the early 1990s by Glyn Roberts (reproduced here with his kind permission). An insight into the reasons for T-T's frustration can be gleaned from listening to the *Strictly T-T* album, which boasts a playfulness and verbal versatility that – unlike Peter Sellers' similar recordings – has largely been forgotten.
20 *Filling the Gap*, p. 27.
21 Terry-Thomas, quoted by Amis, *Memoirs*, p. 178.
22 Recalled by Richard Briers, interview with the author, 7 November 2007.

23 *Terry-Thomas Tells Tales*, p. 110.
24 *Ibid.*, p. 191.
25 Barry Cryer, letter to the author, 29 January 2008.
26 *Terry-Thomas Tells Tales*, pp. 180–1.
27 Eric Sykes recalled for me (15 December 2004) what it was like to work with T-T on *Large as Life*:

> Working at the Palladium in those days, the 1950s, was rather like working under the Gestapo, because there'd be people in the wings watching your every move, and the slightest thing you did 'wrong', such as doing nine minutes instead of your allotted eight, was duly noted and reported back to Management. And so Terry won my undying admiration for standing up to them. He wouldn't be messed about. There was one occasion when he got into trouble because of a fireman. He was a bit late on for his call, so he was in a rush, and he had some steps to go down from his dressing room to the stage, and this fireman was blocking his way. So Terry said, 'Get out of the way, you bastard!' – because he was in such a panic. And, of course, he got reported and the Management came down on him, summoned him to the office, and they said, 'You called this man a bastard. Why?' And Terry just said, 'Well, at the time, I couldn't think of anything stronger!' Typical Terry!

28 Eric Sykes, *Eric Sykes' Comedy Heroes* (London: Virgin, 2003), pp. 170–1.
29 Sarah Miles, correspondence with the author, 17 February 2008.
30 Ken Annakin, interviewed in the mid-1990s by Glyn Roberts (and reproduced here with his kind permission).
31 The characters of Dastardly (voiced by Paul Winchell) and Muttley (whose wheezes were made audible by Don Messick) first appeared in the thirty-four-episode US TV series *Wacky Races* (based, in general terms, on the movie *The Great Race*), which ran originally from 14 September 1968 to September 1970 and then in the seventeen-episode spin-off series of their own, *Dastardly and Muttley in Their Flying Machines* (based on *Those Magnificent Men In Their Flying Machines*), which ran originally from 13 September 1969 to January 1970. As for the original character of Sir Percy, Ken Annakin confirmed to Glyn Roberts that it had been tailor-made for T-T:

> Jack Davies and I certainly created the part of Sir Percy Ware-Armitage for Terry and his side-kick [for] Eric Sykes. I had watched Terry and occasionally had met him socially and felt that he was the perfect English 'bounder' – an aristocrat by birth but completely prepared to cheat everyone and enjoy it. His wide eyes and quivering mouth fit him perfectly for

> this sort of scene and we never wrote a joke which he was not able to squeeze one hundred per cent.

32 *New York Times*, 17 June 1965, p. 27.

33 Eric Sykes, conversation with the author, 15 December 2004.

34 *Ibid.*

35 *Filling the Gap*, p. 116.

36 *Sette volte sette* was probably the movie to which the actor David Lodge was referring when he told Glyn Roberts of his uncredited appearance alongside Terry-Thomas (quoted here with Glyn Roberts' kind permission):

> We worked together in several films, one of which was an Italian film, partly shot in London. We were the only Englishmen in the film – Terry a Det. Inspector and myself as his Sgt. He advised me to claim my fee each day in 'readies', as he termed it, which of course he did and was paid in notes daily. I disregarded his advice and got short-changed by cheque. Every time we met after that he would flash that gap-toothed smile and declare, 'Dear heart, I told you they were an *ABSOLUTE SHOWER!*'

37 *Terry-Thomas Tells Tales*, p. 109.

38 Terry-Thomas had actually attempted to sue for divorce before, at the start of October 1960, but the petition was dismissed by the judge on 10 October because, as T-T's solicitor acknowledged, Pat was contesting the charge. A report in *The Times* (11 October 1960, p. 3) said: 'The husband has decided not to proceed with his petition, and he (counsel) accordingly asked that it might be dismissed. His Lordship said that the suit would be dismissed, and that the wife's costs would be paid by the husband.' Pat agreed, almost two years later, to sue for divorce herself on the grounds of her husband's desertion, and a decree *nisi* was granted on 18 April 1962.

39 Belinda Stevens, speaking on *Legends: Terry-Thomas* (Carlton/ITV, 10 September 2002).

40 *Terry-Thomas Tells Tales*, p. 136.

41 *Ibid.*

42 He confided to his fellow actor David Kossoff on the set of *The Mouse on the Moon*: 'This one's a slipper-warmer.' (Kossoff recalled the comment – 'A splendid use of words' – to Glyn Roberts, with whose kind permission I reproduce it here.)

43 *Terry-Thomas Tells Tales*, p. 144.

44 *Ibid.*, p. 151.

45 *Ibid.*, p. 153.

46 *Ibid.*, p. 82.

47 *Ibid.*, pp. 82–3.

48 *Ibid.*, p. 157.

49 *Ibid.*, p. 156.

50 Marylin Bender's gossipy exposé of the new breed of celebrity, *The Beautiful People*, was published by Coward, McCann & Geoghegan in 1967.

51 Next for Taylor came the La Peregrina pearl for which Burton paid £15,000, followed by a 69.42-carat pear-shaped diamond (dubbed the 'Taylor-Burton Diamond') cut from a rough stone weighing 240.80 carats found in the Premier Mine in 1966 and bought subsequently by Harry Winston.

52 Raymond Burr – a closet homosexual – bought the island in 1963 (primarily to live in relative privacy with his fellow actor and long-term companion Robert Benevides). He would ranch cattle there, farm orchids and invest in improving the lives of the islanders. He sold the island and moved back to the US in 1983.

53 Marlon Brando acquired a 99-year lease on the atoll of Tetiaroa – situated twenty-six miles north of Tahiti – in 1965, envisaging its function in future as part environmental laboratory and part resort.

54 In the mid-1960s, The Beatles asked Alistair Taylor – personal assistant to Brian Epstein and then general manager of Apple Corps – to find them a private island on which to live, partly because 'Harold Wilson's taxing us something rotten' and partly out of frustration at Brian Epstein's various business oversights during the course of the previous few years. Taylor duly found an island – a place called Tsougrias costing £90,000 – that included four beaches, sixteen acres of olive groves, half a dozen tall Greek houses, boats, businesses, and a gently curving bay. British law prohibited its citizens from taking large sums of money out of the country, and the same law applied to spending money on property abroad; one had to purchase currency called property dollars from the British government and pay with those. After applying for the £90,000 in property notes the government initially turned down their request, but eventually agreed (to a maximum of £90,000) and sold them to The Beatles at a premium of a certain percentage. The limit of £90,000, however, meant that there would not be cash available to furnish and improve the island, so Taylor was in negotiations with the government to increase the limit when The Beatles decided to cancel the project. The property dollars were sold back to the government at a profit of six or seven per cent (£11,400) because the premium rate had risen since their purchase. John Lennon then bought two uninhabited islands – known collectively as Dornish – in Clew Bay off the

west coast of Ireland for £1550. (See Alistair Taylor, *Yesterday – The Beatles Remembered* (London: Sidgwick & Jackson, 1988), pp. 82–9, 111–23).

55 *Terry-Thomas Tells Tales*, p. 156.

56 *Ibid.*, p. 110.

57 Ken Annakin, who was the first choice to direct *The Perils of Pauline*, recalled to Glyn Roberts:

> It turned out that the producer [Herb Leonard] really wanted to direct, and what with that and the ridiculously long hours they made us work (14–18 hours a day!) I quit after 18 days. The producer went on to finish it and I believe it didn't look bad. It was a fun idea. I persuaded them to bring Terry over because I could not find an American comic who would be as good as Terry. I shot all his stuff in under a week (mostly on the old MGM lot) and he flew back home.

58 *Terry-Thomas Tells Tales*, p. 112.

59 *Ibid.*, p. 114.

60 *Ibid.*

61 'Which Is the Real Hoar-Stevens?' *Time*, 25 June 1965.

62 *Filling the Gap*, p. 157.

63 The problem with *Private Eye* seems to have arisen back on 7 April 1963, when – during a live appearance on *What's My Line?* – Terry-Thomas sniped at the BBC's popular new satirical show *That Was the Week That Was* for what he perceived as its excessive and unfocussed irreverence. This not only went down rather badly at the BBC, it also acted as a red rag to the satirists, and, on 23 August, *Private Eye* featured a cartoon that contrasted Terry-Thomas's dapper public image with a stumbling and shabbily dressed off-stage alter ego. In stark contrast to his usually easy-going good humour, Terry-Thomas reacted angrily, promptly suing the magazine's company, Pressdram, for libel. Subsequently, in February 1965 in court, it was alleged: 'The plaintiff was naturally extremely angry at what he regarded as a grossly impudent and unwarranted attack upon him and his character. He had not the smallest idea why the defendants should suddenly have chosen him as the subject of a cartoon or why they should have treated him in such a manner.' The magazine, in response, insisted that no offence had actually been meant, claiming, surely a little disingenuously, that the intention had simply been to note that even someone as 'dapper, happy, lively, good humoured and mirth making' an actor as Terry-Thomas was still prone, 'like all other mortals', to the 'emotions, irritations, worries and fatigue which beset us all'. The strange little case ended with Terry-Thomas accepting the assurance that no personal attack had been intended, but he

was still awarded an apology and Pressdram agreed to offer to pay him a sum of money by way of damages and in respect of his costs. (See *The Times*, 9 February 1965, p. 16.)

64 Terry-Thomas, interviewed by Ivan Waterman, *News of the World*, 21 September 1975, p. 5.

65 T-T began his plans to renovate 11 Queen's Gate Mews at the start of 1965. In February, he hired the firm of Merry & King Ltd of Knightsbridge to update and improve the property's plumbing and electrical system, demolish a wine cupboard, create a new large room by removing a partition wall and make various improvements to the kitchen and bathroom. In March, he commissioned the architect Derek Sharp to design a new roof garden (complete with a solarium) and also hired the landscape architect and horticultural specialist Paul Kemble to build and decorate it. The plan was for T-T and his family to leave the house for a vacation in Athens, then a promotional stay in Cannes and a brief visit to Brazil, and then return in June to a nicely remodelled abode. Predictably, however, the project developed a life of its own, and dragged on throughout the rest of the year. On 30 September, clearly exasperated, T-T wrote to Kemble, complaining about the delays, damage and general discomfort caused by the builders:

> Your letter to me when we were in Athens assured me that we could take up residence on such and such a date. When we arrived in England (and I don't have to remind you), we had to spend over three weeks in an extremely unpleasant hotel, not to mention a whacking great bill. I said then and I repeat it, I don't think any of this was necessary, because it was due to the inefficiency, unprofessionalism and disinterestedness of your Manager, coupled with the ignorance of your Foreman, whose ignorance, I might add, manifests itself in the form of arrogant bullying. When you have a man like this you will always have chaos, inefficiency and heart-burn.

As if that was not bad enough, T-T added that, thanks to the absolute shower of a team of workmen, he could no longer get into his own potting shed. (Correspondence courtesy of Richard Hope-Hawkins.)

66 *Terry-Thomas Tells Tales*, p. 161.

67 *Ibid.*, p. 162.

68 *Ibid.*

69 See Susan Elliott and Barry Turner, *Denholm Elliott: Quest for Love* (London: Headline, 1994), *passim*.

70 *Terry-Thomas Tells Tales*, pp. 162, 180.

71 *Monte Carlo … c'est la Rose*, first broadcast in the US on 6 March 1968 by the ABC network.

72 *Terry-Thomas Tells Tales*, p. 163.

73 Georgina Cookson, interviewed by Glyn Roberts.

74 *Terry-Thomas Tells Tales*, p. 167.

75 Trumper Rupert 'Cushan' Stevens was born on 28 August 1968.

76 *Terry-Thomas Tells Tales*, p. 170.

77 Terry-Thomas, interviewed by Ivan Waterman in the *News of the World*, 21 September 1975, p. 5.

78 The forger Elmyr de Hory is remembered now largely thanks to the Orson Welles movie *F for Fake* (1973). Elmyr, who credited himself with having painted nearly one thousand of the classics of modern art, including works by artists such as Matisse, Modigliani and Picasso, was exposed as a forger in 1968 and imprisoned briefly by the Spanish on Ibiza. Welles's movie as a whole was a tribute to the culture of fakery, dealing as well with Elmyr's biographer Clifford Irving. In 1972, Irving was sent to prison and ordered to pay back $765,000 to his publishers when it was determined that his 'authorised' biography of the reclusive billionaire Howard Hughes was actually a fake; Irving had claimed previously that he had tapes, letters and manuscripts from Hughes, and that Hughes had authorised him to write the definitive life. In fact, Hughes – who had not been heard from publicly in over a decade – held a telephone conference to denounce Irving. Irving stood by his story, but experts said that the voice they had heard on the telephone was indeed that of Hughes, and the handwritten documents were deemed fakes. Irving, his wife Edith and his collaborator Richard Suskind were all convicted for their part in the hoax, and Irving spent 14 months in federal prison. See *F for Fake* (Connoisseur Video, 1996: B00004CRRB). Those who have seen the movie (starring Richard Gere) based on Irving's devious antics, *Hoax* (2007), may have been confused by the fact that the action takes place in America rather than Ibiza; this fictional switch was done for production reasons chiefly to do with time and expense.

79 April Ashley had been born a male – George Jamieson – in 1935 in a Liverpool slum, but became a female impersonator in Paris at Le Carrousel (home of the leading drag revue in France) in the mid-1950s before undergoing a sex-change operation in Casablanca on 11 May 1960. She went on to find fame as a top model and hostess in London before anyone knew of her secret, and was often described in the press as 'The Queen of Chelsea'. She married into the peerage in 1963 when she became the wife of Arthur Corbett, the son of the Second Lord Rowallan (and a closet transvestite himself), but when the seven-year marriage ended in divorce,

on 2 February 1970, the case caused a sensation, changing British law. Lord Justice Ormrod – the only man to qualify as a doctor as well as a judge – decreed that although Ashley had a passport and driving license that described her as a woman, the Corbett marriage was null and void because she had been born a male. See Duncan Fallowell and April Ashley, *April Ashley's Odyssey* (London: Jonathan Cape, 1982).

80 *Terry-Thomas Tells Tales*, p. 177.

81 *Ibid.*, p. 174.

82 *Ibid.*, pp. 177–8.

83 Elliott and Turner, *Denholm Elliott: Quest for Love*, p. 190.

84 Leslie Phillips, interviewed by Emma Hawes, *Mail on Sunday*, 9 July 2003.

85 *Terry-Thomas Tells Tales*, p. 172.

86 He could resort, however, to the odd pre-emptive attack. His friend and fellow actor Victor Spinetti, for example, recalled visiting him in Ibiza: 'I said to him, there on top of the hill where he lived, "It is a bit remote here, Terry, what do you do in the evening?" He leant back in his high-backed chair, took a sip of his drink and said, "That's easy, my dear. I go down into the village and tear the hippies off a strip".' (Quotation reproduced with kind permission of Glyn Roberts.)

87 Ingeborg Pertwee, quoted in Bernard Bale, *Jon Pertwee* (London: André Deutsch, 2000), pp. 222–3.

88 Avril Angers, interviewed by Glyn Roberts, 10 February 1994.

89 *Terry-Thomas Tells Tales*, pp. 178–9.

90 *Ibid.*, p. 180.

91 *Ibid.*, p. 179.

92 Terry-Thomas, quoted by d'Arcy, 'Terribly, Terribly Terry-Thomas', p. 33.

93 *Terry-Thomas Tells Tales*, pp. 178–9.

94 Terry-Thomas, interviewed by Michael Parkinson, *Parkinson* (London: Elm Tree, 1975), p. 110.

95 *Terry-Thomas Tells Tales*, p. 169.

96 *Ibid.*, p. 135.

97 *Ibid.*, p. 155.

98 *Ibid.*, p. 170.

99 *Ibid.*

100 Memo, dated 7 November 1963, by Holland Bennett (BBC WAC: Terry-Thomas: TV Artist's File III: 1963–70).

101 The programme was aired on 16 November 1963, and received several favourable reviews, but executives passed on the option to use it as the basis of a series.

102 Letter, dated 23 October 1963, by Terry-Thomas to Michael Mills (BBC WAC: Terry-Thomas: TV Artist's File III: 1963–70).

103 BBC WAC: Terry-Thomas: TV Artist's File III: 1963–70.

104 Handwritten addition to a memo, dated 1 July 1968, by the BBC TV's senior bookings manager, E.K. Wilson (*Ibid.*).

105 Derek Fowlds, quoted by Ross, *The Complete Terry-Thomas*, p. 76.

106 Jonathan Cecil, conversation with the author, 6 March 2008. (See also Cecil's article 'I Once Worked With … Terry-Thomas', *The Call Boy*, Summer 2004, p. 16; copyright Jonathan Cecil.)

107 Terry-Thomas, recalled by Richard Briers, interview with the author, 8 November 2007.

108 *Terry-Thomas Tells Tales*, p. 47.

109 Richard Briers, interview with the author, 8 November 2007.

110 *Ibid.* Briers actually ended up receiving good reviews for his performance in *Cat Among the Pigeons*. Irving Wardle, for example, wrote in *The Times* (16 April 1969, p. 13), 'Mr Briers, the possessor of a strongly developed comic personality, emerges with particular honour from the show in which he drops his usual mask as the helpless innocent and turns on a fine show of resourcefulness and aggression'.

111 See *Terry-Thomas Tells Tales*, pp. 46–7: 'I did ask for him to join me in my TV series … and he was as good as I knew he would be.'

112 Richard Briers, interview with the author, 8 November 2007.

113 Jonathan Cecil, conversation with the author, 6 March 2008.

114 *Ibid.*

115 The show was not helped by being shown on Fridays, as few newspapers in those days bothered to carry reviews in their Saturday editions, preferring instead to concentrate on previews of the weekend schedules.

116 Jonathan Cecil, conversation with the author, 6 March 2008.

117 Terry-Thomas, interviewed by Russell Twisk, 'The Reluctant Globe-trotter', *Radio Times*, 28 November 1968, p. 35.

118 See *Terry-Thomas Tells Tales*, p. 150; Simon Freeman and Barrie Penrose, *Rinkagate: The Rise and Fall of Jeremy Thorpe* (London: Bloomsbury, 1997), p. 146; Auberon Waugh, *The Last Word* (London: Michael Joseph, 1980), *passim*.

119 *Terry-Thomas Tells Tales*, p. 179.

6 An Absolute Shower

1 Born on 27 July 1917, André Bourvil was a French actor best known in his early days for his portrayal on stage and radio of a naïve and gauche peasant farmer, and later for his roles in big-screen comedy – most notably his collaboration with Louis de Funès in the wartime comedy *La Grande Vadrouille* (1966), which also featured Terry-Thomas and went on to break French box-office records with sales of 17 million tickets. In 1968, Bourvil was diagnosed as suffering from a terminal bone-wasting disease called Kahler's syndrome. Against medical advice, he continued working for as long as he could. He died – aged fifty-three – in Paris on 23 September 1970, shortly after completing his contribution to *Le Mur de l'Atlantique*.

2 *Don't Just Lie There, Say Something* was staged at the Metro Theatre in Sydney, Australia, in 1971. It played to full houses on a regular basis, but received merely polite but ambivalent reviews.

3 This episode of *The Persuaders!* – entitled 'The Man in the Middle' – was aired in the UK by ITV on 16 December 1971, and in the US by ABC on 9 October 1971.

4 Terry-Thomas had first appeared on *Desert Island Discs* 13 February 1956 (his luxury, on that occasion, was a horse saddle); his return visit was broadcast on 1 August 1970.

5 The first edition of *Parkinson* was broadcast on 19 June 1971. Apart from Terry-Thomas, the opening show featured interviews with the tennis player Arthur Ashe and the first British paparazzo Ray Bellisario.

6 See *Terry-Thomas Tells Tales*, p. 192.

7 *Monthly Film Bulletin* (vol. 39, no. 466, November 1972, p. 230) judged it 'better than its prototype', but most of the other reviews disagreed.

8 Shanley, 'On Television Tomorrow', p. X21.

9 Terry-Thomas wrote a friendly but lightly chiding letter to Ronnie Corbett on 30 August 1971, noting that Corbett's storytelling style had always struck him as appealingly similar to his own, but adding that, after watching a recent televised performance, he felt that 'the likeness had spread from style to include material'. He singled out a particular monologue as bearing 'an uncanny resemblance' to the 'Bring Back the Cat' story that he included on the *Strictly T-T* LP. 'What I will do,' said T-T, 'is to echo the words of the old actor, Odell, who, when asked to return the loan of a fiver, replied, "I haven't finished with it yet".' (Correspondence reproduced by permission of Richard Hope-Hawkins.)

10 Johnny Carson took over *The Tonight Show* from Jack Paar on 1 October

1962, and remained as its host until his retirement on 21 March 1992; *The Merv Griffin Show* ran from August 1969 to February 1972 on CBS; *The Dick Cavett Show* began on 26 May 1969 on ABC; *Where Do I Sit?* lasted for a mere three shows (from 19 February to 5 March) on BBC2 in 1971; *If It's Saturday It Must Be Nimmo* ran for one series on BBC1 from 24 October to 19 December 1970; and *Parkinson* (as noted above) began on BBC1 on 19 June 1971. The 'half-man, half-desk' phrase is taken from an episode of *The Larry Sanders Show* (see my article, 'Half-man, Half-desk: The Secrets of a Talk-show Host', *Financial Times*, 8/9 April 2000, p. viii).

11 Among the kind of stories that he told Cavett was the one about the young man at a dance:

> There was this chap I knew who, when he was in a dance hall one evening, looked across the room and saw this frightfully pretty girl sitting all on her own. So, naturally, he thought he'd go over and ask her for a dance. Or something. And so he started walking towards her, but, the nearer he got to her, the less he liked the look of her. The light wasn't that good, you know, and his eyes weren't much better, and so he was squinting away, thinking to himself, 'I've made a mistake! What on earth am I going to do? I certainly don't want to ask this girl for a dance. Or anything else!' He was a bit of a rotter, actually. A *stinker*, really. So he thought, 'I must think of something sharpish.' And then, just in time, he got the right idea and went up to her and said, 'Do excuse me, madam, but from the other end of the room I mistook you for my mother!' To which she replied, 'Oh, that's an *awfully* silly mistake for *you* to have made, because *I'm* wearing a wedding ring!'

12 Richard Briers, interview with the author, 8 November 2007.

13 *The Special London Bridge Special* – which featured Tom Jones, Jennifer O'Neill, The Carpenters, Kirk Douglas, Chief Dan George and Hermione Gingold, with brief cameo appearances by Elliott Gould, Lorne Greene, Charlton Heston, Engelbert Humperdinck, George Kirby, Michael Landon, Raquel Welch, Rudolf Nureyev, Terry-Thomas and Jonathan Winters – was broadcast on 7 May 1972.

14 *The Heroes* was released in October 1973 (as *Los Héroes millonarios* in Spain; *Les Enfants de choeur* in France; and *Gli Eroi* in Italy).

15 *Mussolini: Ultimo atto* (1974).

16 *Terry-Thomas Tells Tales*, p. 83.

17 Richard Combs, *The Times*, 26 October 1973, p. 15.

18 Daniel Massey, interviewed by Glyn Roberts (reproduced here with his kind permission).

19 Terry-Thomas, speaking on *Parkinson*, BBC1 19 October 1974; transcribed in Parkinson, *Parkinson*, p. 109.

20 Another factor that probably convinced Terry-Thomas not to risk the exertion was the fact that the proposed fee struck him as far too low: 'I almost fainted when I heard what they wanted to pay,' he told Ivan Waterman during an interview published in the *News of the World*, 21 September 1975, p. 5.

21 It appears that Terry-Thomas sought out an alternative medical opinion as late as April 1975, when the London-based specialist Dr Arthur Unwin examined him and confirmed that he did indeed have Parkinson's Disease (Unwin was interviewed by Glyn Roberts in the early 1990s).

22 An earlier project that came to a premature close was a movie for Paramount called *Easy Come, Easy Go* – in which Terry-Thomas was due to co-star alongside the likes of up-and-coming comedian Mel Brooks. While filming in Chatsworth (in the West San Fernando Valley outside Los Angeles) in August 1965, a freight train that featured in one scene crashed into a flatcar carrying several of the cast and the production team, injuring twelve people (including the director, Barry Shear) and wrecking some valuable equipment. Paramount decided to cash in on the insurance money, pay the actors off and cancel the movie.

23 *Monthly Film Bulletin*, vol. 43, no. 506, March 1976, p. 48.

24 *Ibid.*, p. 63.

25 Terry-Thomas, quoted by Ross, no primary source acknowledged, *The Complete Terry-Thomas*, p. 181.

26 Terry-Thomas was, however, a well-liked member of the cast. Billy Boyle, for example, who played the character called 'Gary', told Glyn Roberts:

> One day we had a very tricky scene very early in the morning. After I had done my piece to camera alone we came around for a reverse on Terry. It was a very difficult bit of dialogue and Terry was having a little difficulty. Although it was the back of my head to camera I stayed there till Terry got it as of course it was magic from him. Shortly afterwards there was a knock on my dressing room door and Terry came in. He held out his hand and said, "Thank you". I was astonished that a "star" such as Terry would thank a rookie like me. I think he knew how in awe of him I was, and for him to recognise I didn't have to stand there while he was doing his dialogue really touched him. That's how sensitive he was to people round him, a real pro.

27 Leslie Phillips, interviewed by David Allsop, *SAGA* magazine, January 2007, p. 96.

28 Leslie Phillips, *Hello* (London: Orion, 2007), pp. 307–8.

29 Bob Kellett, interviewed by Glyn Roberts and reproduced here with his permission. Kellett also recalled his initial trip to see Terry-Thomas at his home on Ibiza and discuss the idea of *Spanish Fly*:

> When I first saw him he was stark naked, diving into the swimming pool at his house. 'Come on in,' he said, laughing. I was over there with my PA and was a little alarmed. We didn't join him in the pool, we sat on the edge and had a jolly chat while he swam on quite unconcerned about it all. Leslie Phillips, who was the co-star with him, had been on tour with a play in Australia and had cut short the run of his play to find, much to his dismay, that there wasn't a script and he was a little bit indignant about the whole thing. I think it was an exercise in how not to make a movie – it was decided by the powers that be that they didn't need a script. They thought they had enough good ideas around to be able to make a funny film without a script.

30 *Monthly Film Bulletin*, vol. 43, no. 505, February 1976, p. 34.

31 *Films Illustrated*, vol. 5, no. 53, January 1976, p. 170.

32 *Monthly Film Bulletin*, vol. 43, no. 505, February 1976, p. 34.

33 Terry-Thomas, interviewed by d'Arcy, 'Terribly, Terribly Terry-Thomas'.

34 *Ibid.*

35 *Terry-Thomas Tells Tales*, p. 98.

36 *Ibid.*, p. 182.

37 *The Times*, 30 November 1976, p. 7.

38 *Terry-Thomas Tells Tales*, p. 183.

39 The plan was for T-T to ski from Littlestone in Kent to Cap Gris Nez to raise money for under-privileged children. A trial run, on 15 July, went well, and he went within a few miles of the French coast, but the actual attempt the following day was abandoned due to the combination of high winds and a rough sea. Another attempt was planned for later in the year, but poor health intervened.

40 Andy Warhol moved to the studio he called 'The Factory' – an old New York loft building located at 231 East 47th Street – at the end of 1963, using it initially for the production of pop art silkscreens and other aestheticised products during the day and for holding parties at night (featuring a notoriously strange combination of artists, poets, rock stars, local eccentrics, amphetamine addicts, Manhattan socialites, full-time party goers and shady drug dealers). Paul Morrissey, who had been making short underground films since the beginning of the decade, met Warhol in the mid-1960s and soon became a production assistant at The Factory. He was the cameraman

on several Warhol films, including *Lonesome Cowboys*; the two co-directed the transvestite comedy *Women in Revolt* (1971) and *L'Amour* (1973). With Warhol as producer, Morrissey made several noteworthy films, most notably his early comedies *Flesh* (1968), *Trash* (1970) and *Heat* (1972), and the distinctly unconventional horror films *Andy Warhol's Frankenstein* (a.k.a. *Flesh for Frankenstein*, 1974) and *Andy Warhol's Dracula* (a.k.a. *Blood for Dracula*, 1974).

41 *Terry-Thomas Tells Tales*, p. 117.

42 *Ibid.*

43 John Preston, *Sunday Telegraph*, 10 December 2000, p. 24.

44 David Robinson, *The Times*, 10 November 1978, p. 9.

45 *Terry-Thomas Tells Tales*, p. 117.

46 Kenneth Williams, diary entry dated 27 July 1977, reproduced in *The Kenneth Williams Diaries*, ed. Russell Davies (London: HarperCollins, 1993), p. 548.

47 Paul Morrissey, speaking in the 'Director's Interview' special feature on the DVD version of *The Hound of the Baskervilles* (Prism Leisure: PPA1580, 2003).

48 *Terry-Thomas Tells Tales*, p. 191.

49 Terry-Thomas appeared on behalf of the Parkinson's Disease Society on Sunday 12 November 1977 on BBC1.

50 *Terry-Thomas Tells Tales*, pp. 192–3.

51 *Ibid.*, p. 191.

52 Terry-Thomas, quoted by Tony Kilmister in the programme for the 9 April 1989 *Terry-Thomas Benefit Gala*.

53 *Terry-Thomas Tells Tales*, p. 193.

54 Frankel, V.H., 'The Terry-Thomas Sign', *Clinical Orthopaedics and Related Research*, 129, November–December 1977, pp. 321–2.

55 See *Terry-Thomas Tells Tales*, p. 159.

56 Derek Jarman wrote to T-T on 20 April 1979 to explain the reasons for cutting the part of Old Prospero (source: the Richard Hope-Hawkins collection).

57 This edition of *This Is Your Life* was broadcast by ITV on 25 December 1979.

58 *Terry-Thomas Tells Tales*, p. 195.

59 Terry-Thomas, quoted in the *Daily Mail*, 9 January 1990, p. 7.

60 *Terry-Thomas Tells Tales*, p. 203.

61 *Ibid.*, p. 199.

62 T-T was not really a political animal, but he was no fan of Margaret Thatcher, either for her right-wing politics or, of course, for her association

with the dreaded Finchley. When, for example, he was planning to ski across the English Channel in 1977, he told reporters: 'The one thing I'll be thinking of on the crossing is how I can avoid meeting Mrs Thatcher' (*Daily Mirror*, 14 July 1977, p. 5).

63 Richard Briers, interview with the author, 8 November 2007.

64 *Terry Thomas Tells Tales*, p. 199.

65 See *Filling the Gap, passim*. The imaginary books, incidentally, have been mistaken for real by some accounts of the life and work of Terry-Thomas – thus inspiring countless fruitless searches through the catalogues of antiquarian booksellers.

66 Recalled by Tony Kilmister in an unpublished mid-1990s interview by Glyn Roberts, reproduced here with his permission.

67 *Terry Thomas Tells Tales*, p. 200.

68 *Ibid.*, p. 207 (see also the comments by Daum quoted by Nigel Dempster in the *Daily Mail*, 10 January 1990, p. 32).

69 *Ibid.*, p. 205.

70 *Ibid.*, p. 206.

71 *Ibid.*, p. 207.

72 His short-lived addresses during this period included 4 Longfield House, Longfield Drive, East Sheen, SW14; and 100 High Street, Marlow, Buckinghamshire, SL7.

73 Smaller contributions were also received from The Royal Theatrical Fund, The Cinema and Television Benevolent Fund and The Grand Order of Water Rats.

74 Richard Briers, interview with the author, 8 November 2007.

75 Tony Purnell, 'Comic Terry's Life of Poverty', *Daily Mirror*, 8 December 1988, p. 7.

76 *Ibid.*

77 Tony Purnell, 'Terry's Torment', *Daily Mirror*, 9 December 1988, p. 9.

78 *Ibid.*

79 Mickey Rooney, in a tribute recorded in 1989 and preserved by Richard Hope-Hawkins.

80 Tony Purnell, 'Terry's Torment', p. 9 and 'Terry's Tonic', *Daily Mirror*, 10 December 1988, p. 9.

81 Richard Hope-Hawkins, interview with the author, 6 February 2008.

82 *Ibid.*

83 Sue Benwell, *A Twitch in Time* (Knebworth: Able, 2002), p. 173.

84 Richard Hope-Hawkins, interview with the author, 6 February 2008.

85 *Ibid.*

86 *Ibid.*

87 *Ibid.*
88 Most of the US interviews were filmed at the King's Head pub in Santa Monica. There was also a related event held in America, sponsored by the Californian radio stations KSRF and KVCM, as well as a special dinner in aid of the American Parkinson's Disease Society.
89 Richard Hope-Hawkins, interview with the author, 6 February 2008.
90 *Ibid.*
91 The Terry-Thomas Trust Fund, set up in 1989, had two initial trustees: Reg Swinson (of the Entertainment Artistes' Benevolent Fund) and John Elliott (then chairman of the Parkinson's Disease Society). A small percentage of the proceeds from the gala event was distributed evenly among the 21 charitable and benevolent organisations represented by Britain's Entertainment Charities Fund.
92 Benwell, *A Twitch in Time*, p. 176.
93 Richard Briers, interview with the author, 8 November 2007.
94 George Cole, London *Evening Standard*, 8 January 1990, p. 3; Richard Briers, in Ross, *The Complete Terry-Thomas*, p. 7; *Guardian*, 9 January 1990, p. 1; *New York Times*, 9 January 1990, p. D23; *Daily Telegraph*, 9 January 1990, p. 17; *Daily Mail*, 9 January 1990, p. 7; *Thames News*, ITV, 9 January 1990.

Epilogue

1 *Terry-Thomas Tells Tales*, p. 208.
2 Comic Heritage held a ceremony to unveil the blue plaque outside 11 Queen's Gate Mews on Sunday, 13 October 1996. It was attended by, among others, Richard Briers, Richard Hope-Hawkins, Herbert Lom, Ian Bannen, Roy Boulting, Bert Kwouk, Bernard Cribbins, Sue Nicholls, Mark Eden, Melvyn Hayes, Ron Moody, Jonathan Cecil, Stirling Moss, Lance Percival, Bernard Cribbins and Paul Daniels.
3 Richard Hope-Hawkins, interview with the author, 6 February 2008.
4 *Ibid.*
5 *Filling the Gap*, p. 136.

Bibliography

Terry-Thomas

Baker, Barry, 'The Most Noble Cad of Them All', *Daily Mail*, 9 January 1990,
   p. 7

Cecil, Jonathan, 'I Once Worked With ... Terry-Thomas', *The Call Boy*,
   Summer 2004, p. 16

d'Arcy, Susan, 'Terribly, Terribly Terry-Thomas', *Films Illustrated*, vol. 6,
   no. 61, September 1976, pp. 32–3.

Flint, Peter B., 'Terry-Thomas, 78, Actor who Satirized Britons', *New York
   Times*, 9 January 1990, p. D23

Florkiewicz, Lynn, 'Terry-Thomas: Bounder of the First Degree', *Best of
   British*, February 2005, pp. 64–5

Harris, Margaret, 'Torment of Terry-Thomas', *The Sun-Herald* (Aus), 8 January
   1989, p. 9

Lewis, Jack, 'Terry-Thomas Takes It Lying Down', *Reynolds News*,
   15 November 1959, p. 11

Purnell, Tony, 'Comic Terry's Life of Poverty', *Daily Mirror*, 8 December 1988,
   p. 7

—, 'Terry's Torment', *Daily Mirror*, 9 December 1988, p. 9

—, 'Terry's Tonic', *Daily Mirror*, 10 December 1988, p. 9

—, 'Farewell to T-T, King of the Cads', *Daily Mirror*, 9 January 1990, p. 7

Ross, Robert, *The Complete Terry-Thomas* (London: Reynolds & Hearn, 2002)

Sykes, Eric, 'Terry-Thomas', *Eric Sykes' Comedy Heroes* (London: Virgin, 2003)

Terry-Thomas, 'The Camera Doesn't Do Me Justice', *Radio Times*, 6 January
   1956, p. 9

—, *Filling the Gap* (London: Max Parrish, 1959)

— with Terry Daum, *Terry-Thomas Tells Tales* (London: Robson, 1990)

Twisk, Russell, 'The Reluctant Globe-trotter', *Radio Times*, 28 November 1968,
   p. 35

Wiseman, Thomas, 'The Dandy on Horseback Says "I Shall Act"', *Evening
   Standard*, 27 April 1955, p. 6

General

Allen, Fred, *Treadmill to Oblivion* (Boston: Little, Brown, 1954)
Allen, Steve, *The Funny Men* (New York: Simon & Schuster, 1956)
Alton, Doug, 'Confessions of a Showgirl', *The Sunday Age* (Aus), 31 January 1993, p. 4
Askey, Arthur, *Before Your Very Eyes* (London: Woburn Press, 1975)
Babington, Bruce, *Launder and Gilliat* (Manchester: Manchester University Press, 2002)
Bale, Bernard, *Jon Pertwee* (London: André Deutsch, 2000)
Beaton, Cecil and Kenneth Tynan, *Persona Grata* (London: Wingate, 1953)
Benny, Jack and Joan Benny, *Sunday Nights at Seven* (New York: Warner, 1990)
Benwell, Sue, *A Twitch in Time* (Knebworth: Able, 2002)
Black, Cilla, *Through the Years* (London: Headline, 1993)
—, *What's It All About?* (London: Ebury Press, 2003)
Black, Peter, *The Biggest Aspidistra in the World* (London: BBC, 1972)
—, *The Mirror in the Corner* (London: Hutchison, 1972)
Bogdanovich, Peter, *Who the Hell's in It?: Conversations with Legendary Film Stars* (London: Faber and Faber, 2004)
Bradbury, David and Joe McGrath, *Now That's Funny!* (London: Methuen, 1998)
Brandreth, Gyles, *Brief Encounters* (London: Politico's, 2003)
Briers, Richard, *Coward & Company* (London: Robson, 1999)
Briggs, Asa, *The History of Broadcasting in the United Kingdom* (Oxford: Oxford University Press, 1961–1979):
  Vol. 1: *The Birth of Broadcasting*, 1961
  Vol. 2: *The Golden Age of Wireless*, 1965
  Vol. 3: *The War of Words*, 1970
  Vol. 4: *Sound and Vision*, 1979
Bygraves, Max, *Stars In My Eyes* (London: Robson, 2003)
Cardiff, David, 'Mass Middlebrow Laughter: The Origins of BBC Comedy', *Media, Culture & Society*, vol. 10, no. 1 (January 1988), pp. 41–60
Cotton, Bill, *The BBC as an Entertainer* (London: BBC, 1977)
—, *Double Bill* (London: Fourth Estate, 2000)
Craig, Mike, *Look Back with Laughter*, vols 1, 2 and 3 (Manchester: Mike Craig Enterprises, 1996)
Cryer, Barry, *You Won't Believe This But …* (London: Virgin, 1998)
—, *Pigs Can Fly* (London: Orion, 2003)

Dunn, Kate, *Do Not Adjust Your Set: The Early Days of Live Television* (London: John Murray, 2003)

Elliott, Susan and Barry Turner, *Denholm Elliott: Quest for Love* (London: Headline, 1994)

Emerson, Ralph Waldo, *Essays and Poems* (London: J.M. Dent, 1995)

Fallowell, Duncan and April Ashley, *April Ashley's Odyssey* (Jonathan Cape: London, 1982)

Farndale, Nigel, 'A woman of parts', *The Sunday Telegraph Magazine*, 17 April 2005, pp. 14–17

Farnes, Norma, *Spike: An Intimate Memoir* (London: Fourth Estate, 2003)

Fisher, John, *Funny Way to be a Hero* (London: Frederick Muller, 1973)

Foster, Andy and Steve Furst, *Radio Comedy 1938–1968* (London: Virgin, 1996)

Freeman, Mickey and Sholom Rubinstein, *Bilko: Behind the Lines with Phil Silvers* (London: Virgin, 2000)

Freeman, Simon with Barrie Penrose, *Rinkagate: The Rise and Fall of Jeremy Thorpe* (London: Bloomsbury, 1997)

Frith, Simon, 'The Pleasures of the Hearth: The Making of BBC Light Entertainment', in Tony Bennett et al. (eds), *Popular Culture and Social Relations* (Milton Keynes: Open University, 1983)

Gambaccini, Paul and Rod Taylor, *Television's Greatest Hits* (London: Network Books, 1993)

Gillett, Philip, *The British Working Class in Postwar Film* (Manchester: Manchester University Press, 2003)

Gilliatt, Penelope, *To Wit* (New York: Scribner, 1990)

Grade, Lew, *Still Dancing* (London: Collins, 1987)

Grade, Michael, *It Seemed Like a Good Idea at the Time* (London: Macmillan, 1999)

Greene, Hugh Carleton, *The BBC as a Public Service* (London: BBC, 1960)

Hudd, Roy, *Roy Hudd's Book of Music-Hall, Variety and Showbiz Anecdotes* (London: Virgin, 1994)

Hughes, John Graven, *The Greasepaint War* (London: New English Library, 1976)

Humphries, Barry, *More Please* (London: Viking, 1982)

James, Clive, *Clive James on Television* (London: Picador, 1991)

Jeffries, Stuart, *Mrs Slocombe's Pussy* (London: Flamingo, 2000)

Josefsberg, Milt, *The Jack Benny Show* (New York: Arlington House, 1977)

Kumar, Krishan, *The Making of English National Identity: Englishness and Britishness in Comparative and Historical Perspective* (Cambridge: Cambridge University Press, 2003)

Lewis, Roger, *The Life and Death of Peter Sellers* (London: Century, 1994)

Lewisohn, Mark, *Radio Times Guide to TV Comedy* (London: BBC, 1998)

McCann, Graham, *Cary Grant: A Class Apart* (London: Fourth Estate, 1996)

—, 'Why the Best Sitcoms Must Be a Class Act', *London Evening Standard*, 21 May 1997, p. 9

—, 'An Offer We Can Refuse', *London Evening Standard*, 2 December 1998, p. 8

—, *Morecambe & Wise* (London: Fourth Estate, 1998)

—, 'Sit Back and Wait for the Comedy', *Financial Times*, 24 November 1999, p. 22

—, 'Half-man, Half-desk: The Secrets of a Talk-show Host', *Financial Times*, 8/9 April 2000, p. viii

—, 'Don't Bury Your Treasures', *Financial Times*, 28 June 2000, p. 22

—, *Dad's Army: The Story of a Classic Television Show* (London: Fourth Estate, 2001)

—, 'Nocturnal Transmissions Are a Turn-off', *Financial Times*, 8 May 2002, p. 18

—, 'You Never Had It So Good or So Funny', *Financial Times*, 13 November 2002, p. 17

—, 'How to Define the Indefinable', *Financial Times*, 20 March 2003, p. 14

—, 'Bob Hope: The Master of Special Delivery Bows Out', *Financial Times*, 29 July 2003, p. 15

—, 'Steptoe and Son', *British Comedy Greats*, ed. Annabel Merullo and Neil Wenborn (London: Cassell Illustrated, 2003), pp. 157–61

—, 'Johnny Speight', *Oxford Dictionary of National Biography* (Oxford: Oxford University Press, 2004)

—, *Frankie Howerd: Stand-Up Comic* (London: Fourth Estate, 2004)

—, (ed.) *The Essential Dave Allen* (London: Hodder & Stoughton, 2005)

—, *Spike & Co* (London: Hodder & Stoughton, 2006)

—, *Fawlty Towers: The Story of the Sitcom* (London: Hodder & Stoughton, 2007)

McFarlane, Brian, *An Autobiography of British Cinema* (London: Methuen, 1997)

—, *The Encyclopedia of British Film* (London: Methuen, 2005)

Mellor, G.J., *The Northern Music Hall* (Newcastle upon Tyne: Frank Graham, 1970)

—, *They Made Us Laugh* (Littleborough: George Kelsall, 1982)

Miall, Leonard, *Inside the BBC* (London: Weidenfeld & Nicolson, 1994)

Midwinter, Eric, *Make 'Em Laugh* (London: George Allen & Unwin, 1979)

Monkhouse, Bob, *Crying With Laughter* (London: Arrow, 1994)

Bounder!

—, *Over The Limit* (London: Century, 1998)

More, Kenneth, *More or Less* (London: Hodder & Stoughton, 1978)

Morecambe, Eric and Ernie Wise, *Eric & Ernie* (London: W.H. Allen, 1973)

Muir, Frank, *Comedy in Television* (London: BBC, 1966)

Murphy, Robert (ed.), *The British Cinema Book* (London: BFI, 2001)

Nathan, David, *The Laughtermakers* (London: Peter Owen, 1971)

Parkinson, Michael, *Parkinson* (London: Elm Tree, 1975)

Pedrick, Gale, 'Laughter in the Air', *BBC Year Book 1948* (London: BBC, 1948), pp. 53–6

Perret, Gene and Martha Bolton, *Talk About Hope* (Carmel, CA: Jester Press, 1998)

Pertwee, Bill, *Promenades and Pierrots* (Devon: Westbridge, 1979)

—, *By Royal Command* (Newton Abbot: David & Charles, 1981)

—, *A Funny Way to Make a Living!* (London: Sunburst, 1996)

Pertwee, Jon, *Moon Boots and Dinner Suits* (London: Hamish Hamilton, 1984)

Pertwee, Michael, *Name Dropping* (London: Leslie Frewin, 1974)

Phillips, Leslie, *Hello* (London: Orion, 2007)

Plomley, Roy, *Desert Island Lists* (London: Hutchinson, 1984)

Priestley, J.B., *Particular Pleasures* (New York: Stein & Day, 1975)

Richards, Jeffrey, *Visions of Yesteryear* (London: Routledge, 1973)

—, *Films and British National Identity* (Manchester: Manchester University Press, 1997)

Rundall, Jeremy, 'They Must Be Joking', *Plays and Players*, February 1967, pp. 55–6

Silvey, Roger, *Who's Listening? The Story of BBC Audience Research* (London: Allen & Unwin, 1974)

Sloan, Tom, *Television Light Entertainment* (London: BBC, 1969)

Sontag, Susan, 'Notes on Camp', (1964), *A Susan Sontag Reader* (Harmondsworth: Penguin, 1982)

Stark, Graham, *Remembering Peter Sellers* (London: Robson, 1990)

Stone, Richard, *You Should Have Been In Last Night* (Sussex: The Book Guild, 2000)

Street, Sarah, *British National Cinema* (London: Routledge, 1997)

Sykes, Eric, *Eric Sykes' Comedy Heroes* (London: Virgin, 2003)

Taylor, Alistair, *Yesterday – The Beatles Remembered* (London: Sidgwick & Jackson, 1988)

Thompson, Harry, *Peter Cook: A Biography* (London: Hodder & Stoughton, 1997)

Took, Barry, *Laughter in the Air* (London: Robson/BBC, 1976)

—, 'Whatever Happened to TV Comedy?', *The Listener*, 5 January 1984, pp. 7–8, and 12 January 1984, pp. 8–9

Tynan, Kenneth, *Profiles* (London: Nick Hern Books, 1989)

Walker, Alexander, *Hollywood, England* (London: Harrap, 1986)

—, *National Heroes* (London: Harrap, 1986)

Watt, John (ed.), *Radio Variety* (London: J.M. Dent, 1939)

Waugh, Auberon, *The Last Word* (London: Michael Joseph, 1980)

Wheldon, Huw, *British Traditions in a World-Wide Medium* (London: BBC, 1973)

—, *The Achievement of Television* (London: BBC, 1975)

—, *The British Experience in Television* (London: BBC, 1976)

Whitfield, June, *… and June Whitfield* (London: Corgi, 2001)

Wilde, Larry, *The Great Comedians* (Secaucus, NJ: Citadel Press, 1973)

Williams, Kenneth, *The Kenneth Williams Diaries*, ed. Russell Davies (London: HarperCollins, 1993)

Wilmut, Roger, *Kindly Leave the Stage: The Story of Variety, 1918–60* (London: Methuen, 1985)

Windsor, Barbara, *All Of Me* (London: Headline, 2001)

Wyndham Goldie, Grace, *Facing the Nation: Broadcasting and Politics 1936–1976* (London: Bodley Head, 1977)

Index